Heraldry & Faith

Ancient Origins of Armorial Bearings and Their Links to Freemasonry

Heraldry
& Faith

Ancient Origins of Armorial Bearings
and Their Links to Freemasonry

Daryl Lamar Andrews

Published in 2023 by
Andrews Press
Chicago, Illinois 60652

Printed in the United States of America

ISBN: 978-0-9835609-6-8

Preface

History is the backbone of who we are. It sets the stage upon which future generations will build and must be set solidly to ensure its stability. Level and stable ground must also be the footing upon which the foundations are laid to ensure that the resulting structure is plumb and level. Inspection must be made upon the materials utilized to build the structures and they must also be carved to the proper specifications. When constructed properly, the resulting structure is a solid edifice capable of lasting lifetimes.

History has typically been constructed along these lines but with bias. Many works have been created and lauded despite its construction on shaky foundations and theories based on superiority complexes. While they have lasted lifetimes, foundational cracks and gaps have appeared over time weaking the edifice. Bias hid truths. Yet, even in the cracks of those theories, the truth continues to creep through providing greater insight into the civilizations of the past while destroying biased interpretations that were meant to denigrate others.

Many in the modern era continue to be surprised at the capabilities of the ancient Egyptians. The mathematical theorem attributed to Pythagoras was widely utilized ages before his birth and taught to him during his studies in Egypt. Crowns and collar jewels worn by modern monarchs find their roots in Africa, Sumer, and other ancient civilizations. They are not modern creations but modifications of the original that fit modern times.

The noble act of filling the cracks solidifies the foundations of history. Continuous searches for more light often force researchers to look backwards to past events as references to confirm the solidity of the structure and to avoid building weak theories atop uncertain ground. The results of these reflections drive introspection and often result in corrections of misinterpretations or biased representations of historical records. Once the gaps are filled, new revelations abound producing new fruit from the healed ground from the research efforts. So, taking a step back to ensure that the targeted ground is solid is critical for forward movement.

Following this pattern is a noble cause. Its intent is progression and not salty regression. This is better illustrated with the story of Lot's wife, Ado, in the Holy Bible relative to the destruction of the cities of Sodom and Gomorrah. Ado turned back to look at the destruction of the cities and was turned into a pillar of salt. Her act was intended to portray her desire as regressive because she appeared to be complicit with the ways of Sodom and backslide. Lot and his daughters, however, remained progressive, avoided backsliding, and embraced that which was to come as directed by God.

True historians do not look backwards to embrace or adopt the ways of old. They look back to ensure that the foundation is solid before building. Lot heeded the directions with full knowledge of the vile history of the cities from personal experience. Aware of Sodom's weak moral foundation, it was not suitable land for bearing spiritual fruit. Therefore, it failed to qualify as stable ground forcing a migration. For only upon solid ground will an edifice stand solidly for ages.

This concept forces noble seekers of light to perform their due diligence in all endeavors to fill the cracks in history's foundations before declaring it prepared for construction. The documented fillers provide a chronology of corrections that define the substances utilized to fill the gaps. The result is a repaired foundation and a solid base upon which future works can be solidly built.

The intent of this work is to fill cracks in the historical foundations of fraternal orders, faiths, histories, and nations of people through examinations of heraldry and faith. The sources of heraldic emblems for Freemasonry and other fraternal organizations extend well beyond the Knights Templar and link to ancient civilizations. The concept of faith is as ancient as the days predating modern religions by millennia, but multiple faiths have also influenced heraldic symbology. Through these avenues, cracks in the historical foundations of heraldry and faith are revealed and substance is being provided to fill them. In doing so, the ground for future research into these practices will be better prepared for construction and produce greater fruits for posterity.

Table of Contents

INTRODUCTION TO HERALDRY 1

    Coats of Arms 7

    Emblems 11

    Heraldic Jurisprudence................................ 20

FOUNDATIONS OF FAITH 33

    Theism of Egypt, Mesopotamia & Palestine 35

    Asian and Indian Theism 60

    Greco-Roman Polytheism................................. 68

    Judeo-Christian Monotheism 76

    Arabian Monotheism and American Effects................. 98

    The Holy Writs...119

SYMBOLIC DEPICTIONS 123

    The Cross 124

    Winged Standards 152

    Celestial and Terrestrial Standards........................... 166

    Modern Symbolism....................................... 170

HERALDIC REGALIA 179

Crowns of Egypt 184

Raiment and Vestments 214

Crook and Flail 233

The Staff and the Sword 239

The Gavel 260

SIGNETS AND LANDMARKS 263

Seals 264

Rings 273

Monuments 280

AFTERWORD 309

APPENDIX 315

Roman Legion Heraldic Inspirations I

Polytheistic Deities with Commonalities III

Leaders of Masonic Bodies & Counterparts IV

General Timeline of Ancient Empires VIII

Timeline of the Origins of Major Faiths LXI

"De Insigniis et Armis" Translation LXIII

Table of Figures

Figure 1 American, Moroccan, Israeli, and Pan-African Flags 5

Figure 2 Coat of Arms 10

Figure 3 Square and Compasses 12

Figure 4 Roman Eagle 13

Figure 5 Contested Warbelton Shield and Modified Gorges Shield 21

Figure 6 Contested Scrope Shield and New Grosvenor Shield 21

Figure 7 Armorial Arms, England, circa 1520AD 23

Figure 8 United Nations Display of Flags 31

Figure 9 Heraldic Emblem of Ashur 37

Figure 10 Map of Egypt and Mesopotamia 1450BC 38

Figure 11 Map of Israel and Judah 52

Figure 12 King Jehu pays tribute to King Shalmaneser III 54

Figure 13 Polytheistic Deities across Old World Nations 74

Figure 14 Kaaba at Mecca 101

Figure 15 Drew Ali, W.F. Muhammad, Elijah Muhammad 110

Figure 16 Noble Drew Ali with flags 112

Figure 17 Table of Holy Writs 120

Figure 18 Trinity of Hinduism 121

Figure 19 Crosses of Christendom 128

Figure 20 The Ankh, Tau Rho Cross and Chi Rho 132

Figure 21 Godfrey de Bouillon 143

Figure 22 Papal and Masonic Hierarchy 147

Figure 23 Emblem of Papacy 150

Figure 24 Table of Roman Legions 153

Figure 25 Roman Standards *166*

Figure 26 32nd and 33rd Degree Eagles *176*

Figure 27 Gold Diadem and a Coronatus *181*

Figure 28 32nd and 33rd Degree Diadems *183*

Figure 29 Atef of Osiris *185*

Figure 30 Crowns of Egypt *186*

Figure 31 Pschent with Nemes of Amenhotep III *187*

Figure 32 Amenhotep III, Tutankhamun and Ramesses IX *189*

Figure 33 Evolution of the Mitre and Papal Tiara *192*

Figure 34 Denars of Emperor Constantine the Great *195*

Figure 35 King Clovis and a Denarius of King Charlemagne *198*

Figure 36 Crowns of Amenhotep III, Richard I & Edward III *198*

Figure 37 Crown of St. Edward *200*

Figure 38 Scottish Rite and York Rite Caps and Crowns *203*

Figure 39 Knights Templar Caps and Chapeaus *204*

Figure 40 Supreme Council Member Crowns *205*

Figure 41 Masonic Top Hat and Shriner Fez *206*

Figure 42 Mehmed the Conqueror and Mahmud II *208*

Figure 43 William J. Florence and John G. Jones *210*

Figure 44 Shrine Logo *211*

Figure 45 Fez and Scottish Rite Crown Comparisons *213*

Figure 46 Mannequin of King Tutankhamun and Relief *218*

Figure 47 Zucchetto *220*

Figure 48 Shendyt, Hebrew Ephod, and Assyrian Tunic *223*

Figure 49 Roman Catholic and Orthodox Cassocks *223*

Figure 50 Pectoral Crosses *225*

Figure 51 Potentate and Past Potentate Jewels *231*

Figure 52 Osiris, Khonsu, Horus and King Tutankhamun *234*

Figure 53 Crosiers of the Orthodox Catholic Church *243*

Figure 54 Templar Arming Sword and Scimitar *250*

Figure 55 Scottish Rite Camp *259*

Figure 56 Judges' Gavel and Masonry Hammer *261*

Figure 57 Sumerian Basha-Enzu Seal and Egyptian Cylinder *268*

Figure 58 Sumerian, Egyptian Scarab, and Hebrew Seals *270*

Figure 59 Seals of King Henry VI and King Henry VIII *272*

Figure 60 Rings of Tutankhamun, Amenhotep I and Sa-Neith *275*

Figure 61 Signets of Marcus Antonius, Tiberius, and Akakios *277*

Figure 62 14th Degree Ring and 33rd Degree Ring *278*

Figure 63 Totem Poles *281*

Figure 64 Obelisk at Temple of Seti I at Abydos *283*

Figure 65 Relief of Seti communing with Amun-Ra *287*

Figure 66 Mastaba and Ziggurat *289*

Figure 67 Washington Monument *291*

Figure 68 Tabernacle of Moses *294*

Figure 69 Herod's Temple *297*

Figure 70 Logos for Masonic Bodies *303*

Figure 71 Security for the Rites *306*

"Heraldry is the fusion of fact and fancy, myth and manner, romance and reality. It is an exuberant union of family, art, and history."

– Charles Burnett

Introduction to Heraldry

Heraldry is the system by which coats of arms and other armorial bearings are devised, described, and regulated. It comprises the practice of devising, blazoning, and granting armorial insignia and the tracing and recording of genealogies.[1] The product is a unique insignia.

Medieval armorial bearings typically align with a family's bloodline or to a royal body and contain specific emblems that serve as unique identifiers.[2] Ancient Rome utilized the eagle to symbolize the Roman Empire. Legions bore the eagle on armor and regalia to clearly identify themselves as aligned with the empire.[3] Those who bore the insignia held allegiance to the owner of the heraldry and were, therefore, considered heralds.

Anciently, heralds were deployed at the command or at the will and pleasure of the chief commander. In Rome, the chief commander was the emperor who delegated authority to his regents and generals to command heralds for the glory of Rome. This was certainly the case in the Roman

---

[1] https://www.merriam-webster.com/dictionary/heraldry, retrieved 6/5/2023

[2] Clark, Hugh, An Introduction to Heraldry, Oxford University, 1829, p.249

[3] Cyrino, Monica Silveira, Big Screen Rome, Wiley, 2006, p.241

War with Palaepolis in 327 BC where Roman Consul Quintus Publilius Philo sent heralds to demand satisfaction from the Greeks bearing heraldry of Rome. Having taken the city due to dissatisfaction, the neighboring city of Neapolis also folded in 326 BC after communications between the heralds and its aristocracy achieved the goal of Roman subordination.[4]

This concept was utilized by Rome's successors, the kings of Europe. Lineage played clear roles in these endeavors as leadership was passed down through bloodlines. Well before European usage, though, this was a common practice of African Empires. So, the concept was not invented in the Dark Ages. It is as ancient as the days.

The art of heraldry though is commonly seen as a practice relegated to times of war. However, it was also heavily utilized during times of peace. In war, a herald would be sent to engage in formal communications with enemy and friendly forces alike to lay terms of warfare or alliance. Heraldry was the code that allowed the messenger

---

[4] Smith, Philip, From the Ascension of Philip of Macedon to the Roman Conquest of Carthage and Asia, The University of California, 1873, p. 291

to be recognized in the dark and in the light. By the same token an army could be considered as a heraldic force representing the plans of a commander. Through either method, the goal of sending a message is achieved.

Heraldic emblems are heavily utilized today by nations and organizations. The typical insignia of a nation is its flag, but other emblems are also leveraged for the same purpose. The Flag of the United States of America consists of thirteen equal horizontal stripes of red alternating with white, with a blue rectangle in the canton bearing fifty small, white, five-pointed stars arranged in nine offset horizontal rows, where rows of six stars alternate with rows of five stars. The fifty stars on the flag represent the fifty states in the union. The thirteen stripes represent the thirteen British colonies that declared independence from Great Britain forming the first states of the union.[5] Although not shown on the flag, the eagle, a Roman symbol, was also adopted as American symbolism. The pyramid topped with the all seeing eye is African in nature but is also adopted as an American symbol like the flag.

---

[5] Herb, Guntram H., David H. Kaplan, Nations and Nationalism, ABC-CLIO, 2008, p. 121

Figure 1 American, Moroccan, Israeli, and Pan-African Flags

The flags of Morocco and Israel are also unique but more simplified. The Moroccan flag is red with a green pentagram at its center. Red signifies bravery, strength, and valor; green represents the Seal of Solomon; and the pentagram represents Islam.[6] The Israeli flag is colored white and blue with the Star of David at its center flanked by blue stripes. These traditional prayer shawl colors of

---

[6] Bordeleau, Andre G., Flags of the Night Sky: When Astronomy Meets National Pride, Springer New York, 2013, p.286

Judaism represent heaven by blue and the earth by white.[7] Faith is the prime denominator between both flags.

The Pan-African flag focuses on heritage. It is a tri-color flag consisting of three equal horizontal bands of red, black, and green. The Universal Negro Improvement Association and African Communities League (UNIA-ACL) formally adopted it on August 13, 1920, in Article 39 of the Declaration of the Rights of the Negro Peoples of the World at its convention in New York City. Red represents the blood that unites all people of African ancestry and has been shed for liberation; black represents the people; and green represents the abundant natural wealth of Africa.[8]

So, flags represent nations, movements, ideals, and other forms of expression that symbolically communicate the values of the respective representative bodies. They are common forms of representation that remain as heraldic staples in modern times. As such, it is of the utmost importance that they are unique.

---

[7] Feisner, Edith Anderson, Ronald Reed, Bloomsbury Academic, 2003, p.192
[8] Kawashima, Masaki, American History, Race and the Struggle for Equality, Springer Nature Singapore, 2016, p.74

Coats of Arms

Many fraternal organizations utilize coats of arms as unique identifiers for their respective organizations. They showcase significant and ornate details which serve as integral parts for unique identification of specific fraternities and sororities. They contain multiple elements which are not limited to but do also include a crest, mantling, a helm, supporters, garter, a motto, and a shield. Members who wear them or carry flags that bear them are, therefore, heralds for the organizations and should take great care in their deportment when adorning them.

Most of these organizations are incorporated providing specific protections under the laws of the United States of America. Their unique naming conventions provides greater protection under the law aiding in the prevention of the emergence of imposters utilizing the same or similar names. Their coats or arms are also trademarked to prevent direct duplication. Following this pathway, Greek fraternities and sororities have minimized avenues for imposter organizations to be formed. While there may be individuals who perpetrate fraudulent affiliation, they are quickly weeded out after due trial and examination.

A method to ensure regularity and mutual support was formulated by Black Greek Letter Organizations (BGLOs). The National Pan-Hellenic Council (NPHC) was organized in 1929 by members of Alpha Kappa Alpha Sorority, Delta Sigma Theta Sorority, Zeta Phi Beta Sorority, Omega Psi Phi Fraternity and Kappa Alpha Psi Fraternity. The initial impetus was due to a lack of recognition by Indiana University of other BGLOs on campus in 1927. Subsequent meetings in 1928 and 1929 produced the NPHC with representation from each of the established fraternities and sororities. The organization was officially organized in 1929 and its constitution adopted on May 10, 1930.[9] Alpha Phi Alpha Fraternity and Phi Beta Sigma Fraternity joined in 1931. Sigma Gamma Rho Sorority joined in 1937 and Iota Phi Theta Fraternity, which was organized in 1963, was added to the council in 1996 increasing the number to nine. This is the source of the nickname for the council – "The Divine Nine".[10]

---

[9] Kimbrough, Walter M., Black Greek 101, Farleigh Dickinson University Press, 2003, p. 35
[10] Ross, Lawrence, The Divine Nine: The History of African American Fraternities and Sororities in America, Kensington, 2001, pp.37-38

The primary motivation of the NPHC is mutual support in undergraduate, graduate, and professional arenas. Through regular communications, the NPHC platform serves as a method to regulate, by general consent, actions performed by the organizations relative to membership indoctrination and other responsibilities. As it relates to coats of arms, most follow the same basic methodologies that incorporate their unique emblems into visual representations of the royalty of their organizations. In maintaining uniformity, they sustain a general framework for operations which is recognized and generally followed by all to date.

Relative to their coats of arms, the typical structure for each coat includes:[11]

- Crests are typically showcased atop the coats and are supported by other structures.

- The crest, separated by a wreath or torse, sits atop the helm or helmet which represents the headgear of the coat.

---

[11] http://cagenweb.org/plumas/nosuchthing.htm#crest retrieved 6/9/2023

- The helm is supported by the shield, which contains additional elements, and secondary supporters to maintain the structural integrity of the coat of arms.

- The coat is decorated with mantle which decorates the helm like the mane of a male lion while garter decorates the shield.

- The entire representation rests upon the motto which is the guiding force for the coat.

Altogether, the entire coat of arms becomes a complete heraldic representation for the respective entity.

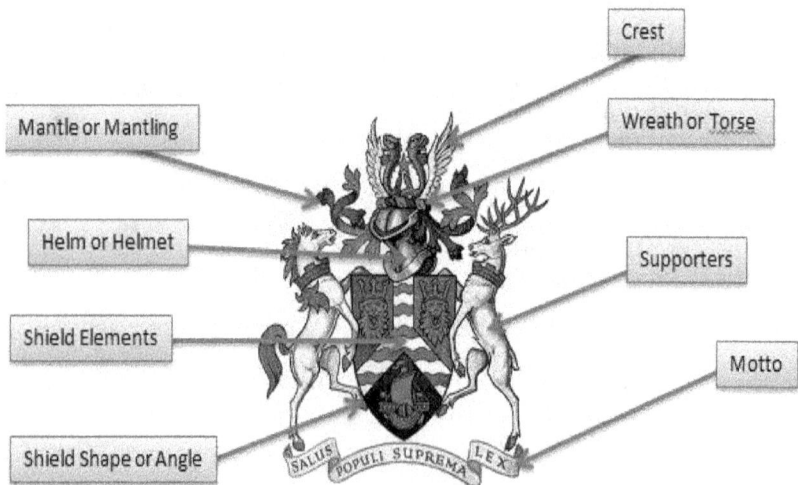

Figure 2 Coat of Arms

Emblems

Many organizations do not necessarily utilize a coat of arms as its primary heraldic representation. However, some utilize unique emblems to identify themselves in a general manner. The lack of specificity, though, can pose challenges allowing imposters to usurp the emblem. If unchecked, the usurpation can remain in place for years to come under the protection of the law.

Although there is no generally accepted coat of arms for Freemasonry, there is a specific emblem that is associated with the organization. The Square and Compass is widely known as a Masonic emblem. It is an insignia which pays tribute to the art and mastery of the science of building and privilege of brotherhood under God.[12] The emblem is not only placed on flags but also on regalia and daily wear to identify members of the Masonic Order. While there are other emblems associated with the fraternity, the Square and Compass is the most acceptable heraldic representation.

---

[12] Mackey, Albert Gallatin, Edward L. Hawkins, An Encyclopedia of Freemasonry and Its Kindred Sciences, Masonic History Company, 1913, pp.708-709

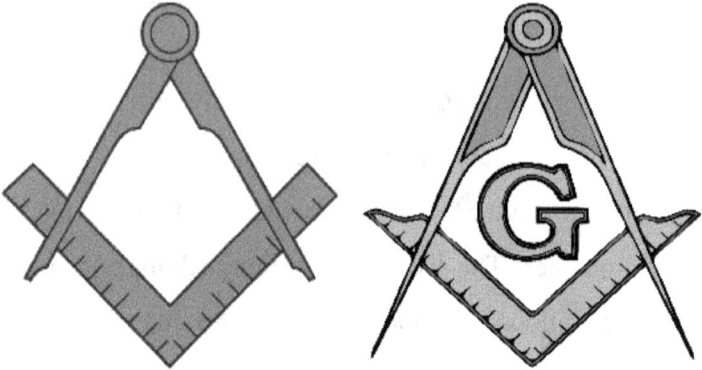

Figure 3 Square and Compasses

It is unfortunate, though, that imposters have also taken advantage of utilizing the emblem for their own gains under the protection of local laws. Some versions of the Square and Compass emblem are trademarked. Yet, the variations remain in the thousands or more. Therefore, lineage is the factor that is utilized to separate imposters from those who legitimately can wear the insignia. Only those from a recognized lineage can be the true heralds for the fraternity.

The manner through which imposters are identified is also through strict trial and due examination. Sadly, due to the naming conventions of Masonic organizations, imposters show no shame and tend to utilize secondary qualifiers to separate themselves from legitimate bodies.

For example, ancient Roman legions were recognized by the letters "SPQR" which equated to "Senate Populus Que Romanus" which translated means "The Senate and People of Rome". [13] There is no secondary qualifier in the naming convention. Only "SPQR" is present preventing confusion. Conversely, the naming convention for a Masonic Grand Lodge does have a secondary qualifier which typically is "F. & A.M." equating to "Free and Accepted Masons" or "A.F.&A.M." equating to "Ancient Free and Accepted Masons". [14] This opens the door for multiple iterations.

Figure 4 Roman Eagle

---

[13] Mouritsen, Henrik, Politics in the Roman Republic, Cambridge University Press, 2017, p.6

[14] Mackey, Albert Gallatin, Robert Ingham Clegg, William James Hughan, Mackey's History of Freemasonry, Masonic History Company, 1921, p.830

It is the secondary qualifier, in many cases, that allows imposter organizations to incorporate under the laws of the land under a unique name. They may call themselves Freemasons even though their lineage does not source to a valid foundation.[15] Local and national entities consider Freemasonry as a private organization. Since the affairs of private organizations are kept private, there typically is no issue or conflict with the local or national statutes unless the laws of the land are broken. As long as the organization meets the qualifications for incorporation, its private lineage is a private matter and irrelevant under the law.

In 1916, the Most Worshipful National Grand Lodge of Free and Accepted Ancient York Masons of the United States of America (FAAYM) filed suit against the Most Worshipful Prince Hall Grand Lodge of Ohio to attempt to prove its legitimacy in a court of law. The court ruled that the National Grand Lodge failed to show lineage to the charter of African Lodge #459, which is the original charter offered to Prince Hall by the Grand Lodge of England

---

[15] Summers, Martin, Manliness and Its Discontents: The Black Middle Class and the Transformation of Masculinity, 1900-1930, University of North Carolina Press, 2005, pp.63-64

(Premier) of 1784. Despite the failure, activities by the National Grand Lodge continued operations without interruption by the law because it was still a unique, private organization. As such, it continued to operate in a clandestine manner forcing the Prince Hall Grand Lodge of Ohio to fend for itself in fraternal circles.[16]

Freemasonry in the State of Illinois found itself in conflict in the 20th Century on account of historical challenges relative to race in that extended from the middle of the 19th Century. The Most Worshipful Prince Hall Grand Lodge, Free and Accepted Masons, State of Illinois could successfully trace its lineage to the charter of African Lodge #459. In 1996, the source was re-affirmed by the United Grand Lodge of England (UGLE), considered the Mother Grand Lodge of Freemasonry. The UGLE is the product of a merger between the Premier and Ancient Grand Lodges of England. The Most Worshipful Grand Lodge, Ancient Free and Accepted Masons, State of Illinois could also trace its lineage to a legitimate Masonic source.

---

[16] Wesley, Charles Harris, The History of Prince Hall Grand Lodge of Free and Accepted Masons of the State of Ohio, 1849-1960, Central State College Press, 1961, pp.189-191

So, in 1998, both organizations, satisfied with their origins of legitimacy, agreed to mutual recognition.[17]

In Illinois, the strict trial and due examination found both organizations in the right and, together, they worked to secure Freemasonry in the state. The nature of the trial and examination ties back to the ability to detect an imposter based on facts. If no evidence exists to confirm that an individual or organization was ever introduced to the Degrees of Freemasonry in a legitimate fashion, then the individual or organization is an imposter.

This designation is black and white but remains as a private distinction only within the fraternal circle. If an organization sources to one who was expelled from Freemasonry, then this is a clear red flag that the organization is illegitimate. Yet, as the designation is a private matter, it is a gray area to the laws of the land.

The Conference of Prince Hall Grand Masters was organized as a method for legitimate Prince Hall Grand

---

[17] Proceedings, Most Worshipful Prince Hall Grand Lodge of Illinois, Official Acts, Grand Master Willie B. Evans Sr., MWPHGL of Illinois, 1998

Lodges to congregate, share ideals, and agree on courses of action collectively to secure the Prince Hall Masonic Order. Its roots trace back to the National Masonic Convention held in the City of Chicago, Illinois on August 23, 1887. Although the convention met multiple times over the course of the next score, they did not meet annually. This would not occur until 1920 when the Conference of Grand Masters (COGM) was officially organized. Annual sessions have remained intact since 1922.[18]

The primary premise of the conference was to secure Prince Hall Freemasonry for posterity through conventions and collaboration. Although each Grand Lodge is autonomous, the exchange of ideas and recommendations have helped to ensure consistency in practices and teachings of Masonic principles. In 1944, the COGM recommended that all seek to incorporate "Prince Hall" in the name of their Grand Lodges. While all could not accomplish the task, it was prompted as a method to clearly identify Prince Hall Affiliated Grand Lodges distinguishing

---

[18] https://www.conferenceofgrandmasterspha.org/single-post/2017/04/22/history, retrieved 6/5/2023

themselves from other so-called Masonic organizations.[19] Subsequent conventions adopted the following goals:[20]

- To discuss together the role of the Freemason in the Great Society; and ways and means of enhancing the image of Prince Hall Masonry.
- To discuss, plan and project methods for building membership and expanding the service of Masonry to the community, state and nation.
- To discuss together the role of the Conference and its importance to Prince Hall Masonry.

These goals remain the clear tasks of the Conference of Grand Masters that survives to this date.

Although there may be good men in illegitimate Masonic ranks, their attachment to a cloudy lineage does not bode well for recognition in the true Masonic ranks. Some may not even know that a break in lineage ever existed in the first place because of the bastardization of the Square and Compass emblem. There are thousands of

---

[19] Morris, S. Brent, The Complete Idiot's Guide to Freemasonry, Alpha Books, 2006, p.63
[20] Ibid

organizations across the United States of America that fall into this category. Therefore, it is critical that heraldry be properly protected and efforts for public education become more pervasive. It is this concept that underscores the importance of a viable and thriving Conference of Prince Hall Grand Masters. Uniting and addressing the private concerns minimizes the risk of diluting the Masonic brand.

While the Square and Compass is a universal emblem, other Masonic Rites, use different armorial bearings to distinguish themselves. The Scottish Rite and York Rite bodies are prime examples. Their male and female affiliations to the Masonic Order are outlined in their constitutions. They reaffirm a connection through specific membership qualifications and many have adopted the "Prince Hall Affiliation (PHA)" monicker in either their names, constitutions, or regalia to solidify the link.

Though various and romantic, in all instances, the heraldry of the Masonic Order, Fraternities and Sororities, and Titulary Houses tie back to ancient orders of royalty and servitude under which like-minded individuals have banded together to achieve some common goal. In Masonic organizations, the bond is further aligned with the belief in a higher power through multiple faiths. This is the substance of heraldry in today's era. Unity serves as the basis and banner upon which organizations thrive and contend today. As such, their banners, which incorporate their heraldry, must be protected and held in high esteem so that they remain consistent and true for posterity.

Heraldic Jurisprudence

Several nations and institutions have adopted laws of heraldic arms to govern the possession, usage, or display of armorial bearings. Trademarks do offer some protection under the current laws in many lands. But the concept sources from a 14th Century treaty on insignias and arms. Jurist and law professor at the University of Padua, Bartolus de Saxoferrato who authored "De Insigniis et Armis" as a framework for the rights to grant and bear arms. The treaty was an effort to document this process and lay out terms and responsibilities for its enactment and enforcement across nations.[21]

---

[21] Woolf, Cecil Nathan Sidney, Bartolus of Sassoferrato:His Position in the History of Medieval Political Thought, University Press, 1913, p.17

Figure 5 Contested Warbelton Shield and Modified Gorges Shield

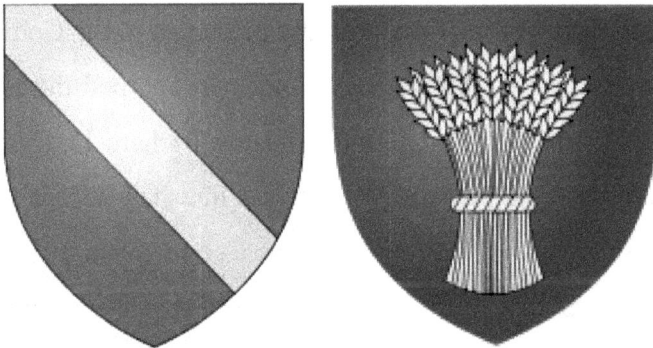

Figure 6 Contested Scrope Shield and New Grosvenor Shield

In the case of Warbelton vs. Gorges in 1347AD in England, a baseline like Saxoferrato's treaty was utilized to settle a coat of arms dispute between John de Warbelton and Theobald de Gorges. Warbelton found issue with Gorges' coat of arms, which was identical to his, at the Siege of Calais in 1346AD. Warbelton presented the conflict to Henry of Grosmont, Earl of Lancaster and

Senechal of England. In 1347AD, Henry convened a Court of Honour consisting of six knights from the siege to hear the claims of both Warbelton and Gorges. Having found Warbelton's claim superior, Gorges was directed to change his arms. In doing so, Gorges added a chevron.[22]

In the case of Scrope vs. Grosvenor in 1389AD in England, the Saxoferrato's baseline was directly leveraged to settle a coat of arms dispute between Richard Scrope and Robert Grosvenor. It was initially presented to the Court of Chivalry in 1386AD because both men adorned the same coat of arms while in service of King Richard II. Despite Grosvenor's claim that his familial line had adorned the coat since his ancestor William the Conqueror in 1066AD, he lost. Scrope's claim was adopted by the Court of Chivalry three years later with the support of King Richard who issued his verdict on May 27, 1390, and ordered Grosvenor to change his arms.[23]

---

[22] Gorges, Raymond, Frederick Brown, The Story of a Family through Eleven Centuries, Illustrated by Portraits and Pedigrees: Being a History of the Family of Gorges, Merrymount Press, 1944, p.37
[23] Rogers, Clifford J., The Oxford Encyclopedia of Medieval Warfare and Military Technology, Oxford University Press, 2010, pp.242-243

Figure 7 Armorial Arms, England, circa 1520AD

King Richard III established a College of Arms in 1484AD in the City of London to manage known coats of arms. King Henry VIII ordered the recording and validation of the arms that were in use in England. The commission to fulfill this directive began in 1530AD and continued through the 17th Century.[24] Those arms which had not been issued appropriately were torn down by the commission who also directed the house on how to proceed to obtain legitimate designations. The results were documented and maintained by the College of Arms by the hands of the following officers:

- Pursuivants

- Heralds

- Kings of Arms

Of the officers, the Kings of Arms were the senior-most officials.

Pursuivants were considered local officials of arms and junior officers in the College of Arms serving as attendants

---

[24] Ibid, p.254

to higher offices. Knights were also able to appoint them. In England, there were four Pursuivants in Ordinary:[25]

1. Rouge Croix

    • Oldest of the four, the office is named after the Cross of St. George or red Crusader cross.

2. Blue Mantle

    • Created by King Henry V, it was designated in service of the Order of the Garter.

3. Rouge Dragon

    • Created by King Henry VII, it represents the royal badge, which is the red dragon of Cadwaldar, a symbol for Wales.

4. Portcullis

    • Also created by King Henry VII, it represents the Beaufort family.

---

[25] Gough, Henry, A Glossary of Terms Used in British Heraldry with a Chronological Table, Illustrative of Its Rise and Progress, J.H. Parker, 1847, pp.256-257

Scotland and Ireland also had designated Pursuivants who were recorded by the College of Arms.

Many Masonic Grand Lodges incorporate the Office of Grand Pursuivant to perform this administrative task at Grand Lodge events. In doing so, the Grand Pursuivant would announce and escort applicants for admission and ensure that all are properly regaled in compliance with general Masonic standards and jurisdictional requirements.[26] It is generally accepted that regalia may hold distinctions that uniquely identify style and rank of office or, for visitors, specific customizations that identify their home jurisdiction. While collar jewels for each office and apron emblems remain consistent across Masonic jurisdictions, it ultimately falls under the Grand Master of the host jurisdiction to determine if customized regalia meets the standard in his domain.

In England, heralds are ranked second in the hierarchy of the College of Arms and are seen as diplomats and messengers between parties. They convey messages within and outside of the college to impacted parties and have

---

[26] The Freemason's Repository, E.L. Freeman & Son, 1895, p.238

historically served as messengers between enemy camps at times of war. There were initially six English heralds:[27]

1. Chester

   - Dating to the 14th Century, this office initially represented Edward, Prince of Wales, the Black Prince.

2. Lancaster

   - Established in 1347AD, this office represented the House of Lancaster.

3. Richmond

   - Established in 1421AD, this heraldic office represented the Estate of Richmond and appointed overseers.

4. Somerset

   - Heraldic office which served the Duke of Somerset.

5. Windsor

   - Heraldic office representing the Order of the Garter since 1348AD.

---

[27] Gough, Henry, A Glossary of Terms Used in British Heraldry with a Chronological Table, Illustrative of Its Rise and Progress, J.H. Parker, 1847, p.16-164

6. York

- Heraldic office representing York and adorning the emblem of the white rose.

At a battle during the Hundred Years War between England and France on October 25, 1415, heralds witnessed and recorded the events. At this particular battle, the English and French Heralds also communicated between the two armies. At the conclusion of the battle, they negotiated all events captured from their records which helped to determine the outcomes of the battle including the victor. With England set as the victor in this battle, the right to name the battle fell to King Henry V who selected the "Battle of Agincourt" as its name.[28]

The King of Arms is the most senior level at the College of Arms. By order of the crown, the King of Arms has the authority to grant armorial bearings and certify the usage of existing ones.[29] The office must be highly effective in marshalling the proper utilization of armorial

---

[28] Rogers, Clifford J., The Oxford Encyclopedia of Medieval Warfare and Military Technology, Oxford University Press, 2010, p.106
[29] Ibid, p.173

bearings which is crucial in maintaining their integrity. In England, there were three Kings of Arms:[30]

1. Garter
   - Principal officer instituted by King Henry V in 1417AD attending to Windsor.
2. Clarenceaux
   - Second ranking officer attending to the East, West, and South of the River Trent.
3. Norroy
   - Third ranking officer attending to the North of the River Trent.

It is the integrity that ensures uniqueness in bearings. The proper lineal usage and dissemination within familial lines among those who are qualified to bear them is critical. As such, all three roles – Pursuivants, Heralds, and Kings of Arms – provide the necessary oversight for the proper protection of heraldic emblems and standards for utilization.

---

[30]Ibid, pp.173-174

Many other nations host similar branches of government that provide heraldic oversight. France had its own College of Arms from 1407 to 1790 but has maintained the National Commission of Heraldry since 1960. Kenya established a College of Arms in 1968. The Canadian Heraldic Authority was established in 1988. These offices controlled the registry of nobility, where applicable, and granted coats of arms to entities for personal, governmental, military, and other purposes.[31] In doing so, they are the heraldic authorities for their respective nations ensuring that integrity is maintained.

The United States of America, on the other hand, does not maintain a specific College of Arms but does work through its Patent and Trademark Office to register unique ownership and symbols to individuals, families, corporations, and other organizations. This is paramount to the identity of the nation whose founding roots are not tied a founding monarchy but to a republic of citizens.[32] As

---

[31] George, Alexandra, Constructing Intellectual Property, Cambridge University Press, 2012, p.283
[32] Fountain, Marc, Coats of Arms: An Introduction to the Science and Art of Heraldry, Modern History Press, 2022, pp.6-7

such, the lack of nobility does not require a College of Arms but does require an authority to ensure uniqueness.

Figure 8 United Nations Display of Flags

The United Nations also does not maintain a College of Arms but does work to ensure that its heraldic emblems are unique and that the heraldry of the nations within its conference, whether democratic republic or monarchy, are documented. This is necessary to ensure that recognized nations receive invitations and are admitted to its proceedings. All flags are represented at the sessions and displayed in alphabetical order by way of its English pronunciation to promote solidarity and identify all who have a voice.[33] It is through this method that heraldic authority is expressed by way of invite-only access.

Although the laws of nations vary within their own respective boundaries, the mode of recognition remains clear and pervasive even across the vast oceans and seas that typically define the boundaries of nations. A nation's flag is its primary emblem of identification and is its soul. No matter what faith a nation acknowledges, its soul is worth protecting.

---

[33] United States Delegation to the United Nations General Assembly, The United States and the United Nations, U.S. Government Printing Office, 1946, pp.5-6

Foundations of Faith

A key factor in the development or selection of emblems for representation is one's individual beliefs or those beliefs of an entity. Many coats of arms are adorned with emblems of faith or figures, whether they be animate or inanimate beings or objects, which represent the soul of the bearer. Other emblems represent the style or rank of the bearer. The collective representation provides a clear picture of who or what the herald represents extending the will and intentions of the benefactor. The way this is done, therefore, forever brands the represented entity in a positive or negative light.

As authority over heraldic representations were managed within respective entities by general codes of conduct or procedures, internal management generally fell in alignment with religion. It was common to see the ankh in Egyptian symbolism and the cross on Christian coats of arms. Therefore, familiarity between nations and their respective coats of arms were instituted through the relationships that were most likely established by way of conflict, trade, historical knowledge, or some other manner of acquaintance.

The dogma adopted by a nation, in most cases, was a predictor of a positive or negative response. A sin in one culture may be acceptable in another. Similar religious dogmas could also have been common ground to establish relationships. As such, a determination, based on customs observed by a herald, can associate the status of friend or foe to the heraldic emblem. Furthermore, Allies did not always maintain coalitions. The best interests of a nation could drive efforts to sway the power dynamic. The acts of the ancient kingdoms can attest to this as their dogma and dictates appeared to drive their actions.

Theism of Egypt, Mesopotamia & Palestine

During the 4th Dynasty of Egypt, Assur, located north of Mesopotamia, was under the rule of the Hurrian Kingdom which was a province under the Hittite empire.[34] Assur endured through the second split of Egypt into Memphis and Thebes and their subsequent reunion in 2125BC.

---

[34] Burney, Charles, Historical Dictionary of the Hittites, Rowman and Littlefield Publishers, 2018, p.139

During this era, Assur grew significantly from trade gaining independence by 2025BC.[35]

Like the Hurrians, the Assyrian religion was polytheistic, but it shifted to a henotheistic system. They believed in the existence of multiple deities but that the god Ashur was superior to the others. Ashur was considered the father of all gods and was, thusly, designated as the god of kings. The emblem of Ashur captured on carvings identify Ashur as a king encircled by an eagle's wings.[36] It became an Assyrian custom for the king to become Ashur's representative and is denoted in the specific heraldry associated with the empire.

Assyria stood independently for four centuries until the Hurrians reclaimed sovereignty in 1680BC. They were ousted by the Mittani who annexed Assyria in 1472BC. Assyria ejected them near 1400BC and conquered the rest of their lands by 1250BC securing the Northern and Central Middle East. By the time of the Israelite exodus from

---

[35] Thomas, Alexander R., Gregory M. Fulkerson, City and County: The Historical Evolution of Urban-Rural Systems, Lexington Books, 2021, p. 172
[36] Ibid, p.202

Egypt, Assyria had conquered Babylon near 1220BC and the Hittites in 1208BC and gained control of the entire Middle East. The Western region of the Middle East was conquered in 1208BC. From this base, the nation extended southward along the Mediterranean coast eventually conquering Phoenicia in 1076BC.[37]

Figure 9 Heraldic Emblem of Ashur

Relative to dogma, the expansion of Assyria fell in direct alignment with its faith. The divine mandate of Ashur was to expand the lands of Assyria giving the king the right to subjugate foreign lands, control their products and bring order to the lands under his rule. The method provided an efficient model for economic control supported by a god

---

[37] Ibid, p.172

under the direction of the god-king.[38] As such, for the masses, the gains of the nation became divine in nature further supporting the role of the king as the official representation of the god.

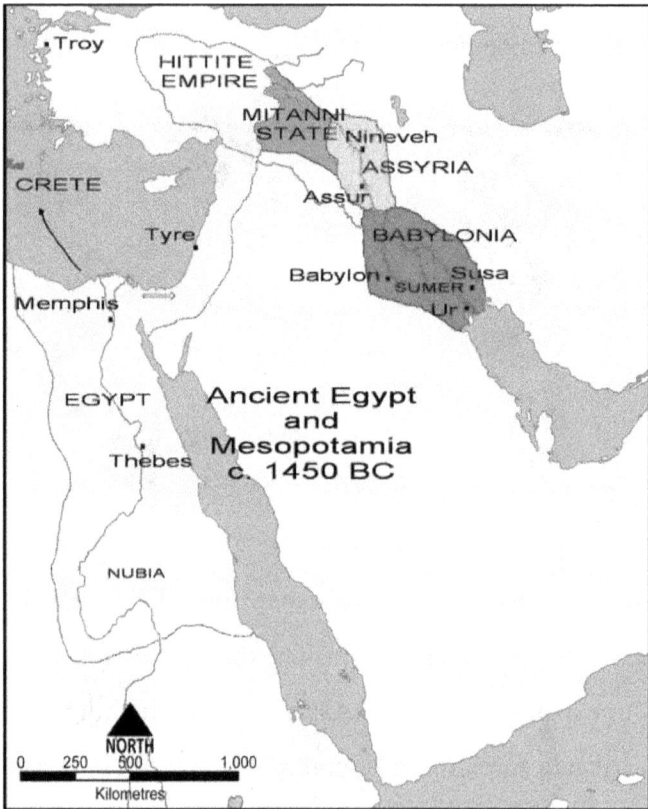

Figure 10 Map of Egypt and Mesopotamia 1450BC

---

[38] Morris, Ian, The Dynamics of Ancient Empires: State Power from Assyria to Byzantium, Oxford University Press, 2008, pp.47-48

Other Assyrian gods were also revered and seen as the primary deities by other cities under the empire:[39]

- Enki, god of water and knowledge, was the patron god of the City of Eridu.
- Enlil, god of the wind, air, earth and storms, was the patron god of Nippur.
- Anu, god of the sky, was the patron god of Uruk. In each locale, the patron god was considered the supreme.

Although Babylon had been conquered, the worship of their gods had not been abolished. In fact, some were adopted and worshipped by the conquered and conquerors after Assyrian domination. Also henotheistic, nine main deities were revered by Babylonians:[40]

- Marduk, considered the supreme being of the nine deities, was the patron god of Babylon and was symbolized by the dragon.

---

[39] Kramer, Samuel Noah, John Maier, Myths of Enki, The Crafty God, Wipf and Stock Publishers, 2020, p.16
[40] Ibid, p.144

- Ishtar, goddess of love and sexuality or fertility, was also worshipped in Uruk as Inanna by Assyrian converts.

- Nabu, god of literacy and wisdom, was the son of Marduk.

- Shamash was the god of the sun.

- Adad, like Enlil, was the god of the storm and rain.

- Tiamat was the goddess of the sea who mated with Apsu, god of ground water, to produce younger gods.

- Ea was the god of water and patron god of the City of Eridu.

- Nergal was the god of war, death and disease who reigned over the underworld.

There were eleven main deities of Ancient Egypt including Osiris, Isis, Horus, Seth, Ptah, Ra (Re), Hathor, Anubis, Thoth, Bastet, and Amun. Of them, the first four held special significance. Osiris, god of the underworld, and Isis, goddess of healing and magic, were husband and wife who birthed Horus. The copulation between Osiris and Isis occurred after the murder of Osiris by his brother,

Seth. Seth, subsequently, dismembered the remains of his brother and scattered them. Isis was able to gather all the remains except for the phallus. While she had power to restore, she could not fully do so without his manhood. As such, he was restored but restricted to the underworld.[41] Seth was the god of chaos and storms. Horus became the god of the sky and was depicted as a falcon. Ptah was the god of craftsmanship, Ra or Re was the god of the sun, Hathor was the goddess of fertility, Anubis was the god who prepared the dead, Thoth was the god of wisdom and writing, Bastet was the goddess of hunting and the moon, Amun was the god of the air.[42]

After the split of Egypt in 2180BC, Ptah became the primary deity of the Northern Kingdom and Amun, the primary deity for the Southern Kingdom. At Memphis, headquarters of the North, Ptah was represented by the Apis or bull. This emblem linked him to Hathor, goddess of

---

[41] Schomp, Virginia, The Ancient Egyptians, pp.54-57
[42] Ibid, pp.26-27

fertility. Together, this symbology situated Memphis as a capitol of strength and beauty.[43]

At Thebes, headquarters of the South, Amun, represented by the ram and the goose, was credited with securing the victory for independence of the Thebans by its strength, courage, and determination. The goose represents the latter. After the reconciliation between Memphis and Thebes in 2125BC, Amun and Ra became the primary deities.[44]

An attempt to shift to monotheism did not occur until the reign of Pharoah Amenhotep IV in 1353BC. He sought to remove Amun or Amen as the primary deity replacing him with Ra, also known as, Aten. Declaring himself as the representative of Aten, he changed his name from Amenhotep to Akhenaten to reflect this and forced monotheism on the Egyptian culture. His wife, Nefertiti, gave birth to several children including a son, Tutankhaten. After the death of the Pharoah in 1334BC and subsequent

---

[43] Shally-Jensen, Michael, Anthony Vivian, A Cultural Encyclopedia of Lost Cities and Civilizations, ABC-CLIO, 2022, p.178
[44] Ibid, p.100

leadership of Tutankhaten, Egypt reverted to its former state. In 1332BC, Tutankhaten changed his name to Tutankhamun as a signet of the restoration of henotheism which remained intact for the centuries that followed. [45]

The dominance of polytheism across the region served as common ground for relations between the Egyptian and Assyrian nations. While the henotheistic leadership may have varied, the similarities between the faiths are recognizable and relatable. Subordinate deities maintained similar representations of character and purpose. As such, it is highly likely that relationships were built upon this common ground making polytheism a signet, in a sense, of like-minded nations and potential allies.

From the 14th Century BC through the 11th Century BC, Egypt and Assyria had formal trade relations and worked through Phoenicia to ship and receive goods from the port of Tyre at the western edge of the Middle East to other domains through the Aegean Sea and Mediterranean Sea.[46] Tyre and Jerusalem were cities that constituted the Land of

---

[45] Ibid, pp.23-25
[46] Ibid, p.181

Canaan which was filled with other polytheistic tribes. After the exodus from Egypt, the land of Canaan became a prime target for the Israelites, a monotheistic tribe, because of polytheism.

A monotheistic nation, Jehovah, the God of Israel, selected the location and directed the Israelite army to take the Land of Canaan. The army was built directly from survivors of the exodus and their subsequent generations after a forty year period of travelling through the wilderness of the Sinai Peninsula. Tabernacles were created as temporary places of worship to indoctrinate and maintain the faith as a unifying force between the Twelve Tribes of Israel. With sustenance supplied by God, the tribes survived, a new generation of soldiers had sprung forth and they were prepared and positioned to take the land promised to them. After the death of Moses, Joshua led them to capture the land which was achieved near 1230BC.[47]

---

[47] Rice, Gene, Africa and the Bible – Corrective Lenses: Critical Essays, Cascade Books, 2019, p.19

Like the Assyrians and Hurrians to the North, the Canaanites were henotheistic. The primary gods of worship were El, Asherah, Ba'al, Yam, Mot, Astronoe, Hadad, Moloch, and Dagon. El was revered as the god of creation.[48] El and Asherah conceived the other gods in the pantheon.[49] Ba'al, god of war, was worshipped specifically by the Canaanites. Astronoe was goddess of misfortune and a consort of Baal.[50] Hadad was god of storms.[51] Mot or Muth was the god of death.[52] Dagon was god of farming.[53] Moloch was god of the sun.[54]

The characteristics of these deities are quite similar to the primary deities of the Assyrians, Babylonians, and Egyptians. El and Asherah hold the same parental qualities of gods as Osiris and Isis. Hadad and the Babylonian god, Adad, were both gods of the storm. Mot and the Egyptian

---

[48] Day, John, Yahweh and the Gods and Goddesses of Canaan, Bloomsbury Publishing, 2010, p.15
[49] Ibid, p.141
[50] Ibid, p.172
[51] Wood, William Carleton, The Religion of Canaan from the Earliest Times to the Hebrew Conquest, Hartford Theological Seminary, 1916, p.68
[52] Ibid, p.268
[53] Ibid, p.77
[54] Holy Bible, Leviticus 18:21

god, Anubis, both ruled the underworld. Moloch, Ra, and Shamash ruled the sun for Canaan, Babylonia, and Egypt respectively. Ba'al, Nargal and Seth were all considered rulers over war. Although the nations were separate and distinct, the similarities in function are undeniable.

Yet, to Israel, there was only one God, Jehovah, who guided them from captivity to the Canaanite lands. The continual challenge with the Israelites, though, was that they regularly slid away from Jehovah despite the successes achieved. This is reasonable to a degree considering that the nation had been under the control of polytheistic nations for centuries. They had gained expertise relative to the nature of the other gods due to massive societal exposure while under foreign rule, forced or unforced. So, shifting from their norm to the worship of a single, predominant deity was a large change.

Ba'al worship, for example, entered Egypt while the Israelites were complicit. Several Israelites adopted the Ba'alistic faith and its practices providing a reason for the decision to create a golden idol during the time of the Exodus. Moses, disgusted and disappointed with Aaron whom he left in command but constructed the idol, destroyed the golden calf.[55] The temptation to backslide was apparently too much for the Israelites to ignore.

Furthermore, the nomadic nature of the tribes did not create a great deal of certainty for them as compared to the solid, stable ground to which many had become accustomed while in captivity. Ironically, it appears that they felt was more secure in subordination to Egypt than their nomadic state. This most likely played a significant role in the psyche of Israel despite Jehovah's role in their deliverance and sustenance in the wilderness.

By the time of the Israelite conquest of Canaan, a new generation of Israelites had come forth to lead and guide the nation. Both Aaron and Moses died before the conquest. Jehovah dictated that they would not enter the promised land because of their lack of full compliance when travelling through the wilderness.[56] So, it was Joshua, a captain of Moses, who led the conquest and established the government of the nation in Canaan.

---

[55] Holy Bible, Exodus 32
[56] Holy Bible, Numbers 20:23-29

After Joshua's death, Judges were installed to maintain order, protect the nation, and promote the faith through prophets and priests. The Judges continually fought off polytheistic nations while the prophets received the word of Jehovah which, in addition to the dogma, was communicated to the citizens through the priests. The grip of the priests, however, did not hold well to the Israelites. Although they had taken the land, the Canaanites were still active throughout the lands. The Israelites, already familiar with polytheism, readily adopted their customs and intermixed faith and familial lines. This angered Jehovah who allowed them to become fodder for their polytheistic neighbors.

Under Judge Othniel's supervision near the turn of the 12th Century BC, the nation was oppressed by Mesopotamia which lasted eight years of his forty-eight years of leadership. The Moabites, neighbors to the Southeast, oppressed them under the term of Judge Ehud for eighteen years of his ninety-eight years of leadership.[57] The Canaanites; Midianites, Arabian neighbors;

---

[57] Holy Bible, Judges 3:9-30

Ammonites, situated north of Moab; and Philistines, Southwest neighbors off the shore of the Mediterranean Sea; all had significant terms of oppression over Israel culminating in over ninety years of subordination. Stability in faith and leadership was not restored until the period of the kings.

After the supervision of Judge Samson, Israel had become frustrated with the leadership model as evidenced by the continual shifts of its citizens from monotheism. As such, they cried out to the Samuel, the prophet, asking for a king to rule over them. Jehovah conceded directing the prophet to hearken to their voices.[58] Saul, the Benjaminite, was subsequently chosen through divine selection as communicated through the prophet.[59] In 1021BC, he was crowned Israel's first king of the region known as Palestine.[60]

Under King Saul's leadership, the twelve tribes reunited under the Kingdom of Israel and worked together to

---

[58] Holy Bible, 1 Samuel 8:19-22
[59] Holy Bible, 1 Samuel 9:17
[60] Taylor, James, The Earth, Xlibris US, 2013, p.92

remove all threats. Though deeply flawed, King Saul and his son, Jonathon, led legions to expel the Philistines from the land. He also led successful campaigns against the Amalekites, Southern neighbor to Philistia. Rather than kill all Amalekites as directed by Jehovah, King Saul detained King Agag as a trophy.[61] This incontinence became his downfall in the eyes of Jehovah who, subsequently, directed Samuel to the house of Jesse to anoint one of his sons as the future king. Of the sons, David was selected and anointed by the prophet.[62] He, however, did not ascend to the throne until Saul's death by his own sword.[63]

Like Saul, King David was also flawed but did achieve significant accomplishments for the kingdom. He designated the City of Jerusalem as the capitol for the Kingdom of Israel. A womanizer who once sent a soldier, Uriah, to the front line of battle to lay with his wife, Bathsheba, David was also most reflective on the impacts of God on his life as noted in the many Psalms he

---

[61] Holy Bible, 1 Samuel 15:18-35
[62] Holy Bible, 1 Samuel 16:1-13
[63] Holy Bible, 1 Samuel 31

authored.[64] He reigned as king for forty years and declared his son Solomon from Bathsheba as successor before his death in 970BC.[65]

King Solomon constructed the first temple at Jerusalem in 966BC which replaced the traveling tabernacles that were erected for worship.[66] Considered the wisest man on earth, he was the last king to rule a unified Israel. His indulgences lead to his downfall.

King Solomon's success in the construction of the temple, renown wisdom, and success in other endeavors, placed him in rare air during his reign. However, his reign did not end without controversy. Taxation was a high issue that complicated matters within the kingdom. It drove a revolt resulting in a separation creating the Kingdom of Israel and the Kingdom of Judah in 931BC.[67] Solomon's son Rehoboam led the Kingdom of Judah which consisted of the Tribes of Judah and Benjamin and was situated in the

---

[64] Holy Bible, 2 Samuel 11
[65] Fee, Gordon D., Robert L. Hubbard Jr., The Eerdmans Companion to the Bible, Eermans Publishing Company, 2011, p.228
[66] Ibid, p.233
[67] Ibid, p.228

South. The remaining ten tribes of Asher, Dan, Ephraim, Gad, Issachar, Manasseh, Naphtali, Reuben, Simeon, and Zebulon, constituted the Kingdom of Israel. They were under the leadership of Jeroboam, a former vassal of Solomon, with its capitol situated in Samaria.[68]

Figure 11 Map of Israel and Judah

---

[68] Ibid, p.236

Although the Kingdoms of Israel and Judah maintained the same monotheistic faith, they were surrounded by polytheistic nations from a territorial perspective in Palestine. The seaports of Gaza, Ashkelon, Ashdod, and Joppa at the Mediterranean Sea in Southwest Palestine was under the control of the Philistines. The seaports of Tyre, Sidon, and Byblos in Northwest Palestine were under the control of the Phoenicians who had been conquered by Assyria in 1076BC. With the Assyrians to the North and Northeast, the Babylonians to the East, and the Egyptians in the South, both kingdoms were precariously situated. Yet, the natural water barrier lessened the immediate risk at Jerusalem and the land to its South.

Trade routes established by King David and King Solomon through Jerusalem were the key methods through which the unified kingdom had expanded well beyond the general borders of Palestine. The Tribe of Judah provided the protection and support particularly around Jerusalem and the Southern region. After the split, however, the Northern Kingdom had immediately become more vulnerable as its reach extended east of the River Jordan to the boundaries of the Assyrian Empire and could no longer lean directly upon Judah for aid.

The Kingdom of Judah in the South was less vulnerable to attacks by Assyria and Babylon because its eastern border was the Dead Sea. This large body of water insulated them from direct land attacks. While the Sinani Peninsula also provided some cover from land attacks by the Egyptians in the South, the ports controlled by the Philistines namely Ashdod and Ashkelon provided key points of focus. Both ports were mouths of tributaries that extended from the Mediterranean Sea to the center of the Southern Kingdom and could have been a viable avenue to land troops and secure ground with Philistine assistance.

Figure 12 King Jehu pays tribute to King Shalmaneser III

All in all, the split of Israel into two separate kingdoms sent a clarion call to the polytheists that Palestine was vulnerable. The split also occurred at a time when Assyria had arguably become the most powerful polytheistic nation. The threats eventually forced Israel to make concessions.

By the 9th Century BC, the Northern Kingdom of Israel was forced to make an alliance with Assyria for survival. In 841BC, King Jehu made such an alliance with King Shalmaneser III to secure support against the Arameans, a Babylonian affiliate to its east.[69] Assyria eventually overran the Aramean states. In 729BC, it finally occupied Babylon securing the bulk of Mesopotamia. Logistically surrounded by enemies and lacking the full support of the Southern Kingdom of Judah, the Northern Kingdom fell to Assyria in 722BC.[70] The tribes that comprised the kingdom are considered the "Lost Tribes" because they were subsequently absorbed by various Assyrian states and their Israelite heritage was lost to a large degree.

---

[69] Lamb, David T., Righteous Jehu and His Evil Heirs: The Deuteronomist's Negative Perspective on Dynastic Succession, OUP Oxford, 2007, p.44

[70] Septuagint: History, Volume 1, Scriptural Research Institute, 2023, pp.171-172

By 721BC, Assyria's foothold in northern Palestine was further secured with an alliance with the Island of Cyprus in the Mediterranean Sea. The alliance centered on the bronze trade. In return, Cyprus became a point through which pressure could be placed upon the Port of Tyre on the west coast of northern Palestine.[71] By the end of the century, Assyria was in full control of the region.

The 7th Century BC was a period of flux for Assyria and increase for Babylon. During the era, Egypt sought to gain a foothold in the region and had constructed an alliance with the Kingdom of Judah, the leaders of the port cities of Sidon and Ashkelon, and the King of Accaron to expel Assyria from the Southeast. King Sennacherib of Assyria launched attacks against the cities crushing the alliance and expelling Egyptian influence from the region by 681BC. His son and successor, King Esarhaddon, extended his father's mission further diluting Egyptian influence. By 677BC, he pushed them back to Egyptian borders.

---

[71] Shally-Jensen, Michael, Anthony Vivian, A Cultural Encyclopedia of Lost Cities and Civilizations, ABC-CLIO, 2022, pp.236-237

Furthermore, he not only raided Egypt in 673BC but finally conquered the empire in 671BC.[72]

After the death of Esarhaddon in 669BC and ascension of his son King Ashurbanipal, Egyptian Pharoah Taharqa reoccupied Memphis and regained control of the delta.[73] While dealing with rising Egyptian fortitude under Taharqa's successor Tantamani, the tide of control in Egypt had begun to shift towards independence. The Assyrians were ultimately expelled from Egypt in 653BC.[74]

Shamash-Shum-Ukin, brother of Ashurbanipal, inherited the kingship of Babylon from Esarhaddon. The brothers engaged in civil war from 652BC to the death of Shamash-Shum-Ukin in 648BC.[75] Kandalu was appointed to fill the leadership void in Babylon through 627BC. Leadership of Assyria fell to Assur-Etil-Ilani in 631BC after the death of Ashurbanipal which was the start of a swift decline for the nation. Within a short period of rule,

---

[72] Ibid, p.237
[73] Ibid, p.41
[74] Pope, Charles N., Living in Truth: Archaeology and the Patriarchs (Part III), DomainOfMan.com, 2020, p.296
[75] Ibid, p.503

the new Assyrian king had proven that he could not maintain full control of his domain. In 626BC, a Babylonian eunuch, Sin-Sumu-Lisir instigated a rebellion overthrowing Assur-Etil-Ilani, securing Babylonian independence, and eventually taking leadership of the Assyrian throne.[76]

Babylonian control over Assyria extended through the middle of the 6th Century BC. Having conquered Philistia in 604BC securing key ports utilized by the Kingdom of Judah, the entirety of Palestine fell under its control. Judah was finally conquered in 586BC bringing an end to the final remnants of the Tribes of Israel. Control of all of Palestine remained intact under Babylonian rule until the Persian Conquest.[77]

Cyrus the Great, King of the Persian Empire, conquered Babylon in 549BC starting an era of expansion of the empire across Mesopotamia which lasted more than two

---

[76] McIntosh, Jane, Ancient Mesopotamia: New Perspectives, Bloomsbury Academic, 2005, pp.107-108
[77] Ibid, pp.108-110

centuries.[78] He allowed Jews to return to Jerusalem to rebuild the city and engage in monotheistic practices which would last through the succeeding centuries.[79] Cambyses II succeeded Cyrus in 530BC. He orchestrated the conquest of Egypt in 525BC but was killed in efforts to stop a rebellion in 522BC.[80] Replaced by Bardiya, who was assassinated the same year, King Darius the Great, ruled the Persian Empire from 522BC and was the first Persian to be heralded as Pharoah of Egypt.[81]

King Darius extended the efforts of Cyrus to a large degree particularly as it related to expansion into India and Asia. In 535BC, Cyrus conquered areas west of the Indus River which had been lost after his death in 530BC. In 518BC, Darius crossed the Himalayas into India and conquered areas in Punjab.[82] He continued to extend the Persian Empire and expand its primary faith, Zoroastrianism, which had already been long established.

---

[78] Ibid, p.113
[79] Ibid, p.113
[80] Briant, Pierre, From Cyrus to Alexander: A History of the Persian Empire, Penn State University Press, 2002, p.59
[81] Ibid, p.99
[82] Ibid, p.140

The teachings of Zoroaster are monotheistic and purport that there is a never-ending battle between good and evil. The supreme deity is Ahura Mazda whose nemesis is an evil spirit, Ahriman. The faith supports the free will of believers but promotes the Threefold Path of Asha which focuses on "good thoughts", "good words", and "good deeds". Following this path, Cyrus allowed other faiths like Judaism and Hinduism to publicly promote their dogma and doctrine.[83] King Darius also followed suit during his term of leadership.[84] This pattern, relative to the tolerance of multiple faiths, became the standard practice under Persian leadership.

Asian and Indian Theism

Hinduism had been an active part of Indus Valley Civilization culture since before 2000BC. The Indus Valley was situated South of Mesopotamia and East of Egypt across the Arabian Sea.[85] To Hindus, God is universal, and

---

[83] Boyce, Mary, A History of Zoroastrianism Under the Achaemenians, Brill, 2015, p.62

[84] Ibid, p.119

[85] Eliot, Charles, Hinduism and Buddhism: A Historical Sketch, Volume 1, E. Arnold, 2008, p.51

everyone is divine. Brahma, originally a mortal, is the original God and is the entity who created good, evil and life, from his own essence including other gods, demons, ancestors, and men with Manu being the first man.[86] This concept affirms that Hinduism essentially is pantheistic placing a focus on universal beliefs.

Karma is based upon the principal of cause and effect. The energy placed in the universe returns to the giver which may result in individuals returning to a lower state in their next life if negativity was predominant.[87] Moksha refers to the belief in the possibility of universal freedom and liberation from the earthly bounds.[88] Samsara refers to the cycle of birth, death, and rebirth and that all living beings experience the process of reincarnation.[89] These beliefs were passed through oral tradition through 1500BC and were documented in Vedas, revelations of sages that were revealed in meditative states.[90]

---

[86] Ibid, p.48
[87] Ibid, pp.194-195
[88] Ibid, p.44
[89] Ibid, p.L
[90] Ibid, p.40

Rituals were also incorporated to maintain a connection with the Hindu gods created by Brahma including Soma, the plant god; Agni, the god of fire; Brhaspati, the priestly god; Indra, the warrior god; Vayu, and Rudra, the storm and wind gods; Dyaus, the sky god; Varuna, god of the cosmos; Mitra, god of the night; and Vishnu, the pervade.[91] From the rituals, believers would receive insights when meditating by way of spiritual communion and act according to ten principles:[92]

1. Satya (Truth)
2. Ahimsa (Non-violence)
3. Brahmacharya (Celibacy, non-adultery)
4. Asteya (No desire to possess or steal)
5. Aparighara (Non-corrupt)
6. Shaucha (Cleanliness)
7. Santosh (Contentment)
8. Swadhyaya (Reading of scriptures)
9. Tapas (Austerity, perseverance, penance)
10. Ishwarpranidhan (Regular prayers)

---

[91] Ibid, pp.330-332
[92] Kapur, Kamlesh, Hindu Dharma-A Teaching Guide, Xlibris, 2023, pp.121-123

The principles served as the basis for a new revelation of Hinduism in the 6th Century BC named Buddhism.

Born in Lumbini in the 6th Century BC, Siddhartha Gautama, a royal prince, attained enlightenment at Bodh Gaya driving him to leave his royal estate and travel through India to share his revelations. Gautama's revelations were not caste restrictive which found him teaching particularly to citizens of the lower castes through his travels across the Indus Valley.[93] Monastic orders were established from devoted believers who promoted the aspects of the faith.

Gautama's revelation centered around the concept of Nirvana. He promoted that there was a balance between indulgence and asceticism which leads to freedom from ignorance, craving, rebirth, and suffering. These concepts were taught through the Noble Eightfold Path which is a type of mental training consisting of eight ethical and meditative practices - Right View, Right Resolve, Right

---

[93] Ibid, pp.115-117

Speech, Right Action, Right Livelihood, Right Effort, Right Mindfulness, and Right Concentration: [94]

- Right View refers to the acknowledgment of the four noble truths of reality. The Truth of Suffering refers to the ongoing state of dissatisfaction endured by all living beings. That suffering arises from causes or conditions that may or may not be controlled is the Truth of the Origin of Suffering. The Truth of Cessation is an affirmation that there is a possibility to reach a state where suffering has ceased. The Truth of the Path further affirms that there is a path that can be followed to reach cessation. Acceptance of these truths is a belief in their reality which limits suffering.

- Right Resolve focuses on maintaining the correct perceptions of reality. Suffering occurs when reality is not accepted. Resolving oneself thusly promotes Right Speech and Right Action. The intentions of words and actions towards upliftment rather than destruction led to greater connections will all.

---

[94] Ibid, pp.117-118

Together, they promote a Right Livelihood in which no one is intentionally harmed and that one does not over utilize resources. In doing so, others are not harmed if resources are utilized as needed.

- Right Effort refers to the continual journey of cultivating goodness and practicing those things which cause happiness. Right Mindfulness aids in guiding efforts. Awareness of situations around practitioners through self-examination and examination of one's surroundings, one may be able to adequately reflect on the full scenario and respond accordingly. In doing so, a positive and aware mental attitude should provoke an adequate response in dealing with reality now and beyond.

- Right Concentration refers to maintaining a keen focus on the object of meditation and developing a stable mind. By avoiding detrimental thoughts during meditation, the mind naturally flows to points of positivity through which constructive revelations can be forged.

An ethical focus through Right Action, Right Speech, and Right Livelihood develops practical, ethical responses as the norm for practitioners. Meditating through Right Mind, Right Effort, and Right Concentration, helps to define the object upon which meditation is focused. Wisdom through Right View and Right Resolve helps to ensure that the correct insights are revealed and that the appropriate action is applied to produce positive outcomes. Mastery of these concepts produces Nirvana or freedom from suffering.[95]

The teachings of Buddha were spread primarily through trade over the Silk Road from India through China and beyond. They spread quickly because it was communicated through the caste of the common people who outnumbered citizens of higher castes. The three classes included:[96]

- Upper Class – Rulers, warriors, priests and scholars
- Middle Class - Merchants, traders, and farmers
- Lower Class – Peasants and untouchables

This spread constituted Gautama's revelation, in essence, to open the door of religious freedom to all.

---

[95] The Pacific World: Journal of the Institute of Buddhist Studies, The Institute, 2005, p.98
[96] Heirman, Ann, Stephan Peter Bumbacher, The Spread of Buddhism, Brill, 2007, p.147

Gautama attained Parinirvana or was freed from earthly suffering in death in 483 BC. His followers began to organize a religious movement granting the name Buddha or "awakened one" as his final epithet. The First Buddhist Council at Rajgriha in 400BC produced the Vinaya Pitaka or guidelines for Buddhist monks and Sutta Pitaka or teachings of Buddha up to that term. The Second Buddhist Council at Vaishali in 383BC was engaged to recognize and resolve differences between subdivisions of the faith.[97] In doing so, a united cadre of Buddhists maintained the integrity of the faith.

The Indian campaign of Alexander the Great between 327BC and 325BC found the Indus Valley Civilization under Macedonian Rule. However, his further efforts to push eastward were thwarted as his soldiers refused to engage armies of Eastern India that were five times or more its size. Alexander's army, then, moved Southeast and then back to Macedonia.[98] Throughout his campaign, there was

---

[97] Baruah, Bibhuti, Buddhists Sects and Sectarianism, Sarup and Sons, 2000, pp.37-38
[98] Ibid, p.5

no diminishment of the Buddhist faith. It had, in fact, grown.

By the 3rd Century BC, Buddhism had become so extensive the Ashoka the Great, third Emperor of the Mauryan Empire, declared Buddhism as the state religion of India and promoted the spread of the faith beyond its borders after the Third Buddhist Council at Pataliputra in 250BC.[99] The Abhidhamma Pitaka or "higher teachings" was added centuries later.[100] The complete Dharma – Vinaya Pitaka, Sutta Pitaka and Abhidhamma Pitaka - comprise the Tripitaka, the sacred text of Buddhism.[101]

Greco-Roman Polytheism

The 6th Century BC also bore witness to the rise of the Republic of Rome whose origins extend to the 8th Century BC. Its foundations are considered the destruction of Troy and the bloodline of Aeneas, a survivor of the Trojan War. His journey by sea across the Mediterranean Sea, by the

---

[99] Ibid, p.16
[100] Ibid, p.100
[101] Ibid, p.98

command of the gods, drove him to the shores of Italy. These survivors became the progenitors of Rome.

Located at the Northwest tip of Asia Minor on the Aegean Sea, Troy was the setting for the Trojan War of the Greeks which was considered to have occurred by historians like Herodotus near 1200BC.[102] On the surface, the war was fought due to the abduction of Helen, wife of King Menelaus of Sparta, a Greek contingent located on the Southern tip of Greece, by Paris of Troy. The Greek nations banded together to assault Troy for Helen's return initially but found the land to be of great strategic importance because of its location near the Northeastern edge of the Aegean Sea. With Troy as a port of access in the Northeast and a prosperous trading center, they would not only be able to mobilize the entire western coast of Asia Minor but also control the mouth of the Black Sea which extended across the entire North shore of Asia Minor.[103] So, the aim changed from a personal conflict over Helen to a war for regional dominance.

---

[102] Thomas, Carol G., Craig Conant, The Trojan War, University of Oklahoma Press, 2007, p.64
[103] Ibid, p.29

Relative to the Gods, the Trojan War accomplished multiple objectives. It was utilized to justify henotheistic hierarchy and settle a dispute between goddesses. The goddess Athena supported the Greeks with the assistance of Hera, Poseidon, Hermes, and Hephaestus. The god Ares supported the Trojans with assistance from Apollo, Artemis, and Aphrodite. The sides were set based upon a contest driven by the god Zeus to identify the most beautiful of all the goddesses. Paris was selected to make the choice unwittingly. He chose Aphrodite due to her promise to deliver Helen of Sparta who was considered the most beautiful woman in the world. But to obtain her, Paris had to steal her from King Menelaus of Sparta, which he did.[104] This act from the contest of the gods started the war.

The war lasted ten years with a Greek victory. As the Trojans were eventually slayed, few survived and escaped to secure the Trojan race. Of them, Aeneas was aided by Aphrodite and Apollo who carried him away from certain death in battle from Diomedes. A relative of King Priam of Troy, Aeneas escaped by sea taking a Southern route along

---

[104] Ibid, p.113

the Eastern coast of Asia Minor to Crete avoiding the Greek combatants with the assistance of the god Poseidon. From Crete, they traveled westward on the Mediterranean to Sicily and Carthage and then Northeast up the Adriatic Sea to Alba Longa, the eventual home of Rome.[105]

By the 8th Century, Alba Longa had become a prominent city in the Latin League. It is from this site that mythical twins Romulus and Remus were born by Rhea Silvia, a vestal virgin who was impregnated by Mars. Natural leaders, both had groups of followers, and both had resolved to build a city of their own together. After a dispute between the brethren on the location of the city, Remus was slain by his brother. Romulus, subsequently, founded Rome as his namesake city atop the site known as Palatine Hill near 750BC.[106] This constitutes the mythical beginnings of Rome.

Early Rome was ruled by kings with the first being Romulus. He ruled through 716BC. Numa Pompilius, his brother-in-law, succeeded him by serving as king from

---

[105] Ibid, pp.73-74
[106] Nardo, Don, Roman Mythology, Lucent Books, 2012, pp.53-55

716BC to 672BC. Tullus Hostilius followed and was succeeded by Ancus Marcius in 640BC. After the death of Ancus Marcius in 616BC, Lucius Tarquinius Priscus ruled until his assassination in 578BC where his son-in-law, Servius Tullius, seized the kingship. Also assassinated in 534BC, Servius Tullius was succeeded by the grandson of Lucius Tarquinius Priscus, namely, Lucius Tarquinius Superbus. He ruled through 509BC and consolidated the leadership of the Latin League, which comprised multiple nations on the central Italian peninsula.[107]

Despite the power held by Lucius Tarquinius Superbus, he was considered a tyrant who drove Rome into a state of flux. In 509BC, Lucius Junius Brutus led a revolt against the monarchy in efforts to overthrow him.[108] After succeeding, he laid the groundwork for the creation of the Centuriate and Tribal Assemblies to secure the new republic and facilitate legislation. In doing so, the Republic of Rome was formed.

---

[107] Ibid, p.21
[108] Ibid, p.23

With an alliance forged with the Latin League, Rome continued to expand across the entire Italian Peninsula during the period when the Persian Empire expanded its territory further eastward into Asia. By 400 BC, Rome had grown into a powerful entity but remained in conflict with its surrounding neighbors over control of the peninsula. After defeating and subduing Latin neighbors in 338BC, the might of Rome had grown at the same time that the might of the Persian Empire had begun to falter.[109]

The conquests of Alexander the Great in 329BC obliterated the Persian Empire ceding control of Asia Minor, Mesopotamia, Egypt, and ground gained in Asia to the Greeks. Alexander did not seek to eliminate the faiths in the region though. He, in turn, allowed them to operate without a pause like Cyrus the Great did, even adopting some of their practices as his own, which is most likely due to the common thread of polytheism Many of the gods of the Greco-Roman arena matched the primary gods of the

---

[109] Crawford, Michael Hewson, The Roman Republic, Harvard University Press, 1993, pp.36-38

Persian Emprie which also aligned with specific
Mesopotamian deities:[110]

Attributes	Greco	Roman	Egyptian	Babylonian
King of the gods - *sky and thunder*	Zeus	Jupiter	Amun	Marduk
Queen of the **Gods** *- marriage, and womanhood*	Hera	Juno	Isis / Hathor / Mut	Ishtar
God of the sea	Poseidon	Neptune	Hetmehit (goddess)	Tiamut (goddess)
Goddess of the harvest	Demeter	Ceres	Isis	Nabu (god)
Goddess of wisdom and war	Athena	Minerva	Neith/Isis	Nabu (god)
God of light, sun, archery, and arts	Apollo	Apollo	Horus	Shamash
Goddess of the hunt	Artemis	Diana	Bastet	Ninurta (god)
God of war	Ares	Mars	Anhur	Nergal
Goddess of love	Aphrodite	Venus	Hathor/Isis	Ishtar
God of the Underworld	Hades	Pluto	Osiris	Nergal
God & Goddess of fire and craftsmanship	Hephaestus & Hestia	Vulcan & Vesta	Ptah / Anuket	Enki
Messenger of the Gods	Hermes	Mercury	Anubis / Thoth	Nabu
God of festivity	Dionysus	Bacchus	Shezmu	Ishtar

Figure 13 Polytheistic Deities across Old World Nations

---

[110] Smith, William, A New Classical Dictionary of Greek and Roman
Biography, Mythology and Geography, Harper & Brothers, 1854, p.953

So, the Greco-Roman and Mesopotamian faith structures were quite similar and, though Alexander's reign was relatively short-lived, his dominance lasted through his death in 323BC in Babylon.[111] After which a period of unrest endured resulting in Greek sects of the Empire.

The 3rd Century BC found Egypt, Southern Palestine, Crete, and seaports along the Mediterranean under the control of the Ptolemies, a Macedonian Greek state.[112] Mesopotamia, Northern Palestine, and West Asia were under the control of Seleucus I, King of the Seleucid Empire, another Macedonian Greek state.[113] Asia Minor was also separated into Greek states while Macedonia directly controlled the remaining Greek states except for those on the Italian Peninsula. Rome secured those states after the Battle of Beneventum in 275BC. King Pyrrhus of Epirus was forced to return to Greece due to the heavy losses at Tarentum.[114]

---

[111] Ibid, p.58
[112] Ibid, p.62
[113] Ibid, p.132
[114] Ibid, p.6

Roman conquests continued through the next two centuries. By 63BC after the capture of Jerusalem, Roman Provinces included Carthage at Northwest Africa, Asia Minor, and Northern Palestine. Roman Protectorates included Southern Palestine and Northern Mesopotamia, and as well as control over the Mediterranean, Aegean, and Adriatic. Attributing all victories to the influence of multiple deities, polytheistic dominance reigned supreme for a time.

Judeo-Christian Monotheism

In lieu of polytheistic domination, monotheistic sects still survived. Judaism remained active despite pressures to diminish its influence particularly in the Palestine region. The tolerance of Alexander fell to the wayside to a large degree. While it was common to allow pagan practices in Jewish territories within the region, the Jews, denounced them forcing the hand of the Seleucid rulers. The clashes escalated into the Maccabean Revolt in the 2nd Century BC.

Seleucid King Antiochus IV sought to repress Judaism to quell reverberation of its internal conflicts in Jerusalem in 168BC. He placed the city under direct Seleucid control commandeering the temple and allowing pagan practices within its walls. The family of Judah Maccabee gathered supporters in 167BC and retook the city. With enough support to hold the city, the Maccabees cleansed and rededicated the temple. They rebuffed repeated Seleucid attempts to retake the city forcing them to cease efforts. The city was ceded back to Jewish authority in 160BC.[115]

The death of Judah Maccabee from battle in 160BC and restoration of Jewish authority, found him seen as a messiah of sorts. His brother Jonathan succeeded him as the leader of the sect and maintained control. His leadership gained Jerusalem its status as a vassal state in 152BC. With external support from Rome and by the hands of Simon Thassi, another brother of Judah, the Hasmonean Dynasty was established in 141BC to oversee Judea.[116]

The Hasmoneans reigned Jerusalem without conflict until 67BC. Internal conflicts ensued between the sons of Alexander Jannaeus and Salome Alexandra. Hyrcanus, the

---

[115] Rabow, Jerry, 50 Jewish Messiahs, Gefen Publishing House, 2022, pp.168-169
[116] Eshel, Hanan, The Dead Sea Scrolls and the Hasmonean State, Eerdman's Publishing Company, 2008, pp.10-11

eldest, sided with the Pharisees in their specific beliefs in the resurrection of the dead and an afterlife. Aristobulus, sided with the more popular Sadducees, who held strongly to the key tenets outlined by the Torah. The Torah was received directly by Moses from God at Mt. Sinai during the exodus of the Israelites from Egypt. It is comprised of five books namely the Be-reshit, Shemot, Va-yikra, Be-midbar and Devarim, which correspond to Genesis, Exodus, Leviticus, Numbers and Deuteronomy. These books primary focus on the history and laws of Judaism and do not support the immortality of the soul and the realm of angels and spirits. As such, the brothers fought for the throne to lead the nation.[117]

Hyrcanus was crowned King of Judea in 67BC but Sadducee support for Aristobulus proved to be problematic. Incidents between the brethren forced the elder to abdicate the throne at the threat of his life in 66BC. Outraged with the outcome, Antipater, an influential Pharisee, convinced the elder to reclaim the throne with the military support he arranged through Rome. Accepting the support, Hyrcanus

---

[117] Ibid, p.11

laid siege on Jerusalem with support from Emperor Pompey routing Aristobulus in 63BC. After Hyrcanus paid tribute to Rome, Judea was reduced to a vassal state subordinate to the Roman Empire.[118]

In 40BC, Herod was appointed King of Judea by Rome but Antigonus, the existing leader, resisted. In 39BC, Herod arranged to wed Mariamme, granddaughter of Hyrcanus to gain favor which was unsuccessful. Armed with forces, Herod returned, captured Jerusalem, and sent Antigonus to his execution to Mark Antony in Rome in 37BC.[119]

Herod immediately sought to secure the throne against Hasmonean contestation. Hyrcanus, who had retreated to live with Babylonian Jews, returned in 36BC at Herod's request as a guest. He was treated with respect to subversively gain his trust until he could be placed in a position to justify detrimental action. In 30BC, Hyrcanus was charged with treason for plotting against the King of Arabia. He was publicly condemned to gain Judean

---

[118] Gilman, Daniel Coit, Harry Thurston Peck, Frank Moore Colby, The New International Encyclopaedia, Volume 10, Dodd, Mead, 1906, p.412
[119] Ibid, pp.11-13

support, and summarily executed.[120] Mariamme, Herod's wife and female Hasmonean relative, also became the victim of trumped up charges and was executed in 29BC. His granddaughter Herodias, and her daughter, Salome, were exiled to Gaul eliminating potential contenders.[121]

Although known as a builder due to his impressive works in refurbishing and expanding the temple, his need to maintain power was insatiable. He ordered the massacre of innocent Judean infants after hearing word near 6BC from the Magi that a king would be born in Bethlehem. By his order, boys two years old and under in Bethlehem and its vicinity were slain over a period of four and five years between 6BC and 1BC to further secure his state as king.[122] An infant in the age range at the time, Joseph and Mary fled the vicinity with their son, Jesus to save his life after receiving word from an angel. This incident is the basis for modern time acronyms for the common era (CE) and Anno Domini (AD), the traditional birth year of Jesus.

---

[120] Ibid, p.412
[121] Ibid, p.14
[122] Ibid, p.12

The Ministry of Jesus is estimated to have begun near 27AD. After being baptized in the Jordan River by John the Baptist, his ministry reached points across Palestine including Galilee, Decapolis, Samaria, and Judea. Jews were the primary target. Disciples who worked to learn and preach the message were gathered. Aware of his impending demise, Jesus admonished them to preach but be prepared for the challenges to come. In 30AD, Jesus was crucified at Golgotha outside of Jerusalem, resurrected three days later, and ascended to heaven.[123] His life, death, resurrection, and ascension is the basis of the Christian faith. After the death of Jesus, the disciples scattered but continued their labors resulting in the baptism of new converts.

Through the efforts of Mark, the faith extended into Egypt by 33AD. Through the efforts of Paul, a convert from 34AD, the faith extended throughout Greece.[124] The followers were first referred to as "Christians" in Antioch in 42AD after eight years of practice by the Disciple Peter

---

[123] Richey, Lola S., Who is Jesus? Essential Facts of Jesus Christ, Author House, 2012, pp.10-11
[124] Vidmar, John, The Catholic Church Through the Ages: A History, Paulist Press, 2005, pp.19-21

in 34AD. The Church of Antioch was expanded by the hands of Paul and Barnabas. It incorporated Jews who had accepted the new covenant and gentiles, after baptism. James, stepbrother of Jesus and leader of the Church of Jerusalem, was the progenitor of converting gentiles into the new faith. At the Council of Jerusalem in 49AD, Paul supported James' method as the quintessential practice for expansion of the faith and promoted it.[125]

By 63AD, the faith had extended swiftly and significantly across the Mediterranean region. Letters issued by Paul, James and others to the churches helped to maintain their connectivity despite geographical distances. The recording of their actions also provided a historical track-record of their labors for prosperity. Effective communication was the superstructure for the growth of the faith. Its popularity, however, made Christians targets for persecution. The Great Fire of Rome occurred in 64AD under the term of Emperor Nero. Intended to be a controlled fire to clear space for a major construction project, the fire ran out of control. After six days of

---

[125] Ibid, p.24

burning, two-thirds of Roman settlements and businesses had been destroyed negatively impacting the economy to a significant degree. Nero laid the blame, baselessly, on the Christian sect.[126]

Other persecutions were more direct. James, brother of John, had already been slain by order of Herod Agrippa, King of Judea, prior to his own death in 44AD. Emperor Nero ordered the beheading of the Apostle Paul in 64AD after the Great Fire of Rome. The crucifixion of the Apostle Peter upside down followed.[127] With no apparent opposition from the Jews, Judea was complicit in these actions as they did not blow back on the kingdom. However, inaction on their behalf was short lived.

During the Christian Persecutions, a series of Jewish Revolts occurred between 66AD and 135AD. The source of the first revolt in 66AD was protestation of oppressive taxation. After funds were seized from the treasury of the Jewish temple by Roman Governor Cestius Gallus by force, rebel forces gathered and attacked the Syrian Legion

---

[126] Ibid, p.25
[127] Ibid, pp.25-26

under the control of the governor. With the Syrian Legion defeated, tensions escalated forcing Nero to charge Roman General Vespasian to squash the rebellion. Armed with four legions, he conquered Galilee in 67AD and drove the rebels out of Galilee to Jerusalem by 68AD.[128]

In June of 68AD, Nero, feeling backed into a corner by the Senate and other conflicts, committed suicide. He was quickly succeeded by three leaders – Galba, Otho, and Vitellus - who all died by murder or suicide in 69AD. After which, Vespasian was recalled to Rome by the Senate to serve as emperor. He turned the campaign against the Jews over to his son, Titus who breached. Jerusalem in 70AD.[129]

Although Jerusalem was lost, rebel efforts continued. The advances of Titus forced them to retreat to the mountain fortress of Masada. Situated atop a high plateau on the Dead Sea, the Roman siege began in 72AD with an aggressive construction campaign. Siege ramps were built along with other implements to breach. Surrounded, the

---

[128] Rudich, Vasily, Political Dissidence Under Nero: The Price of Dissimulation, Taylor & Francis, 2005, p.190
[129] Ibid, p.191

inhabitants of the fortress had no hope of escape. At the breach of the walls in 73AD, the Jewish forces, who had already resolved themselves to defeat, committed mass suicide concluding the first Roman-Jewish War.[130]

Titus succeeded his father as emperor in 79AD. He died from a fever at the age of forty-one two years later and, his brother, Domitian, succeeded him in 81AD.[131] Under his term, Rome reverted to a monarchy in which the Senate was publicly disrespected and ignored.[132] This stance was a stark contrast between him and his predecessors who valued republic rule. Yet, he moved forward focusing on internal dominance instead of expansion.

Caesar Domitian was a pure polytheist who adhered to traditional Roman beliefs. Representing himself as Jupiter, he was transformed into a religious figure which did not bode well for other faiths. He established an imperial cult and deified his father and brother, constructing the Temple

[130] Tucker, Spencer C., The Encyclopedia of Arab-Israeli Conflict: A Political, Social, and Military History, ABC-CLIO, 2008, pp.668-669
[131] Wilson, Marvin R., Our Father Abraham: Jewish Roots of the Christian Faith, Wm. B. Eerdman's Publishing,1989, p.75
[132] Strauss, Barry, The Caesars: Roman Emperors from Augustus to Constantine, Simon & Schuster, 2020, p.145

of Vespasian and Titus as shrines of worship.[133] These acts found him hated among public officials. His disdain for other faiths was also very clear and direct. Christians continued to be flagged as the source of many of Rome's problems and the Roman citizenry supported this concept in many ways.

The Jewish community also held disdain for Christians and other faiths outside of its spectrum. The Birkat HaMinim of 85AD clearly outlines Jewish sentiment for those who did not follow Judaism:[134]

For the apostates (meshumaddim) let there be no hope and uproot the kingdom of arrogance (malkhut zadom), speedily and in our days. May the Nazarenes (ha-nazarim/nosrim/notzrim) and the sectarians (minim) perish as in a moment. Let them be blotted out of the book of life, and not be written together with the righteous. You are praised, O Lord, who subdues the arrogant.

---

[133] Ibid, pp.145-146
[134] Wilson, Marvin R., Our Father Abraham: Jewish Roots of the Christian Faith, Wm. B. Eerdman's Publishing,1989, pp.65-66

This prayer of disloyalty curses on non-Jews including atheists, polytheists, Nazarenes or Christians, and other sects. So, faith had become heraldic representation of the enemy in the eyes of Rome and the Jews.

By 95AD Domitian had exiled several Christians to Patmos, a prison colony, including the Apostle John, the site of his revelation of the apocalypse. Shortly thereafter, Domitian was assassinated in 96AD.[135] Emperor Nerva briefly reigned until 98AD naming Trajan, a military general, as his successor.[136] While Christian persecution continued particularly as it relates to guilt and punishment of accused crimes, Trajan shifted the priority on judgment based upon facts and not prejudiced conjecture stating that persecution based on unproven charges was "contrary to the spirit of our times."[137] While he sought to level the fairness factor, persecution in prosecutions remained intact.

---

[135] Strauss, Barry, The Caesars: Roman Emperors from Augustus to Constantine, Simon & Schuster, 2020, p.148
[136] Ibid, p.149
[137] Haddad, Robert M., The Case for Christianity: St. Justin Martyr's Arguments for Religious Liberty and Judicial Justice, Taylor Trade Publishing, 2010, p.15

Trajan's top priority was on the external expansion of Rome. He eventually controlled all lands with access to the Mediterranean Sea from the entire Iberian Peninsula to Palestine. In addition, the whole of Asia Minor, Egypt, Palestine, and Mesopotamia were under Roman control. At the time of his death in 117AD, his successor, Hadrian inherited a massive domain which is the likely cause for halting the expansion of the empire under his reign.[138]

Hadrian's focus shifted back to internal matters and protection against foreign enemies at Rome's borders. He shored up the Roman army and erected barriers around settlements. Construction on a wall as a defensive fortification between Britain and unconquered Caledonia began in 122AD. The completed wall took six years to construct and extended nearly from the west to the east coast of England. It was flanked by a ditch or vallum to its south which ran parallel to the wall for further security.

---

[138] Ibid, pp.15-16

Frontier boundaries were also constructed as defensive barriers and boundary markers against German tribes.[139]

The Jewish Revolt of 132AD also required Hadrian's direct attention. Lead by Simon Bar Kochba, the source was unresolved tension from the First Jewish Revolt. Construction of the City of Aelia Capitolina and a Temple of Jupiter upon the ruins of Jerusalem from the First Jewish Revolt reignited the Jewish sentiments.[140] This drove Bar Kochba to gather Jewish forces and fight.

Bar Kochba was seen by many Jews as the messiah that they had been waiting for. Rabbi Akiva Ben Yosef directly linked him as the messiah to references from the Torah:[141]

> *He hath said, which heard the words of God, and*
> *knew the knowledge of the most High, which saw*
> *the vision of the Almighty, falling into a trance, but*
> *having his eyes open: I shall see him, but not now: I*
> *shall behold him, but not nigh: there shall come a*

---

[139] Strauss, Barry, The Caesars: Roman Emperors from Augustus to Constantine, Simon & Schuster, 2020, pp.191-192
[140] Ibid, p.306
[141] Holy Bible, Number 24:16-17

Star out of Jacob, and a Scepter shall rise out of Israel, and shall smite the corners of Moab, and destroy all the children of Sheth.

This assertion was utilized in a failed attempt to steer Christians from Jesus as the Messiah to Bar Kochba to attain additional support. However, the swift actions by Hadrian to invade Judea in 134AD were too much to combat. By 135AD, after sustaining heavy Roman and Jewish losses, Judea was lost. In 136AD, political ramifications to suppress Judaism and expel Jews from Jerusalem were adopted. The final blow was the renaming of Judea to Syria Palestina.[142]

The messianic debate between the Christians and the Jews had always been a point of conflict. The Jews never accepted Jesus as the Messiah in Isaiah's prophecy:[143]

Yet it pleased the LORD to bruise him; he hath put him to grief: when thou shalt make his soul an offering for sin, he shall see his seed, he shall

---

[142] Ibid, p.306
[143] Holy Bible, Isaiah 53:10-12

prolong his days, and the pleasure of the LORD shall prosper in his hand. He shall see of the travail of his soul and shall be satisfied: by his knowledge shall my righteous servant justify many; for he shall bear their iniquities. Therefore, will I divide him a portion with the great, and he shall divide the spoil with the strong; because he hath poured out his soul unto death: and he was numbered with the transgressors; and he bare the sin of many, and made intercession for the transgressors.

Alternatively, Jesus prophesied of false prophets to his disciples. He noted that "false christs and false prophets will arise and perform signs and wonders, to lead astray, if possible, the elect."[144] The politicization of the events surrounding Jesus during his period minimized the possibility of divine ordinance to Jews. It is also likely that Bar Kochba fell victim to the same mindset for Christians seeing it as a ploy for support.

---

[144] Holy Bible, Mark 13:22

The spread of Christianity was also a confirmation to many of the messianic state of Jesus. By the 3rd Century, the faith had spread from Rome to Asia Minor, Egypt, Greece, and Gaul. By the 4th Century, large Christian communities existed in these areas despite local and large scale persecution. Persecution reached a pinnacle under the term of Roman Emperor Diocletian and his progenitors.

Diocletian followed the pattern of Emperor Decius who required the tributes from all inhabitants under Roman rule. Like Trajan, Decius deified himself and ruled with an iron thumb. Not accepting the deified stated of Decius and refusing to comply with the orders of tribute and sacrifice to him and other Roman gods, Christians were arrested, tried for non-compliance, and summarily executed. This was the fate of Fabian, a bishop in Rome in 250AD.[145]

Emperor Valerian followed Decius' pattern of persecution. In 257AD, he required all Christian church leaders to participate in pagan rituals and disallowed public Christian meetings. A year later, he ordered the execution

---

[145] Bunson, Matthew, A Dictionary of the Roman Empire, OUP USA, 1995, p.153

of all Christian lay persons in Rome and extended the order across the provinces. Cyprian, Bishop of Carthage, was arrested on September 1, 258 AD, tried, convicted of sac religion, and executed two days later.[146] Many attribute his capture and torture by the Persian Empire in 260AD as recompense for these acts.[147] Valerian was the first Roman emperor to be taken alive by an enemy.

The attempts of Decius and Valerian were ultimately implemented to halt the expansion of the Christian church. The power of the faithful appeared to outweigh the rule of Rome and the fate of Valerian could likely have served as an impediment to persecutory practices by the emperors that followed. This was not the case for Diocletian when he became emperor in 284AD. Almost immediately, he took stances against Christians and other religions that did not align with traditional Roman polytheism. He purged the army of Christian soldiers to avoid conflicts between faith and direct orders in the line of service.[148] He condemned

---

[146] Ibid, p.122

[147] Ibid, p.51

[148] Strauss, Barry, The Caesars: Roman Emperors from Augustus to Constantine, Simon & Schuster, 2020, pp.280-281

Manicheans, members of a Parthian Christian sect founded by the messianic prophet Mani, to death by edict to squash the new faith before it could spread.[149] Surrounding himself with supporters, he sought to eliminate the scourge of non-traditional faiths and restore Rome to its former glory.

As Rome had become a monolith, Diocletian also decided to split the empire into the Western and Eastern Empires in 286AD. Diocletian abdicated in 305AD. As the Eastern Empire had become expansive, its independent rulership in alliance with the Western Empire would better position Roman dominance for ages. Emperor Galerius of the Eastern Empire was a Diocletian supporter while Emperor Constantius I of the Western Empire was more independent. Maxientius, a general who did not support the split, was declared emperor of Italy with the support of the Praetorian Guard in 306AD.[150] Thus, the start of the 4th Century found three emperors in power.

---

[149] Gardner, Ian, Samuel N.C. Lieu, Manichaean Texts from the Roman Empire, Cambridge University Press, 2004, p.116
[150] Strauss, Barry, The Caesars: Roman Emperors from Augustus to Constantine, Simon & Schuster, 2020, pp.290-291

While Galerius continued persecutory practices against Christians and Maxientius sought to cleanse Italy, Constantius favored the approach of acceptance. Upon his death, his son, Emperor Constantine, who maintained similar values, succeeded him over the Western Empire but this conflicted with Galerius who elevated Licinius. Conflicts between the emperors endured until 312AD. Constantine defeated Maxientius and was convinced that it was divine Christian intervention that sealed his victory. In doing so, he converted to Christianity and secured the leadership of the Western Empire.[151]

Licinius was elevated to co-Emperor of the Eastern Empire along with Maximinius after the death of Galerius in 311AD.[152] With governing lines drawn, the truce did not last lost. A civil war between them in 313AD found Licinius the victor and sole ruler of Eastern Rome. In collaboration with Constantine, a joint edict, Edit of Milan, was issued granting religious freedom.[153]

---

[151] Ibid, p.296
[152] Ibid, p.291
[153] Ibid, p.299

Between 314AD and 321AD, a series of conflicts between Constantine and Licinius drove them to come to a final conclusion on rulership of Rome as a whole. Civil war erupted in 314AD when Licinius appeared to show support for an attempt to overthrow Constantine from the throne. A year later, at the Battle of Mardia, an appointee of Licinius, Valens, again attempted to overthrow Constantine. With the execution of Valens after a humiliating defeat, a truce was again resolved. Finally, in 321AD, after Constantine pursued ravaging Samaritans and, subsequently, ravaging Goths into Licinius' territory twice, Licinius claimed that Constantine had broken the truce placing the empires at war. Constantine's victory over Licinius at the Battle of Adrianople in 324AD secured the Western and Eastern Empires under a single Emperor.[154]

A Christian, Emperor Constantine was still an advocate of religious freedom but saw the need to create more structure around Christianity. In 325AD, he convened a Council at Nicea from which the doctrine of the Holy

---

[154] Bunson, Matthew, A Dictionary of the Roman Empire, OUP USA, 1995, pp.237-238

Trinity whereby God the Father, the Son (Jesus as God incarnate), and Holy Ghost (God in spirit) were equal. This Nicene Creed was accepted as the basis for Christian belief throughout the empire but was not without controversy. The Aryan belief was that Jesus was subordinate to God.[155] Yet, the Nicene Creed prevailed.

Other sects believed in the holiness of Jesus but maintained the stance of Judaism that Jesus was not the messiah, and one was still yet to come. Many messiahs would appear, but Moses of Crete claimed to be that messiah for whom the Jews were awaiting near 448AD. His arrival aligned with the timeline outlined by the Talmud, near 440AD, and he convinced many Christians to leave their worldly possessions and follow him back to Palestine to reclaim the land. Upon reaching a promontory point overlooking the Aegean, several followed his directive to jump over the cliff and were either drowned, crushed by the rocks on the shore, or saved by Cretan fisherman. Moses

---

[155] Strauss, Barry, The Caesars: Roman Emperors from Augustus to Constantine, Simon & Schuster, 2020, pp.303-304

slipped away with their effects. Most of the survivors eventually converted to Christianity.[156]

Although the faith had spread significantly, the message was not congruent across the Christian diaspora. Jesus was considered a holy man by all but not necessarily equivalent to God in all cases. But the focus on God as the highest, expanded monotheism and dispelled polytheistic views to a large degree in lands that were former strongholds of multiple gods. However, the lack of clarity and inconsistency in the actions of the faithful also caused a problem which was the basis for the rise of Islam.

Arabian Monotheism and American Effects

Islam is the evolution of Judaism with respect for Jesus who is proclaimed as a holy man. It is the fulfillment of the Abrahamic legacy outlined in the Torah through the bloodline of Ishmael. It proclaims the Prophet Muhammad as the last apostle of God due to his formation of the new faith and divine ordination by Allah, God of Abraham, on

---

[156] Rabow, Jerry, 50 Jewish Messiahs, Gefen Publishing House, 2022, pp.17-18

consecrated ground.[157] It accepts Jesus as a prophet but not the equivalent of God. It also accepts that Jesus was born of the Virgin Mary through divine copulation.[158] Furthermore, Muslims or followers of Islam, do not believe in the existence of the Holy Trinity but that Allah is singular and God alone.[159] Muhammad's role, therefore, was to be the last messenger of God and provide a new revelation on monotheism and promote surrendering oneself to God so that his will can be accomplished on earth.

Upon taking the mantle of leadership, Muhammad's efforts and travels drove him to settle at the cave at Mt. Hira situated outside of the City of Mecca in 609AD. The cave was the site where he received revelations from Allah through the Angel Gabriel in 610AD.[160] Over a period of twenty-three years, the revelations were captured constructing the Holy Qur'an or the "new song" proclaimed by Isaiah in the Holy Bible. Designated as the

---

[157] Gabriel, Mark A., Jesus and Muhammad: Profound Differences and Surprising Similarities, Charisma House, 2004, p.80
[158] Ibid, p.95
[159] Holy Qu'ran, Surah 5, Al Maidah, 77
[160] Hall, Manley Palmer, Twelve World Teachers: A Summary of Their Lives and Teachings, Philosophers Press, p.187

messenger of the new song, Muhammad advanced the Faith of Islam.

Muhammad's viewpoint of deity was controversial to his tribe, the Quraysh, which was polytheistic and henotheistic. He attributed the thriving condition of Mecca solely to the beneficence of Allah, the God of Abraham and sought to sanctify the Kaaba in the name of Allah through Islam.[161] As his revelations from Gabriel continued, he privately sought support in Mecca. However, by 613AD, he had gained sufficient support from the Banu Hashim and a multitude of followers which prompted him publicly to preach and seek converts to the new faith.[162] In 617AD, the Quraysh boycotted and persecuted the Hashim Clan for this stance, but it failed. By 619AD, Islam had grown significantly. But, the same year, Muhammad lost his first wife Khadijah and his uncle Abu Talib, his protector.[163] These sorrows were followed by the Isra and Miraj.

---

[161] Holy Qu'ran, Surah 106:1-4
[162] Mallah, Hashim Yahya, The Governmental System of the Prophet Muhammad, Dar al-Kotob al-Ilmiyah, 2008, pp.21-22
[163] Ibid, p.26

Figure 14 Kaaba at Mecca

The Isra refers to the spiritual and physical journey of Muhammad who traveled from Mecca to the Temple Mount at Jerusalem on the back of a Buraq or winged heavenly beast to engage in prayer with prophets. The Miraj refers to his subsequent ascension into heaven from Jerusalem where he met prophets at the seven levels of heaven including Adam, John the Baptist, Jesus, Joseph, Idris, Aaron, Moses and Abraham. He received instructions for the faithful and was, subsequently, returned to

Jerusalem and then carried to Mecca in 620AD.[164] The single day's journey still bears great significance because Jerusalem had already been considered as holy ground through Judaism. Mecca, by virtue of the Isra and Miraj, became held in the same regard making both Mecca and Jerusalem key religious sites for Islam.

Persecution, though, against Muslims remained constant even though Muhammad's spiritual night journey had become renown. By 622AD, the skirmishes between the Muslims and Quraysh intensified forcing Muhammad to leave Mecca and migrate to Medina. By 624AD, the conflicts had escalated into a full-fledged war. The Battle of Badr of 624AD found the Muslims victorious in raids over the Quraysh Meccan forces.[165] Their success, despite being outnumbered, led to more converts to Islam.

The Battle of Uhud in 625AD found the Muslims defeated by a superior force. Jewish tribes in Medina were partially blamed for the loss and accused of treachery as

---

[164] El-Neil, Ibn, The Truth About Islam, Strategic Book Publishing, 2008, p.147
[165] Ibid, p.149

many Quraysh still maintained Judaism as its core faith.[166] Accusations continued after the Battle of the Trench in 627AD. The siege by the Quraysh of Medina resulted in a stalemate. Banu Qurayza, a Quraysh Jewish leader in Medina, was accused and convicted of conspiracy and, subsequently, beheaded. The Treaty of Hudabiyyah of 628AD effectively ended the war with terms including:[167]

1. Cease in hostilities at Medina;
2. Restoration of Hajj privileges;
3. Ban of Meccan Muslims from settling in Medina;
4. Acceptance of Medina Muslims to join Meccans.

The intent of the treaty was twofold. It was meant to create peace and prevent Medina from returning to a Muslim stronghold. However, after a breach of the treaty by the Quraysh in 630AD, Muhammad's forces conquered Mecca. By the time of Muhammad's death in 632AD, Islam had extended across the Arabian Peninsula.[168]

---

[166] Ibid, pp.150-151
[167] Ibid, pp.152-153
[168] Ibid, pp.155-156

From this period until the Holy Wars, the scimitar ruled the region through the Rashidun Caliphate. They extended Islam beyond Arabia to the Middle East and Northeast Africa. The first Caliph was Abu Bakr, a prominent leader under Muhammad. Umar, who succeeded him, was assassinated by a slave in 644AD. Uthman, who was elected by a council of elders, was murdered in 656AD. Ali took control and was considered the first Imam. However, he was murdered in 661AD.[169]

The Umayyad Caliphate controlled the region from 661AD to 750AD and preferred ethnic Arabs lead the Caliphate extending Islam deeper into the Middle East and westward to Portugal, Spain and all of Northern Africa. They separated the empire into provinces and shifted management to appointed governors. Due to poor management, multiple rebellions ensued resulting in the Abbasid Caliphate overthrowing the Umayyads in 750AD forcing their retreat to Spain.[170]

---

[169] Porterfield, Jason, The Islamic Golden Age and the Caliphates, Rosen Publishing Group Inc., 2016, pp.10-14
[170] Ibid, p.52

The Abbasids ruled with challenges of their own through the Holy Wars. The first Caliph, al-Saffah, served only four years in leadership and is responsible for extending Islam to Central Asia and making it the premier faith in the region. He was succeeded by the founder of the City of Baghdad, al-Manur, who served from 754AD to 775AD. Peace reigned under the terms of his successors al-Mahdi and al-Hadi, through 786AD. However, a rival dynasty was organized under the term of Harun al-Rashid ending Abbasid stability.

The Idrisid Dynasty was founded by Idris ben Allah, grandson of Muhammad who was forced to flee to Morocco, under Berber control, due to his stance taken at the Battle of Fakhkh. The selection of Harun al-Rashid was challenged by the Muhammadian bloodline. After failing to secure the throne, Idris fled to the Berbers who made him an Imam. By 788AD, he was elevated to Emir as Idris I.[171]

Idris conquered large portions of Morocco. By the time of his death three years after installation, he had founded

---

the City of Fez in 789AD and secured most of Morocco except for its westernmost points that bordered the Atlantic Ocean. He was succeeded by his son, Idris II. Although born after the death of Idris I, the dynasty maintained control through administrative Berber leadership until Idris II was old enough to lead. Under his term of leadership, the City of Fez had become the capital in 808AD, and additional Moroccan ground had been conquered.[172]

Although strong in Morocco, the Idrisid Dynasty was still not more dominant than the Abbasids. Yet, by the end of the 9th Century, many internal challenges occurred within the Abbasid Dynasty. Under al-Mu'tasim and al-Wathik, the leadership had become significantly weakened.[173] They lost more control over the court from progressive Turkish influence. The assassination of al-Mutawakkil by the Turks in 861AD gave the Turks leverage over his successor, al-Muntasir.[174] After his short lived reign, al-Muntasin found himself in a civil war with

---

[172] Ibid, pp.50-52
[173] Patton, Walter Melville, Ahmed Ibn Hanbal and the Mihna: A Biography of the Imam, Cosimo Classics, 2010, p121
[174] Ibid, pp.130-131

his eventual successor al-Mu'tazz. Having fled Baghdad in 865AD, al-Muntasin lost the throne. Al-Mu'tazz was quickly disposed of by the Turks in 869AD.[175] This chaos consumed the Caliphate well into the 10th Century giving rise to the Fatimids who created a Caliph of their own.

The Fatimid Caliphate was established in 909AD by Muslims who traced their lineage to Fatima, daughter of the Prophet Muhammad. Under the leadership of al-Mahdi Billah, the Fatimids took control of North Africa along the Mediterranean from Tunisia to Egypt. In 970AD, they conquered Palestine and controlled lands including Jerusalem. By 973AD, Egypt had come under its control. With the Umayyads, who fled to Spain, under the control of the Fatamids, they took Morocco in 974AD expelling the Idrisids.[176] So, like the challenges of heritage and heraldry to the control of the line of Abrham, blood was shed again within bloodlines for control of the lands of the Southern Mediterranean and North Africa.

---

[175] El-Hibri, Tayeb, The Abbasid Caliphate: A History, Cambridge University Pres, 2021, pp.140-143
[176] Ibid, pp.291-294

The 11th Century found the Fatamids in constant conflict with the Muslim Turks, Abbasids, and Christians. By 1055AD, the Turks had control of Baghdad.[177] Turkish control extended to Jerusalem by 1071AD.[178] Conflicts were abundant for the next twenty years but, by the start of the Crusades in 1096AD, the Fatamids had regained control of Jerusalem for a short time.[179] The Crusaders took Jerusalem in the name of Christianity in 1099AD.[180]

The First Crusade weakened both the Fatimids and the Turks depleting their resources to a large degree. The Abbasids took advantage of the period replenishing their strength but, other clans did the same and rose to create competing Caliphates of their own. The Almohad Empire, for example, was established in 1121AD.[181] Their influence spread quickly across North Africa because of the anti-Abbasid stance. However, by the early 12th Century, the Abbasid armies were rebuilt, and the leadership was

---

[177] Lev, Yacob, State and Society in Fatimid Egypt, Brill, 2022, p.50
[178] Ibid, p.44
[179] Ibid, p.48
[180] Ibid, p.97
[181] Bennison, Amira K., Almoravid and Almohad Empires, Edinburgh University, Press, 2016, pp.57-58

focused on restoring the dynasty as the most prominent Caliphate. In doing so, Baghdad was retaken in 1157AD. Under the leadership of Saladin, the Fatamids were finally overthrown in 1171AD and the control over the South Mediterranean was restored to the Abbasid Caliphate shortly thereafter.[182]

The 13th Century resulted in several leadership transitions. After the death of al-Nasir in 1225AD, the Abbasid Dynasty lost the sultanate to the Mamluks. The Mamluks fell victim, however, to the Mongols in 1258AD and sacked Baghdad.[183] This ended the Abbasid Dynasty whose fall signaled the end of worldwide Arab-Muslim control by a single Caliphate. It also opened the doors for others to secure the faith along with their expansion efforts like the Ottomans who did so in 1299AD.[184] Islam spread through the Balkans and Northern Europe with Ottoman conquests extending the faith through the 20th Century.

---

[182] Abun-Nasr, Jamil M., A History of the Maghrib in the Islamic Period, Cambridge University Press, 1987, p.66
[183] Ibid, p.76
[184] Ibid, p.109

Figure 15 Drew Ali, W.F. Muhammad, Elijah Muhammad

Islam also made its way as an organized faith to the United States of America in the 20th Century. Two American-born men were the primary drivers of the influx. Noble Drew Ali founded the Moorish Science Temple and Elijah Muhammad founded the Nation of Islam. Through their hands, Islam would flourish in America.

Timothy Drew was born on January 8, 1886, in North Carolina, USA, of humble origins.[185] At the age of 16, he joined a Romani band of gypsies who took him overseas to Egypt, and the Middle East. A master magician, he engaged

---

[185] Ancestry.com. Illinois, U.S., Deaths and Stillbirths Index, 1916-1947, Provo, UT, USA: Ancestry.com Operations, Inc., 2011

in the tutelage of a sage who introduced him to Islam.[186] From this basis, Drew became a devoted Muslim with a vision for its extension in America upon his return.

In 1913, Timothy Drew became Noble Drew Ali, having changed his name to signify adoption of Islam as his faith and doctrine. His doctrine was developed while overseas including lost revelations to the Holy Qur'an. Combined with other revelations from Ali, a bolstered Koran was developed serving as the religious text adopted by the Moorish Science Temple of America, which was founded in Newark, New Jersey, USA, in 1913.[187]

The doctrine was a fusion of Orthodox Islam and Christianity which also promoted independence and African liberation as influenced by the movement of Marcus Mosiah Garvey.[188] The Holy Koran of the Moorish Science Temple supplements the Holy Qur'an with

---

[186] Miyakawa, Felicia M., Five Percenter Rap: God Hop's Music, Message, and Black Muslim Mission, Indiana University Press, 2005, p.10

[187] Ed. Wilmore, Gayraud S., African American Religious Studies: An Interdisciplinary Anthology, Duke University Press, 1989, p.292

[188] Gomez, Michael A., Black Crescent: The Experience and Legacy of African Muslims in the Americas, Cambridge University Press, 2005, p.226

narratives on the fall of man per the Holy Bible, the resurrection of Jesus, and a prophesy communicated by Allah to Noble Drew Ali himself. Ali further preached the direct linkage of African Americans to the Moors of Morocco and its surrounding vicinity and advocated that African Americans return to the original faith of their forefathers – Islam.[189]

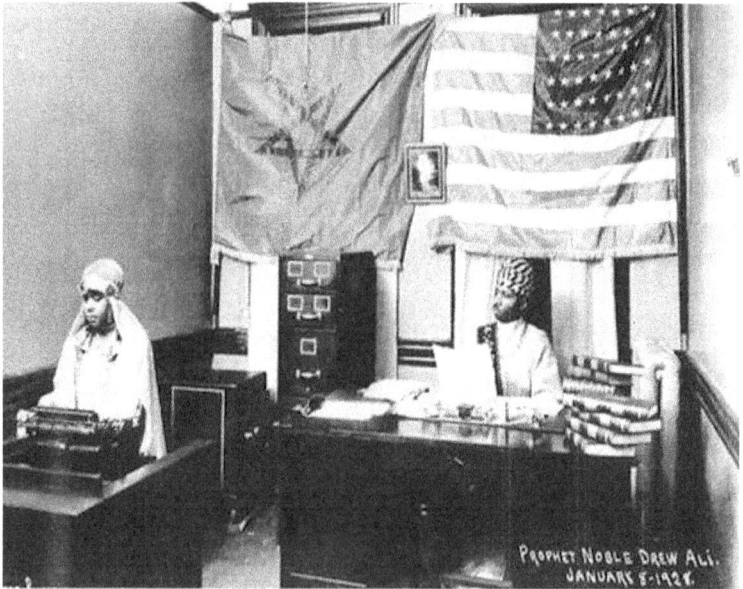

Figure 16 Noble Drew Ali with flags

---

[189] Ibid, pp.215-217

Considering the racial climate in the United States of America at the time of Ali's ascent, the growth attained by his organization could be considered tremendous. He met with multiple racial challenges at all social and political levels and, for a time, successfully rebuffed internal challenges to his leadership. The charismatic way he endured the challenges served as the source of the massive expansion of his movement in America.

Ali was confronted directly by United States President Woodrow Wilson for his beliefs and discouraged. After demanding that the government return the Moorish flag taken from his people, Wilson is said to have acknowledged its existence. The events surrounding its possession by the government tie to the first United States President, George Washington, who disavowed them after the Revolutionary War in contrast to the trust held with the Emperor of Morocco, Sidi Mohammed. It is purported that this was done because the Moorish consorts of Washington were colored and could be enslaved along with American slaves. It is believed by many historians that the flag was that of Washington's Moorish consort, a free man who was often captured in paintings and caricatures of Washington, that

Ali requested and received from Wilson.[190] This was considered a major victory in the early stages of the faith.

In 1914, Ali experienced a challenge to his leadership by Abdul Wali Farad Muhammad Ali. also known as Wallace Farad Muhammad, of Newark, New Jersey. Wallace, who was also a Muslim, sought to win converts to Islam in the same vicinity as Ali however Ali's progressive stance relative to the African American community resonated greater than Wallace's did at the time.[191] Many blacks who migrated to the north by way of the Great Migration filled his flock. As such, the challenge by Wallace, initially, fell short but picked up steam after the death of Ali in 1929.

Prior to his death, Ali was successful in branding Moorish Science and leading it in the same manner as a caliph over a caliphate. He had a strong base of loyal members who also perpetuated the faith locally and abroad.

[190] Dew, Spencer, The Aliites: Race and Law in the Religions of Noble Drew Ali, University of Chicago Press, 2019, p.87
[191] Misiroglu, Gina, American Countercultures: An Encyclopedia of Nonconformists, Alternate Lifestyles, and Radical Ideas in U.S. History, Taylor & Francis, 2015, p.86

Despite the strength of his organization, he continued to experience challenges to this leadership. In 1929, he was arrested in Chicago accused of the death of his business manager, Claude Green, over a financial dispute. As Ali was not in Chicago at the time of the murder, he was clearly innocent. Yet, after being arrested, he was incarcerated and died mysteriously after being released from police custody months later.

By the time of his death in 1929, the organization had more than 30,000 members nationwide. While many remained, Wallace's message began to resonate as Ali's death left a great void. It is from this void, that the Nation of Islam benefitted. The charismatic leadership of Wallace and teachings were similar to those of Ali which helped him to fill the void and gain converts. As such, in 1930, he organized the Nation of Islam in Detroit, Michigan, USA, and worked to expand.[192]

In 1931, Elijah Poole, an assistant to Wallace who changed his name to Elijah Muhammad, moved into a

---

[192] Ibid, p.86

leadership role of the Nation of Islam in Detroit. Within a very short period of time, he was named Chief Minister of the nation and preached the message of the nation with great appeal drawing many into the fold. In 1934, he was sent to Chicago, Illinois, USA, to establish a center in the city. He was particularly successful in drawing many from the Second Great Migration in Chicago. The same year, Wallace disappeared which thrusted Elijah to the forefront.[193]

The Nation of Islam contained key components that were critical to its early success and remain critical to its sustaining power. The message remained consistent in that independence through faith and knowledge of self through racial pride were key tenets. A university was created to teach Islamic doctrine as well as the tenets of the organization. The Fruit of Islam was established to secure the faith.[194] Together, these components addressed the race

---

[193] Misiroglu, Gina, American Countercultures: An Encyclopedia of Nonconformists, Alternate Lifestyles, and Radical Ideas in U.S. History, Taylor & Francis, 2015, p.86
[194] Ibid, pp.86-87

issues of the day by promoting economic self-sufficiency and providing the infrastructure to accomplish this goal.

Members were encouraged to change their names to incorporate "X" along with a traditional Muslim name to signify their affiliation to the new faith. As many African Americans had a lineage to Slavery and took their names from the slave masters, changing the last name to "X" also signified a permanent break in the chains and unshackling of the historical yoke of oppression.[195] The programs implemented by the nation also helped to uplift the downtrodden and provide opportunities for economic insolvency. It is from these members that nation would prosper and extend itself, though, not without controversy.

Malcolm X became a prominent minister of the nation in the 1950s and continued to rise in prominence because of his dynamic method of preaching and ability to speak truth to power effectively. Primarily based in New York City, New York, USA, his audience was not only citizens in the local vicinity but also to the nation.[196] It was his

---

[195] Ibid, p.87
[196] Ibid, pp.87-88

commentary on the assassination of President John F. Kennedy in 1963 that drew national criticism not only in American society but also in the ranks of the nation. He stated, relative to the assassination, that it was "a case of chickens coming home to roost."[197] He was subsequently expelled from the nation by Elijah which drove him to transition to Orthodox Islam and make a hajj or pilgrimage to Mecca to connect with the faithful. Shortly after his return, he was assassinated in 1965 before he could express a new song to the faithful.[198]

Elijah continued to drive the Nation of Islam until his death in 1975. The nation, however, had also split into two sects. One which followed the traditional practices as outlined by Elijah and the other, the American Muslim Mission following the orthodox tenets presented by Malcom X. Under the direction of Louis Farrakhan in the 1970s, the Nation of Islam expanded further in

---

[197] Gomez, Michael A., Black Crescent: The Experience and Legacy of African Muslims in the Americas, Cambridge University Press, 2005, p.351

[198] Misiroglu, Gina, American Countercultures: An Encyclopedia of Nonconformists, Alternate Lifestyles, and Radical Ideas in U.S. History, Taylor & Francis, 2015, p.88

communities across America at a great rate lifting the faith to higher heights following the same pattern as Elijah.[199] His efforts and the activities of the nation remain in high regard in the modern era in the United States.

The Holy Writs

Each of the faiths had associated Holy Writs that communicate the story of the supreme being or beings and, in most cases, testimonials and prophecies presented by divine interaction. The Holy Writs themselves were more than just spiritual works or canonical utterings and prescriptions upon clergy. They contained examples of the way believers should live their lives as well as historical references of key events of the faith. Whether the deity was Ra, Yahweh, God, Allah, Brahma, or another, interaction with a supreme being was revealed in some form as an affirmation of the existence of a higher power. The writs, in essence, also became heraldic emblems of the faiths and signets of adoption of specific deities.

---

[199] Ed. Wilmore, Gayraud S., African American Religious Studies: An Interdisciplinary Anthology, Duke University Press, 1989, p.297

Faith	Holy Writ(s)		
Kemetism (Egypt)	Hieroglyphics	Tablets	
Zoroastrianism (Mesopotamia)	Tablets	Avesta	
Judaism	Tanakh Kabbalah	Talmud Midrash	Haggadah
Hinduism	Vedas	Upanishads	Puranas
Buddhism	Pitakas		
Christianity	Bible	Apocrypha	
Islam	Qur'an	Hadith	Koran (Moorish Science)

Figure 17 Table of Holy Writs

Of the faiths, polytheism appeared to be more prevalent in ancient times. The Egyptians and Mesopotamians including the Assyrians and Babylonians worshipped multiple deities as showcased on hieroglyphics and recorded upon tablets. A similar hierarchical structure existed between each of these affirming henotheism in their polytheistic beliefs. Although there was an attempt to Pharoah Akhenaten to shift to monotheism in Egypt, it was short-lived. As such, these nations held closely to polytheistic faiths making it the cornerstones of their lives.

Figure 18 Trinity of Hinduism

Monotheism was initially driven under the faith of Judaism which evolved into Christianity after the new dispensation of Jesus and Islam after a new revelation from Muhammad. All three faiths, Judaism, Christianity, and Islam, reference a single, omnipotent god in their religious texts. Although Christianity morphs Jesus, the Holy Spirit, and God into a triune deity, the dogma and practices support monotheism ensuring alignment with the faith.

While Hinduism and Buddhism share the same source, their paths are slightly different. According to Hindus, Brahma created the universe, Vishnu preserves Brahma's creation, and Shiva, the destroyer, transforms creation. They constitute the Hindu trinity. This aligns with polytheistic beliefs. On the other hand, Buddhists do not directly acknowledge a belief in many gods but do believe in the existence of the supernatural and that the universe is eternal and constantly evolving. This beliefs constitutes pantheism attributing divinity to all beings in the universe. As such, all beings are divine.

So, whether, polytheistic, monotheistic, or pantheistic, all faiths acknowledge the existence of a supreme being, a creator of the universe and everything within it. These beliefs are typically expressed in the imagery adopted by the specific faiths which often adorn their respective emblems as a visual indicator of faith. These emblems were often utilized for further heraldic representation and, as a result, became the substance of recognition for nations and faiths throughout the various lands. As such, if a word goes unspoken but heraldry is in place, one's status or relation will always be known in the dark or in the light based on the imagery.

Symbolic Depictions

Faith was a key factor in the selection of images to represent the specific beliefs of religions. There are several emblems which clearly outline religious affiliations of heralds. In the modern era, the most popular is the cross.

The Cross

The cross is a universal emblem which signifies the faith of Christianity. It is also a heraldic emblem which has been adopted by the Scottish Rite of Freemasonry and York Rite of Freemasonry. It is also linked to a long history of other emblems with their own specific meanings. Some are holy while others are terrestrial. However, when combined, their linkage and meaning provide the clear representations and significance to the respective rite.

Two heralds of God are the sources of key emblems of the Ancient and Accepted Scottish Rite of Freemasonry. Melchizedek is chronicled in the Old Testament of the Holy Bible. Jesus is referenced in the Old Testament and chronicled in the New Testament of the Holy Bible. He is also represented in the Holy Qur'an. Both were steadfast in their duties to God in Salem and Jerusalem respectively and are worthy of emulation.

King Melchizedek, High Priest of Salem, was the keeper of God's tabernacle. Salem translates to "peace" and is referred to as the "City of Peace".[200] By God's authority, Melchizedek, the Herald, was empowered to grant blessings. He blessed Abram whose faith drove him there to seek the blessing on Salem's consecrated ground. After receiving the blessing, he reciprocated with a tithe.[201] To many Biblical historians, this is the blessing that affirmed God's prior promise to Abram that he would be the father of nations.[202]

Regarding the promise, God fulfilled it through Hagar and Sarai. As Sarai had grown in age and believed herself to be barren, she gave her maid servant, Hagar, to Abram to have a child. From Hagar, Ishmael was born.[203] After which, God changed Abram's name to Abraham, had an angel to touch Sarai to make her fertile, changed Sarai's name to Sarah, and declared to Abraham that she would

---

[200] Thornton, John, A Journey to Salem, T. Ward & Company, Second Edition, 1834, p. 55
[201] Holy Bible, Genesis 14:19-20
[202] Holy Bible, Genesis 12
[203] Holy Bible, Genesis 16:11-15

bear him a son to be named Isaac.[204] Isaac was born accordingly.[205]

Abram translates to "exalted father". Abraham is the plural representation denoting "exalted father of many". Sarai's name was, likewise, changed by God to Sarah. Sarai translates to "princess" whereas Sarah translates to "mother of nations".[206] To many Christians, Isaac is the object of God's promise. To others, Ishmael is the object. A holistic view offers that both fulfilled God's promise as the faiths of Judaism and Islam represents the multitude of nations.

For Christianity, Isaac's bloodline eventually produced David who was designated for King of Jerusalem by Nathan, God's herald.[207] Jerusalem translates to "foundation of peace" or "vision of peace".[208] It is from this bloodline that Jesus is born.[209] While Jesus' birth is agreed upon between the Christian and Muslim faiths, their

---

[204] Holy Bible, Genesis 17
[205] Holy Bible, Genesis 21:3
[206] Holy Bible, Genesis 17:5,16
[207] Holy Bible, Matthew 1:1-6
[208] Thornton, John, A Journey to Salem, T. Ward & Company, Second Edition, 1834, p. 55
[209] Holy Bible, Matthew 1:6-25

account on death differ. Both concur on the divine origin of Jesus's conception and birth.[210-211] According to the Holy Qur'an, Jesus ascended from the earth by Allah with an exemplar crucified instead.[212] According to the Holy Bible, Jesus was crucified first at Calvary and then resurrected in Jerusalem while under Roman rule.[213] His life, death and resurrection, is the foundation for everlasting peace for Christians as Jesus, the eternal Melchizedek, the eternal High Priest, brought forth the New Dispensation.

The representation of Jesus' sacrifice in Christianity is the cross. Portrayals of it drove variations of the cross in heraldic representations. The most common is the single-barred cross. However, there are variances in its meanings. For example, the empty cross represents a resurrected Jesus to some. To others, it represents an implement of Jesus' death. A crucifix is a representation of the cross with Jesus' body affixed.

---

[210] Holy Qu'ran, 19:16-34
[211] Holy Bible, Matthew 1:18-23
[212] Holy Qu'ran, 4:157-158
[213] Holy Bible, Mark 15:25

Figure 19 Crosses of Christendom

Another representation is the Cross of Jerusalem. It consists of a single-barred cross surrounded by four other crosses to represent the crucifixion of Jesus. The surrounding crosses represent the wounds to the hands, feet, and side of Jesus in addition to the headplate.[214] A two-barred cross was subsequently introduced to highlight the horizontal extension of Jesus' arms and the area in which the feet of Jesus were nailed. A three-barred cross was also introduced to not only identify the locations where the hands and feet were pierced but also the location of the nameplate which stated "INRI" was affixed.[215] "INRI"

---

[214] Hickman, Hoyt L., United Methodist Altars: A Guide for the Congregation, Revised, Abingdon Press, 2011, pp.105-106
[215] Stillson, Henry Leonard, William James Hughan, History of the Ancient and Honorable Fraternity of Free and Accepted Masons and Concordant Orders, Fraternity Publishing Company, 1890, p.783

translates to Jesus of Nazareth, King of the Jews.[216] These portrayals became heraldic symbols for the faithful.

The triple-barred cross finds its roots in Salem, an ancient, Middle Eastern town mentioned in several passages of the Holy Bible in several passages. It is referenced in the Holy Bible in several locations the Old and New Testaments:

- *In Genesis 14:18—"And **Melchizedek** king of Salem brought forth bread and wine: and he was the priest of the most high God."*

- *Psalms 76:1-3— "In Judah is God known: his name is great in Israel. In Salem also is his tabernacle, and his dwelling place in Zion. There brake he the arrows of the bow, the shield, and the sword, and the battle. Selah."*

- *Hebrews 7:1-2—"For this **Melchizedek**, king of Salem, priest of the most high God, who met Abraham returning from the slaughter of the kings,*

---

[216] Hickman, Hoyt L., United Methodist Altars: A Guide for the Congregation, Revised, Abingdon Press, 2011, p.107

and blessed him; To whom also Abraham gave a tenth part of all; first being by interpretation King of righteousness, and after that also King of Salem, which is, King of peace; Without father, without mother, without descent, having neither beginning of days, nor end of life; but made like unto the Son of God; abideth a priest continually."

These scriptures equate Salem with "power" and "peace". The scriptures also identify Melchizedek as the King of Salem or the King of Peace. He was a chief priest of God, and, in the peace of God, he maintained peace and authority in managing the domain through the wisdom and guidance of the Most-High God. It is by this same token that leaders who bear the emblem of the Cross of Salem are also held accountable for those whom they serve by leading.

Modern day Kings of Salem are situated with the power and authority to maintain peace despite the storms that may cross their paths. As such, it is of critical importance that modern leaders be like Melchizedek. As a chief priest, he was worshipful and transformed those instructions into practical actions in the effective leadership of his people.

The term "worshipful" is a term that should be familiar to all of the bodies within the Masonic diaspora. It does not just apply to the Blue Lodge, but it applies to every house. To some it is just a title or style attached to the head of a Lodge. To others, it is a term of action describing the position that the leader of the body should be in. Worship to our heavenly father up above shall yield wisdom and direction which are key components to the substance of good leadership. In the minds of many, these qualities are the substance of things hoped for in all good leaders. The evidence of which was shown in the respect given to Melchizedek. Consider that Abram, father of many nations and devout worshippers to God, gave Melchizedek a tithe.[217] It was Abraham's faith in God that delivered Ishmael and Isaac who would birth many nations. His respect for a chief priest of God, the King of Salem, provides evidence to the works of Melchizedek.

Many scholars consider Melchizedek as a forerunner to Christ. The Holy Bible affirms that Jesus was considered a

---

[217] Holy Bible, Genesis 14:20

priest in the Order of Melchizedek.[218] The Cross of Salem, the Cross of Peace, is also an ever present reminder of their efforts. Christ gave Christians the opportunity for everlasting life which is the New Dispensation. Melchizedek's efforts fell under the Old Dispensation and the promise changed with the sacrifice of Christ.[219]

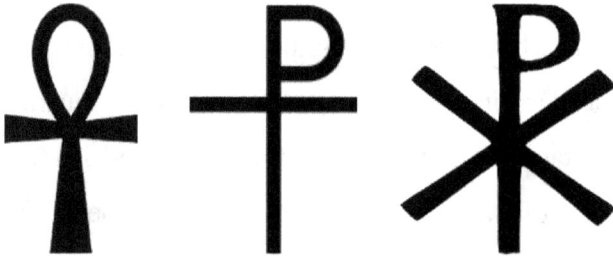

Figure 20 The Ankh, Tau Rho Cross and Chi Rho

The Ankh is an ancient Egyptian symbol which symbolized the life force of the universe. It predates Christianity by millennia as evidenced by its presence on hieroglyphs found on the relief of Pharoah Amenemhet I of the 12th Dynasty and Queen Hatshepsut of the 29th Dynasty of Egypt.[220] The Goddess Nut is often carved and painted

---

[218218] Holy Bible, Hebrews 7:13-17
[219] Barrett, Benjamin Fiske, Lectures on the New Dispensation, Called the New Jerusalem, Michigan and Northern Indiana, Associated of the New Church, 1855, pp.186-187
[220] The Metropolitan Museum Journal, Volume 5, 1972, pp.9-12

with the Ankh in hand as the Goddess of Cosmology who provided protection for the dead entering the afterlife.[221]

The Copts or Egyptian Christians of North Africa were converted to Christianity by Mark, the Evangelist, in the First Century after the death of Jesus.[222] Mark established the Church of Alexandria from converts in the region who utilized familiar symbols like the ankh to express their newfound faith through emblems that Coptic citizens would quickly understand. The ankh already represented the life force which was an eternal prospect as it was commonly believed that the soul lived on beyond the earthly plain. As such, the Copts changed the meaning of the symbol to fit the narrative of the New Dispensation offered by the sacrifice of Jesus Christ.[223] To be a Christian, one must simply be born again to have access to eternal life.

The Tau Rho Cross visually resembled the ankh but was born from its example. The "T" or Tau in Greek

---

[221] Willis, Roy G., World Mythology, H. Holt, 1993, p.40
[222] Morgan, Robert, History of the Coptic Orthodox People and the Church of Egypt, Friesen Press, 2016, pp.9-10
[223] Natan, Yoel, Moon-o-theism, Volume 1, Y. Natan, 2006, p.577

simply represents the cross of the crucifixion of Jesus. The "P" or Rho represents victory. The cross was typically displayed with the Greek letters of alpha and omega on the left and right underneath the tau. When combined, it is a full representation of the cycle of life of Jesus' terrestrial life, death, and resurrection from the cross into eternal life.[224]

The Chi Rho Cross was intended as a sign of providence over the army of Constantine. Towards the end of the 3rd Century, the Roman Empire had been split into three states. By the early 4th Century, Maxentius, Constantine and Licinius led the competing states resulting in several battles for power. At the Battle of the Milvian Bridge on October 28, 312AD against Maxentius, Constantine was commanded in a vision to mark the sign revealed to him on the shields of his soldiers as they engaged in battle. The emblem appeared to be a modified Tau Rho Cross in which the Tau bar was replaced by the Chi or "X" figure. Having followed the command, he defeated Maxentius, and it was later revealed to him that

---

[224] Hurtado, Larry W., The Earliest Christian Artifacts: Manuscripts and Christian Origins, Eerdmans Publishing Company, 2006, pp.146-147

the sign was a representation of Jesus on the Cross. It was this revelation that drove him to commit to Christianity and utilize the Chi Rho Cross as his standard.[225]

After years of conflicts and battles, Constantine defeated Licinius at the Battle of Adrianople on July 3, 324AD.[226] The victory consolidated the entire Roman Empire under his rule. Constantinople was founded in his namesake in 330AD as the new Capitol of Rome and Christianity was declared the official religion of the Eastern Roman Empire. Until his death in 337AD, Constantine's efforts in promoting the faith were tremendous.[227] Gaining converts after conquests and missionary efforts to spread the gospel were key methods that were implemented to effectively facilitate the spread. Constantine's leadership drove the Chi Rho Cross to become not only one of the most recognizable emblems of Christianity but also one that symbolizes his sovereignty. Collectively, they testify to victory through the divine providence of God under the path of Jesus Christ.

---

[225] Drake, H.A., Constantine and the Bishops, John Hopkins University Press, 2002, pp.188-189
[226] Ibid, p.235
[227] Ibid, p.393

In the Scottish Rite, the powers of a good Sovereign Grand Commander are properly managed through his supplication by way of being worshipful. Prayer and supplication to the creator ensures that peace prevails and that there is a strong direction for the organization. So, like Melchizedek, the Grand Commander is as Sovereign over the jurisdiction of the Scottish Rite as Melchizedek was over Salem. Likewise, with his leadership directed by the Most-High God, peace is maintained creating a holy foundation for future growth in the same manner that Jesus' sacrifice of earthly glory and ambition laid the pathway for eternal life.

In etymological terms, Salem and Jerusalem appear to hold similar meanings. Salem is translated as "foundation of peace" and Jerusalem as "city of peace."[228] Together, they both set the stage for Prince of Peace, Jesus. The blessing of Abram by Melchizedek at Salem laid the foundation. King David of the Abrahamic line became the King of Jerusalem extending the foundation upon which the

---

[228] French, Bill, Lessons from Heaven's Borderland, Xulon Press, 2005, p. 225

New Dispensation of Christianity was presented at Jerusalem. In doing so, it proclaimed the sovereignty of Jesus not only as the "Prince of Peace" but the sovereign dispenser of Christian salvation.

Relative to the Scottish Rite, Sovereign Grand Commanders, bearers of the Cross of Salem in slanted form, who align with this lineage of faith are also set to build upon solid ground should they follow the lead of God in the execution of the cardinal virtues of the Masonic Order. Fortitude is required to lead through trying times to restore peace. Prudence is critical in regulating actions, seeking truth and applying wisdom to life's daily situations. Temperance in leadership is crucial in maintaining balance carefully weighing key factors in the decision making processes. Rendering justice without distinction of rank and grade was one of the most admirable traits of King Solomon, son of King David.[229] Stellar execution of all four of these virtues with God's guidance is a sign of one who rules well.

---

[229] https://www.hillsborough25.org/masonic_noble_virtues.html, retrieved 6/5/2023

The un-slanted cross is used symbolically by faiths to represent the leader in the same religious light as Melchizedek. The Pope's triple roles as leader of worship, teacher, and community leader are represented thusly. It aligns him with St. Peter whose powers and responsibilities were temporal, spiritual, and material. These align with the three theological virtues of faith, hope, and charity.[230] Even though Freemasonry is not a religion, these same three principles are the cornerstone of the Order.

The Cross of Salem is also used to represent leaders of a Grand Commandery of Knights Templar. Templars of old committed themselves to the protection of the Holy Land while Templars of new era commit themselves to the protection of the faith. In like manner with the Pope, faith is the key principle which is marked by the emblem.

The key focus of the York Rite is spirituality. The faiths of Abraham and Jesus, namely Judaism and Christianity respectively, are both represented in the Capitular, Cryptic and Chivalric Degrees. Under the

---

[230] The Ecclesiastical Review, Volume 44, American Ecclesiastical Review, 1911, p.161

direction of a Grand High Priest, the Capitular Degrees of Holy Royal Arch Masonry are inculcated and conserved. Under the direction of a Grand Thrice Illustrious Master, the Cryptic Degrees of Royal and Select Masters are inculcated and preserved. Both are based upon the Old Testament of the Holy Bible. Under the direction of a Right Eminent Grand Commander, the solidarity of the Christian faith is directed like the solidarity of the Knights Templar of the Holy Wars to preserve the rite.[231] Leadership in these bodies and the Symbolic Lodge are selectively honored as Knights of the York Cross of Honor for their service.[232] As such, it is keenly clear that the focus of this Rite is faith-based.

As the focus of the Scottish Rite is philosophical yet spiritual, this provides a hint as to why the Cross of Salem may be represented in a slanted fashion for the Sovereign Grand Commander. Despite the final position of the cross, the messages of power and peace through both orders ring

---

[231] Morris, Brent S., The Complete Idiots Guide to Freemasonry, Alpha Books, 2006, pp.92-99
[232] Ibid, p.127

loudly and clearly. Representing those virtues through actions will ensure peace and order in leadership.

The two-barred cross or the "Cross of Lorraine" is known in many circles as the Cross of the Army of Godfrey de Bouillon, Duke of Lower Lorraine and Defender of the Holy Sepulcher. Godfrey de Bouillon was the son of Count Eustace II of Boulogne and Ida of Lorraine, daughter of Godfrey the Bearded (Godfrey III), Duke of Lower Lorraine. Lorraine had been segregated into Upper and Lower sections under the Holy Roman Empire long ago and placed under the direction of separate Dukes. The father of Godfrey III, Gothelo I, had been granted the Duchy of Lower Lorraine in 1023 and Upper Lorraine in 1033 which, effectively, consolidated the Duchy under a single leader.[233] A powerful Duchy with experienced soldiers and leadership, its consolidation was viewed as a threat to the Holy Roman Empire which set into action several events that lead to multiple transitions of leadership in the domain.

---

[233] Woodward, Bernard Bolingbroke, William Leist Readwin Cates, Encyclopaedia of Chronology, Lee and Shepard, 1872, p.875

Henry III actually came to power in 1039 after the death of his father, Conrad II of Germany.[234] He was crowned emperor of the Holy Roman Empire by Pope Clement II who had, himself, been nominated by Henry to the papal crown. After the death of Pope Clement II, in 1047, Henry nominated Pope Benedict IX in 1048, and after his death during the same year, nominated Pope Damasus II who died within a month of elevation. As such, Henry selected Pope Leo IX in 1049 as a puppet tool to control the Empire.[235]

After the death of Gothelo in 1044, control over both Duchies were to be segregated to Godfrey III and Gothelo II by order of the Emperor, Henry III. According to scholars, this was due to fear of a united Lorraine. Outraged by the decision, Godfrey III started a twelve year rebellion in 1044. This drove the emperor to appoint Frederick of Luxembourg as Duke of Lower Lorraine in 1046 and Adalbert as Duke of Upper Lorraine in 1047. Eustace took on the cause of his father-in-law's rebellion in 1048. As a result of his participation in the rebellion and from claims

---

[234] Ibid, p.875
[235] Ibid, p.955

that his marriage to Ida was within a prohibited degree of kinship as both were descendants of King Louis II of France, Eustace was excommunicated from the Holy Roman Church within months of his declaration by Pope Leo IX in 1049.[236]

Although the rebellion devastated Lower Lorraine, it had outlasted Pope Leo IX and the Emperor. Pope Leo died in 1054 and was succeeded by Pope Victor II. The new Pope was at the side of Emperor Henry III when he died in October of 1056. As the guardian of and advisor to the new emperor Henry IV, who was only six years old at the time, Pope Victor II worked through the youth to restore peace throughout the Holy Roman Empire. In doing so, Godfrey was exiled to Tuscany to serve as Margrave and, after the death of Pope Victor II in 1057, he was appointed Duke of Spoleto through the work of his brother, Pope Stephen IX, who succeeded Pope Victor II.[237]

As Duke of Spoleto, Godfrey became very powerful politically and utilized his relationships to become a

---

[236] Ibid, p.875
[237] Clare, Israel Smith, Mediaeval History, Union Book Company, 1906, pp.1938-1941

political cornerstone in Northern Italy. His success in expelling antipope Benedict X during the term of his brother and political intervention in regional conflicts under succeeding Popes had gained him control of Loguordo and Pisa and prominence in Rome. His service through this period found him being recalled as Duke of Lower Lorraine by Emperor Henry IV after the death of Frederick in 1065 and Margrave of Antwerp which was under Frederick's control.[238]

Figure 21 Godfrey de Bouillon

---

[238] Ibid, p.1941

As Duke of Lower Lorraine, Godfrey rebuilt his castle at Bouillon and maintained his status as Margrave of Tuscany until his death in 1069. Godfrey IV, the hunchback, succeeded his father as Duke of Lower Lorraine and Margrave of Tuscany and Antwerp. After his death in 1076, Lower Lorraine was transferred to Conrad II, Tuscany to Matilda and Antwerp to Godfrey de Bouillon. Conrad ascended to King of Germany in 1087. After Conrad's ascension, Godfrey de Bouillon, once again, became Duke of Lower Lorraine.[239] It is through this line of succession that he came to power.

A devout Christian and accomplished warrior, Godfrey was a prominent figure in the First Crusade. He took out loans on his castle at Bouillon and on his other lands to finance the Crusade called on by Pope Urban II in 1095. In doing so, he gathered Knights from across Europe to liberate Jerusalem, the Holy Land, from Muslim control and aid the Byzantine Empire which was under Muslim attack. By 1097, multiple armies had arrived at Constantinople, which was the Capitol of the Byzantine

---

[239] Ibid, p.875

Empire along with Godfrey's Crusaders. Together, they marched into battle. After three years of war, the Crusaders captured Jerusalem and established Crusaders states. [240]

The Army of Godfrey of Bouillon adopted the heraldic, two-barred cross to denote its fealty to the Holy Roman Church of the Holy Roman Empire as the three-barred cross had been adopted by the Pope, the representative of the Holy Roman Church. When engaging in battle, the Cross of Lorraine was worn in red to represent the willingness of the Knights under Godfrey's command to shed their blood in defense of Christ and the Church. As a result of their efforts, Godfrey was heralded as the Defender of the Holy Sepulcher and installed as King of Jerusalem in 1099. He had a short reign as king controlling Jerusalem, Acre, Ascalon, Arsuf, Jaffa and Caesarea. He died on July 18, 1100, in Jerusalem and was buried at the Church of the Holy Sepulcher.[241]

The symbols that were utilized by the Army of Godfrey de Bouillon and the Knights of the First Crusades have

---

[240] Clare, Israel Smith, Mediaeval History, Union Book Company, 1906, p.2059
[241] Ibid, p.2063

remained stable throughout the centuries across the Holy Roman Empire and active within the ranks of the church and Rites of Freemasonry. Like the Cross of Salem, the Cross of Lorraine and Cross of Jerusalem are used today as hierarchical symbols within the Roman Catholic Church. They are also used in Freemasonry as symbols of authority in the York and Scottish Rites.

The Cross of Lorraine is utilized by Cardinals or officers of the Roman Catholic Church to represent their fealty and willingness to push forth in the name of the church. It was worn as an emblem on the arms of Rudolphus, Archbishop of Canterbury in 1114.[242] It is also said to have been instituted as a heraldic emblem by Frederick Barbarossa, Emperor of Rome, in 1190. It is also used to identify officers of Knights Templar Commanderies in the York Rite of Freemasonry.[243] The slanted version is adorned by Sovereign Grand Inspectors General of the Scottish Rite of Freemasonry to signify their fealty to the

---

[242] The Monthly Packet of Evening Readings for Members of the English Church, Volume 10, Johan and Charles Mozley, 1855, p.146
[243] The Monthly Packet of Evening Readings for Members of the English Church, Volume 10, Johan and Charles Mozley, 1855, p.146

Rite as active, emeritus or past-active members under the direct leadership of the Sovereign Grand Commander.[244]

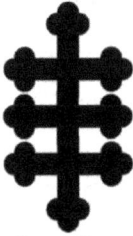

Papal Cross

Godfrey

Soldiarity

Scottish Rite Leaders

Scottish Rite Management

Scottish Rite Soldiarity

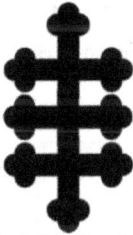

York Rite Leaders

York Rite Management

York Rite Soldiarity

Figure 22 Papal and Masonic Hierarchy

---

[244] The New Age, Volume 26, Supreme Council, 33°, Ancient and Accepted Scottish Rite of Freemasonry of the Southern Jurisdiction, U.S.A., 1918, p.152

The Cross of Jerusalem was adorned by soldiers during the Crusades in red during the Holy Wars to symbolize their willingness to shed blood and give their lives on behalf of the church. Soldiers under the command of Godfrey de Bouillon were of the first to fight for the faith in this manner.[245] This emblem is heraldry for Knights Templar who have directly adopted the Christian faith which lasts to this date.[246] However, as the Scottish Rite endeavors to understand all faiths philosophically, the cross was selected to represent a free church within a free state with respect to all faiths. It is also used as jewels for subordinate level leadership.

Between the Roman Catholic Church and the Scottish Rite, the leadership structure is also similar. As the Pope oversees a consortium of Cardinals for consultation and decision making for the Holy See or the ecclesiastical jurisdiction of the Roman Catholic Church, the Sovereign Grand Commander oversees a consortium of Sovereign Grand Inspector Generals, members of a Supreme Council,

---

[245] Aspiration, Representation and Memory: The Guise in Europe, 1506-1688, Taylor & Francis, 2016, p.31
[246] Shaw, Jeffrey M., Timothy J. Demy, War and Religion: An Encyclopedia of Faith and Conflict, ABC-CLIO, 2017, p.76

to execute the affairs of the Rite. Honorary members of the Supreme Council or Grand Inspector Generals are crowned based on degrees of service but do not have the same rights as active or emeritus members. Their privileges are extended at local levels. Likewise, bishops, priests and other church officers have limited ability at the Holy See but full authority at the local levels to which they have been assigned.[247]

So, from a hierarchical perspective during the Holy Wars, the triple-barred cross represented national leadership under the pope, the double-barred cross represented local leadership under leaders like Godfrey de Bouillon, and the Cross of Jerusalem or likenesses thereof represented the rank and file who dedicated themselves wholly to the cause. The emblems translated well into the Rites of Freemasonry and still stand today. Thus, making the style and rank of leadership readily apparent.

---

[247] Keeler, Helen, Susan Grimbly, 101 Things Everyone Should Know About Catholicism, Adams Media, 2005, Part 2, No. 38

Figure 23 Emblem of Papacy

For the Roman Catholic Church, this Ecclesiastical Heraldry is further symbolized in its Coat of Arms through the keys to heaven entrusted to St. Peter:[248]

> *"And I will give unto thee the keys of the kingdom of heaven: and whatsoever thou shalt bind on earth shall be bound in heaven: and whatsoever thou shalt loose on earth shall be loosed in heaven."*

The keys are gold and silver to represent the power of loosing and binding in heaven (gold) and on earth (silver)

---

[248] Holy Bible, Matthew 16:18-19

through the papacy. The cord with the bows that unites the grips alludes to the bond between the two powers. Collectively, they represent the "Keys to the Kingdom". The triple crown represents the pope's functions as supreme pastor, teacher, and priest. The gold cross on the triple crown symbolizes the sovereignty of Jesus.[249] In totality, the pope represents the keeper of the keys on earth.

The Crosses of Jerusalem, Lorraine and Salem and their variations have a direct connection to a belief in God through Jesus Christ as they each represent specific facets of Christ's sacrifice. However, like Christ and like Mohammed, the fundamental duty of believers is to meet the demands of God and the crosses signify that responsibility. This is a key component to the heraldry of the cross. It is a reminder of the primary premise echoed by the author of the Book of Ecclesiastes in the Holy Bible - "let us hear the conclusion of the whole matter: Fear God

---

[249] Bell, Gary R., How Good is Good Enough for God?, WestBow Press, 2017

and keep his commandments: for this is the whole duty of man."[250]

Winged Standards

Like the cross, the standards of the legions of ancient Rome historically bore multiple animals like eagles, boars, and wolves to represent the souls of the specific legions. Mythical beasts were also associated with some and paraded in battle. The specific standard represented the essence of the legion or "genius legionis" and the legion would do anything to protect it.[251]

Some standards were also aligned with deities or "genius loci" as protective spirits. Multiple divisions were associated with specific legions which is the basis for the association of multiple animals, mythical creatures, and deities into a single legion. These beliefs were not only critical to unification within the ranks but also meaningful relative to reputation potentially striking fear into the opposition before taking to the fields of battle.

---

[250] Holy Bible, Ecclesiastes 12:13
[251] D'Amato, Raffaele, Roman Standards and Standard Bearers, Bloomsbury Publishing, 2018, pp.27-28

Standards of Roman Legions[252]

Legion	Animal	Mythical	Deity
I	Boar, Bull & Ram	Capricorn & Pegasus	Minerva
II	Boar & She-Wolf	Capricorn & Pegasus	Mars & Hercules
III	Bull & Stork		
IIII	Lion, Bull & Ram	Capricorn	
V	Elephant, Eagle & Bull		
VI	She-wolf & Bull	None	Twins
VII	Bull		Castor & Pollux
VIII	Bull		
VIIII	None		Neptune
X	Bull, Boar & Dolphin		Neptune
XI	Dolphin & She-wolf	Capricorn	Neptune & Twins
XII	None	Lightning Bolt	None
XIII	Lion & Eagle	Capricorn	Castor & Pollux
XIIII	None	Capricorn	None
XV	None		Apollo
XVI	Lion	Pegasus	None
XX	Boar	Capricorn	None
XXI	None	Capricorn	None
XXII	Wolf & Bull	Capricorn	Hercules
XXVIIII	Eagle with Lion in talons		
XXX	Dolphin	Capricorn	Jupiter & Neptune

Figure 24 Table of Roman Legions

---

[252] The British Magazine, Volume 29, John Turrill, 1846, p.334

The eagle became the earmark animal standard for Rome by the hands of Consul Gaius Marius in 107BC.[253] To this day, the eagle with the emblazoned letters "SPQR" (Senatus Populus Que Romanus in Latin translates to "the senate and the people of Rome") still embodies the once great Roman empire because the eagle has grand qualities that could be emulated by every soldier and leader.[254] Specific attributes are highlighted with specific parts of the eagle's body. Each quality represented by the body part relates to specific portions of leadership and service.

The eye of the eagle often represents vision and a keen focus on leadership and service.[255] A good leader is a good servant as he must focus on utilizing the skills of those for whom he is accountable to benefit the whole. A good servant is a good leader as he must focus on the task at hand and serve as a director to see it through to the end. Like the construction of buildings, if the cornerstone is not laid on level ground, the structure will not be erected in a

---

[253] Mommsen, Theodor, The History of Rome, Volume 3, C. Scribner's Sons, 1905, p.462

[254] Mouritsen, Henrik, Politics in the Roman Republic, Cambridge University Press, 2017, p.6

[255] Rogers, Janine, Eagle, Reaktion Books, 2014, p.28

plumb fashion. As such, great focus must be taken early on to reduce the possibility of negative, long-term effects.

An eagle's eyes are also enhanced by sets of lenses. When an eagle is flying towards the sun, a lens protracts to protect the eyes. When an eagle seeks prey, a lens retracts to allow for sharper vision. The conical shape of the pair of eyes allows for an increased field of vision and the ability to see even the smallest prey.[256] This superior vision allows the eagle to take deeper looks at situations and see past the apparent as with all great leaders in the history of mankind.

Compared to the human eye, the eagle eye is far superior. Visual acuity is the eye's ability to separate details of an object without any blur. The normal or a 'good' vision for a human is 20/20. Eagles, however, have retinas with cones and have a much deeper fovea—a cone-rich structure in the back of the eye. These give them a visual acuity of an impressive 20/5, or 20/4 which allows

---

[256] Capainolo, Peter, Carol A. Butler, How Fast Can A Falcon Dive?, Rutgers University Press, 2010, p.41

them to hunt even the tiny prey from hundreds of feet up in the air.[257]

Eagles can see colors more vividly than humans can. They can even see ultraviolet light and pick out more shades of one color. Their ability to even see the UV light allows them to see the bodily traces left by their prey.[258] Mice's and other small prey's urine is visible to the eagles in the ultraviolent range, making them easy targets even a few hundred feet above the ground.

Human eyes are positioned at the front of the heads, giving us a binocular vision and a peripheral vision of just 180 degrees. We can only see complete images when we use both eyes, as closing one will block a portion of vision that was visible with that eye. The use of both eyes gives us the ability to determine the depth of field and helps us realize the speed of any moving object. Unfortunately, our peripheral vision is quite poor.

---

[257] https://www.insightvisioncenter.com/human-vision-vs-eagle-vision/ retrieved 6/6/2023
[258] Capainolo, Peter, Carol A. Butler, How Fast Can A Falcon Dive?, Rutgers University Press, 2010, pp.41-42

On the other hand, an eagle's eyes are rotated towards the front of the head and are angled 30 degrees from the midline of the face. This allows them to have a 340 degree field of vision.[259] Their peripheral vision is quite impressive greatly assisting their predatory practices.

The ability to switch between seeing things that are near and far requires quick changes in the lens of the eyes, which is known as accommodation. As humans age, the muscles required to change the shape of the lens get stiff and become less effective, requiring us to wear glasses to see distant and nearby things equally clear.[260] However, the eagles not only have a lens that changes the shape to accommodate the changing distance but even their cornea can change shape to better focus on near and far objects. Considering these factors, eagle eyes are far superior to the eyes of humans. It is highly unlikely that the human eye will ever excel to the point of an eagle's due to its position and construction. While poor vision can be enhanced with

---

[259] Ibid, p.42
[260] Yanoff, Myron, Jay S. Duker, Ophthalmology, Mosby Elsevier, 2009, p.52

visual aids, the human eye can never be as efficient as an eagle's.

An eagle's wings stretch far and wide and, when flexed by the strength of its faithful breasts, it has the strength to carry objects that weigh significantly greater. Its claws hold the power to grasp and to prick prey. A full sized eagle can easily carry away a lamb. Once captured, the eagle's beak is hard enough to penetrate its prey.[261] It is by its mouth and its claws that life and death on its prey are dispersed. With all great leaders, the life and death of their organizations are typically measured from the tongue.

The eagle is also unique as it can fly higher than any other bird. It can do so because of all the aforementioned attributes. Anciently, it was considered a messenger of the gods because its abilities far outweighed its counterparts. It can also swoop faster than any other bird and defeat any bird which comes in its path. The eagle is the clearly the king of the skies because it has mastered the skies. As such, it flies over terrain majestically with no fear as a representation of its courage and strength. A clear

---

[261] Watson, Jeff, The Golden Eagle, Bloomsbury Publishing, 2010, p.81

representation of infinite power, its majesty and mastery symbolize immortality of the soul.[262]

Historically, great leaders have shown great balance when wielding power. Several have moved majestically while exhibiting mastery in service. It was their "eagle" vision that allowed them to focus on specific aspects which gained their successes. It was their strength that allowed them to carry heavy burdens which may have seemed impossible to the average man. It was their patience that prevented wasted motion. It was their foresight that prompted them to hold off on force.

Many see Dr. Martin Luther King Jr. and the Honorable Barak H. Obama as eagle-like men. African Americans certainly benefitted from the introduction of the Civil Rights Act of 1964 and the Voting Rights Act of 1965 which were driven by the efforts of Dr. King.[263] The election of Obama to the highest office of the United States of America in 2008 despite arduous challenges and high profile challengers was certainly a moral victory for many

---

[262] Ibid, p.360
[263] Kotz, Nick, Judgment Days, Houghton Miflin Harcourt, 2005, p.333

American citizens.[264] Americans were presented government sponsored options for healthcare through the Affordable Care Act of 2010 that would not have been available. Its intent was to help the helpless.[265] Both King and Obama mastered the terrain of their respective days and ages to secure solutions for those whom they protected and served. In doing so over tremendous odds, their eagle status is cemented.

The way both succeeded though wreaks of a sense of majesty. They flew majestically over troubled terrain, grasped the challenges in their claws and achieved victories through stellar leadership. Their architected plans satisfied the outcries of citizens justifying the specific moves taken. The number of lynchings and voices from the number of uninsured were heard. So, how can a good leader lead effectively without serving by listening to followers?

Consider that none of the movements of the Civil Rights Era would have succeeded without eagle men and

---

[264] Andrews, Daryl L., Personification of Hope: A Legacy of National African American Political Leadership, Andrews Press, 2012, p.
[265] Morris, John C., Martin K. Mayer, Robert C. Kenter, State Politics and the Affordable Care Act, Taylor & Francis, 2019, p.1

women to stay focused on specific missions. Without accomplishing the missions, the vision could not have become a reality. As such, despite the role, "leader" or "follower", eagle qualities are critical to success at the vision and mission levels.

An eagle leads by example. Here are seven habits of eagles that are typically associated with organizational leadership and were likely utilized by these heroes:[266]

1. **Eagles flock together:** Eagles enjoy living at high altitudes and do not mix with other birds because they cannot fly at the same altitude. Any mixture with other birds is used as an opportunity to find something to eat or to take something away from them. Only eagles can match other eagles.

2. **Eagles see their prey or enemies a long distance away:** Eagles place themselves in positions where they can see prey and where they can easily see danger coming their way. Their nests are typically

---

[266] https://www.cscslions.org/dr-derenzo-s-blog/7-habits-of-eagles-leadership-lesson retrieved 6/6/2023

high enough so that predators cannot reach but close enough where its superior vision can spot prey.

3. **Eagles do not eat dead things:** Eagles take up challenges and do not waste time on things with no movement. They do not associate with scavengers who feed off the dead.

4. **Eagles love the storm:** Eagles can fly into storms because they are uniquely crafted to do so. They typically USE the storm to gain higher heights in flight. The pressure of the storm lifts them up while flying through allowing the eagle to fly higher with less energy. Like all good leaders, the challenge of the storm allows that eagle to fly to greater heights.

5. **Eagles test before they trust:** After a female eagle and male eagle have mated, they stay mated for life because trust has been earned. The female eagle will run the male eagle through a series of tests before choosing him as her mate. Once faithfulness has been proven, trust has then been earned.

6. **Eagles train their children to maturity:** Mature eagles ensure that their offspring are protected until

they are ready to move forward on their own. Under the cover of protection, the children are in the venue of preparation. Like internships in corporations, neophytes are trained under the corporate umbrella with some restrictions. As such, when college studies have concluded and the restrictions are removed, they are more likely to move forward successfully in the corporate world.

7. **Eagles retire until new feathers grow:** Older eagles with worn feathers retire to high places to replenish. A sabbatical is a common practice with faith leaders and professors who provide opportunities for them to replenish physically, mentally, and emotionally. New learnings are typically achieved and allow them to return armed with new information and refreshed.

When considering all the qualities of the eagle, it is understandable why the Roman leaders flocked to this animal to represent its legions.

The qualities of the stork or pelican held different representations for nations and faiths. In Greek and Roman mythology, the stork served as a model leader and caretaker. The stork and the bull were associated with the 3rd Roman legion, as such, because it served as a protective force in North Africa as well as a corps of engineers. They were primarily responsible for constructing roads and aqueducts providing for the army's ability to sustain itself and mobilize.[267] By urbanizing areas, Rome was able to create, maintain, and control cities and vassal states.

To the Christian, Jesus is often represented as a pelican because pelicans were known, according to legend, to feed their young with their own blood for sustenance. As Jesus shed his blood for mankind, his blood is seen as sustenance for the faithful and lens through which God, the father, hears his children.[268] As such, the pelican is typically represented surrounded by its brood who are dipping their beaks into their mother's wounded breast. According to Albert Mackey, "It is said, if it be true, that the pelican kills its young, and grieves for them for three days. Then she wounds herself, and with the aspersion of her blood

---

[267] Elliott, Simon, Roman Britain's Missing Legion, Pen & Sword Books Limited, 2021, pp.11-12
[268] O'Collins, Gerald, Jesus Our Redeemer: A Christian Approach to Salvation, OUP Oxford, 2007, p.188

resuscitates her children."[269] For Christians, Jesus' blood resuscitates and clears away sin providing an opportunity for the dead to be resurrected along with the just.

To the ancient Egyptians, the pelican is revered as a protector and a guide. Pelicans are natural protectors against snakes whom they can scoop and swallow with ease. In the underworld, it is seen as an emblem of safe passage for the dead guiding them to the light and scooping evil spirits away. In doing so, the dead soul, represented by the falcon, may travel safely to God.[270]

The owl is associated with divine wisdom and, like the falcon, is also a symbol of the soul. An owl's vision can penetrate darkness allowing it to see in the dark and in the light. Wisdom is attained from superior insight which becomes the guiding force to its actions. In fact, an owl's vision is sharper at night. An owl's hoot at night, however,

---

[269] Mackey, Albert Gallatin, Edward L. Hawkins, An Encyclopedia of Freemasonry and Its Kindred Sciences, Masonic History Company, 1913, pp.640-641
[270] Hart, George, The Routledge Dictionary of Egyptian Gods and Goddesses, Routledge, 2005, p.125

symbolized that death was forthcoming.[271] With the eyes placed int he forefront, it has 360 degrees of vision compared to 340 degrees of vision of an eagle, whose eyes are placed at angles.[272] Therefore, its ability to navigate in light or darkness is superior indeed.

Celestial and Terrestrial Standards

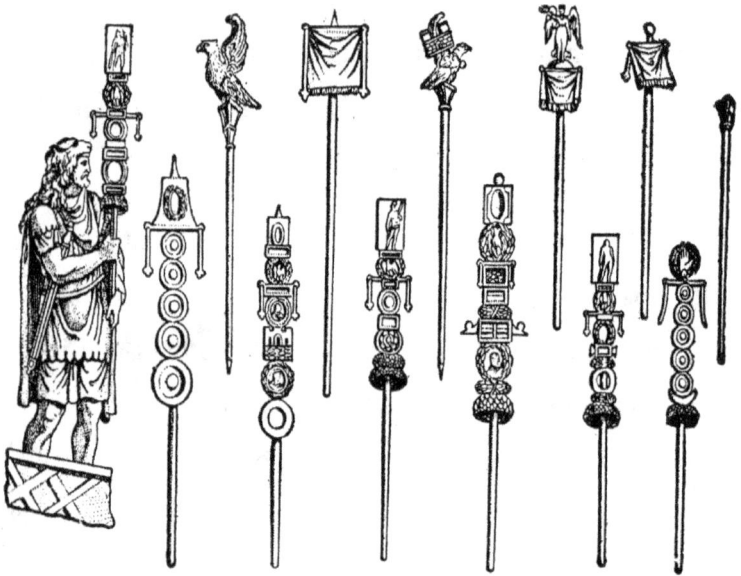

Figure 25 Roman Standards

---

[271] Dobson, Eleanor, Nichola Tonks, Ancient Egypt in the Modern Imagination, Bloomsbury Publishing, 2020, p.222
[272] Berger, Cynthia, Owls, Stackpole Books, 2005, p.7

Pegasus, according to mythology, was a winged horse born from the blood of Medusa. Its ability to fly to Olympus and roam across terrestrial planes made it the choice animal for the gods Poseidon and Athena.[273] Roman Legion I adopted it as its mythical standard to promote its ability to swiftly attack its enemies on land or through the sky.

Landbound animals were particularly revered due to their toughness and barbarism during times of war. Several embodied ferocity and swiftness on terrain. The dexterity and determination of others aligned with loyalty, calmness, and bravery under pressure. These characteristics embodied the quintessential soldier particularly in Rome.

Legions which adorned the standard of the boar were considered the most barbaric. Preferring clubs to swords, fighting was not done necessarily by precision but with the brute force of a berserker. Barbarism was the common characteristic associated with boar standard bearers.[274] The

---

[273] Dixon-Kennedy, Mike, Encyclopedia of Greco-Roman Mythology, Bloomsbury Academic, 1998, p.239
[274] Geary, Patrick J., Readings in Medieval History: The Early Middle Ages, University of Toronto Press, 2010, p.77

ram and goat were also similarly heralded due to their ferocity, determination, and dexterity.[275] Stubbornness is a key factor that is associated with determination. By this same token, the bull or Minotaur were similarly set aside for those legions that were particularly barbaric. A favorite of the goddess Venus, strength, stubbornness, and dexterity were beautiful qualities because they are key attributes in achieving victory in war.[276]

While ferocity is a key attribute associated with the wolf, it is also the prime characteristic of other animals and gods. The association with the founders of Rome or the Twins is the she-wolf. The she-wolf protected and nurtured Remus and Romulus, raising them in the wild. Ironclad legions often bore this standard as their primary task was protection. Mars was also the celestial representation of the wolf.[277] Lions were also associated with legions to express their majesty and strength. Vespasian selected the lion for

---

[275] Werness, Hope B., The Continuum Encyclopedia of Animal Symbolism in Art, Continuum, 2006, p.342

[276] Keppie, L.J.F., Legions and Veterans: Roman Army Papers 1971-2000, Franz Steiner Verlag, 2000, p.202

[277] Preble, George Henry, History of the Flag of the United States of America, A. Williams, 1880, p.55

his Legion to commemorate the strength of the god
Hercules.[278]

Speed and agility are attributes that are often associated
with calvary units in the military. As calvary units rode on
horseback for swiftness and ferocity, the units often
adorned the horse as its standard on land.[279] Swiftness on
the seas were also the prayers of the various seamen aboard
ships of war. As such, the dolphin became a key standard
for vessels that served in the same manner as modern
destroyers which navigated the seas with deadly agility.[280]
The Capricorn or the sea goat was a standard for ramming
vessels designed to inflict maximum damage upon enemy
ships by direct and forceful contact.[281] Swiftness and
deadly power were the key factors exemplified by these
standards.

The gods were also worshipped for safe passage along
the seas which is the basis for prayers of grace and

---

[278] Dando-Collins, Stephen, Legions of Rome: The Definitive History
of Every Imperial Roman Legion, St. Martin's Publishing Group, 2012,
p.130
[279] Ibid, p.196
[280] Ibid, p.128
[281] Ibid, p.128

domination by the bearers of the respective standards. Neptune, Roman god of the sea, was worshipped to ensure protection from the storms of the sea as well as doom for enemy ships with whom they may come in contact. Mars, Roman god of war, was worshipped for strength and power during battle. Apollo was worshipped for speed and accuracy with weapons of war. In addition to these key gods, others were also worshipped for grace and protection.

Modern Symbolism

The Scottish Rite Eagle or double headed eagle represents the same code for Scottish Rite Masons as it did for the Romans. In fact, it doubles down on the qualities as a two-headed eagle is its symbol. It remains the rallying symbol because the qualities represented by the eagle have transcended the ages and are still relevant today. Hence, the eagle remains as the quintessential representation of power and leadership.

The symbol most widely recognized in the Ancient and Accepted Scottish Rite of Freemasonry is the Double-Headed Eagle of Lagash. It is one of the oldest Royal Crests in the existence. This symbol had been in use at least a thousand years before the Hebrew Exodus from Egypt and more than two thousand years before the building of King Solomon's Temple. Records indicate that in the early days of modern Freemasonry the Double-Headed Eagle was first used around 1758 by a Masonic body in Paris. That Masonic body was known as "The Emperors of the East and West" which controlled the advanced Degrees then in use. These degrees are slated as the precursor of the Ancient Accepted Scottish Rite.[282] According to Mackey, the degrees of the Council of Emperors of the East and West numbered twenty-five. With the first nineteen matching those which currently exist in the Scottish Rite, the remaining six were incorporated into the Scottish Rite per the Constitutions of 1762 including:[283]

- 20° - Grand Patriarch Noachite
- 21° - Key of Masonry
- 22° - Prince of Lebanon

[282] Mackey, Albert Gallatin, Edward L. Hawkins, An Encyclopedia of Freemasonry and Its Kindred Sciences, Masonic History Company, 1913, p.241
[283] Scottish Rite, Council of Deliberation, NY, Transactions of the Council of Deliberation for the Bodies of the AAS Rite, in the State of New York, 1884, pp.29-32

- 23° - Knight of the Sun
- 24° – Kadosh
- 25° - Prince of the Royal Secret

The organization established subordinate bodies in France and Germany but endured controversy. In 1760, the Knights of the East was organized in France as a clandestine rival to the Order placing the state of the degrees in flux. However, despite years of disputes between these organizations and the Scottish Rite, the latter survived.[284]

Like the Holy Roman Empire, the kingdom of the Scottish Rite of Freemasonry is called the Holy Empire. Scottish Rite Masons represent the military arm of the empire. The kingdom is dedicated to the principles of the Rite which amplifies and elaborates upon the cardinal virtues of Freemasonry through Ineffable, Historical, Philosophical, Traditional and Chivalric Degrees. These degrees are grouped and categorized to convey specific objectives and meanings of the virtues of Freemasonry.

---

[284] Mackey, Albert Gallatin, Edward L. Hawkins, An Encyclopedia of Freemasonry and Its Kindred Sciences, Masonic History Company, 1913, p.241

Developed years ago, they are categorized and organized as follows:[285]

- The Lodge of Perfection - "Ineffable Degrees":
  - $4°$ - Secret Master
  - $5°$ - Perfect Master
  - $6°$ - Intimate Secretary
  - $7°$ - Provost and Judge
  - $8°$ - Intendant of the Building
  - $9°$ - Elect of Nine
  - $10°$ - Elect of Fifteen
  - $11°$ - Sublime Elect of Twelve
  - $12°$ - Grand Master Architect
  - $13°$ - Master of the Ninth Arch
  - $14°$ - Grand Elect, Perfect and Sublime Mason

- The "Historical & Philosophical Degrees" cover the Fifteenth through the Eighteenth Degrees. While some jurisdictions group the Fifteenth and Sixteenth Degrees under the Council of the Prince of Jerusalem, others group all four degrees under the Chapter of the Rose Croix.

---

[285] Ibid, p.672

- o 15° - Knights of the East or Sword
- o 16° - Prince of Jerusalem
- o 17° - Knight of the East and West
- o 18° - Knights of the Rose Croix

- The lessons taught in the 18th Degree are that man must have a new Temple in his heart where God is worshipped in spirit and in truth and that he must have a new law of love which all men everywhere may understand and practice. This degree affirms the broad principles of universality and tolerance. The pelican represents these beliefs. The "Traditional and Chivalric Degrees" cover the Nineteenth to the Thirty-Second Degrees. While some jurisdictions group the nineteenth to the thirtieth Degrees under the Council of Kadosh and the Thirty-First and Thirty-Second Degrees under the Consistory, others consolidate them all under the Consistory:

  - o 19° - Grand Pontiff
  - o 20° - Grand Master of All Symbolic Lodges; or Master ad Vitam
  - o 21° - Noachite or Prussian Knight

- 22° - Knights of the Royal Axe; or Prince Libanus
- 23° - Chief of the Tabernacle
- 24° - Prince of the Tabernacle
- 25° - Knight of the Brazen Serpent
- 26° - Prince of Mercy
- 27° - Knight Commander of the Temple
- 28° - Knight of the Sun
- 29° - Knights of St. Andrew
- 30° - Knights Kadosh
- 31° - Grand Inspector Inquisitor Commander
- 32° - Sublime Prince of the Royal Secret

In these degrees are found the definitions of good men and good leaders. When transformed into practical action, they convert the thoughts of good men into stones that can be utilized to build a strong tower on the foundation of peace. By doing so, they extend the kingdom physically and spiritually and open pathways for future growth.

The Thirty-Third Degree is an Honorary Degree bestowed upon deserving Fraters. Those chosen few are saluted as Grand Inspectors General with honorary membership in the Supreme Council. Sovereign Grand

Inspectors General hold actual membership as part of the governing class of the Rite.[286]

Figure 26 32nd and 33rd Degree Eagles

The primary standard for the Scottish Rite, the double-headed, is adorned in multiple ways based on the rank of the member. Generally, the symbolic meaning of this symbol is that of duality which resolves itself in unity. As man is composed of both body and spirit, he is both temporary and eternal. Both good and evil exist in the

---

[286] Ibid, p.672

world and good men must perpetually espouse good while opposing evil. It also reminds us that knowledge comes both from study and insight; and that our obligations are both to ourselves and to others; that both faith and reason are necessary.

For Thirty-Second Degree members or Sublime Princes, the double-headed eagle features the motto, pendant from the hilt of the sword to the point and displaying the Latin "spes mea in deo est", which translates "My Hope is in God". Centered in a triangle at the breast of the eagle is the number "32". For Thirty-Third Degree members, the motto in Latin reads "deus meumque jus" which translates "For God and My Right". The eagle is also affixed with a crown and centered, in a triangle at the breast of the eagle, is the number "33".[287] Outside of the triangles and mottos, the coronated eagle is the key differentiation between Thirty-Second and Thirty-Third Degree members. The corona or the crown is a distinct honor afforded by the Supreme Council. Only Grand Inspectors General are

---

[287] Mackey, Albert Gallatin, Edward L. Hawkins, An Encyclopedia of Freemasonry and Its Kindred Sciences, Masonic History Company, 1913, p.495

eligible for the responsibilities associated with the parent organization.

All in all, the various symbols of the Scottish Rite do not easily reveal their meanings. There may be many meanings to any one symbol. Only after thought and reflection do they fulfill their function and begin to trigger ideas in the mind. With the strength and grace of eagles, protection and nourishment of the pelican, may those ideas be transformed into action for the betterment of the world.

Heraldic Regalia

"In the Scottish Rite, the caps indicate the consecration of one's physical and spiritual (material and intellectual) attributes to the betterment of humanity. On the one hand, the caps are an inheritance from our chivalric tradition, as similar ones were associated with European Orders of Knighthood, where they evolved from the Arming Bonnet, worn under the helmet. On the other hand, they are also worn as a type of prayer cap, a tradition which also survives in some religions. Thus, the caps are a constant reminder that the physical must be subject to the spiritual and that, like knights, we must valiantly endeavor to maintain honor and virtue by applying the Moral Sense and Reason."[288] While Arturo de Hoyos' assertion is certainly an honorable description of the cap or the crown, its origins go further than the European Order of Knighthood. In fact, they can be traced as far back as ancient Egypt.

The English word "crown" sources from the Latin word "corona". The "corona" was typically fashioned as a "coronatus" which translates into a "wreath". Among the Greeks and Romans, a coronatus or laurel wreath was given

---

[288] De Hoyos, Arturo, Scottish Rite Ritual Monitor and Guide, Washington DC: The Supreme Council, 33°. SJ, 2010, p.135

as an honor for athletic contests or a reward for military accomplishment. While the coronatus was typically comprised of grass, flowers, and twigs, it evolved in materials and purpose.[289] They were later comprised of gold and precious stones and worn like diadems to identify status.

Figure 27 Gold Diadem and a Coronatus

The diadem was introduced to the Greeks as a symbol of royalty by Alexander the Great (356 BC–323 BC). During his conquests he adopted local customs and practices as a method to ensure that the conquered lands

---

[289] Hunter, Robert, The Imperial Encyclopaedia Dictionary, Dictionary and Cyclopaedia Company, 1901, p.1126

would remain in line.[290] The diadem was considered Persian in nature. The Achaemenid Empire utilized them on turbans to identify their king as was done for King Darius III. Persian princes also tied diadems to their turbans to identify their royal lineage.[291] This practice was a clear method to identify sovereignty within this nation.

Diadems, themselves, are considered precursors to the modern crown. A diadem was fashioned in a complete circle covering the browband of the head of its wearer. It was adorned with jewels or other precious items in many cases but was a sign of honor and royalty. King Saul of Israel wore his diadem in battle. [292] The coronatus, however, did not fully cover the browband of the head of the wearer. The front portion of it was opened allowing for its edges to settle directly above the eyebrows while revealing the frontal brow of the wearer. As time passed, it evolved into a diadem-like crown.[293] The convergence of

---

[290] The Holy Bible According to the Authorized Version: Hebrews to Revelation, C. Scribner's Sons, 1890, p.533
[291] Rufus, Quintus Curtis, Histories of Alexander the Great, OUP Oxford, 2009, p.177
[292] Smith, William, Horatio Balch Hackett, Ezra Abbot, Dr. William Smith's Dictionary of the Bible, Hurd and Houghton, 1888, p.597
[293] Ibid, p.2855

the diadem and corona is the basis for the general construction of the crowns of the Ancient Accepted Scottish Rite.

Relative to Supreme Councils, its actual and honorary members, 33rd Degree members, are crowned and designated with special headgear that emulates a wreathed diadem. The headgear also bears the double-headed eagle or heraldic emblem of the Scottish Rite. Non-wreathed diadems identify 32nd Degree members.

32nd Degree Non-wreathed   *33rd Degree Wreathed*

Figure 28 32nd and 33rd Degree Diadems

As it relates to the crowns of members of Supreme Councils, there are additional modifications that designate actual and honorary members as well as leadership. Sovereign Grand Commanders bear the Cross of Salem on their crowns as a sign of leadership in place of the double-headed eagle. Some Supreme Councils designate that the Cross of Lorraine is born upon their crowns as a sign for actual members. Others maintain the usage of the double-headed eagle but leverage different color schemes as designations. These factors are determined by the Supreme Councils themselves and are documented within the Constitution and Bylaws of the respective bodies.

Crowns of Egypt

The concept of placing the heraldic emblem of the Rite front and centered on crowns is one that did not originate with Alexander the Great. While the eagle, as an emblem of majesty, vision and power was long heralded by the Holy Roman and Prussian Empires, it was not affixed to diadems. This practice is attributed to the Ancient Egyptians pre-dating the Greco-Roman representations.

Pre-historic Egypt constitutes the period prior to the early dynasties of Egypt and is considered as an era of the gods due to the myths associated with the times. Osiris was a key figure among the gods and came to personify fertility and the resurrection of the dead. He was slain by his brother Seth who built a trap that bound him in a sarcophagus. After placing it in a river, Osiris eventually drowned. Isis, wife of Osiris, found his body and copulated after temporarily resurrecting him.[294] Seth, then, found the body of Osiris, severed it into pieces and scattered them across Egypt. This was done to deny Osiris a proper burial and prevent life for him in the underworld. Isis eventually found all the pieces except the phallus and buried them. The burial gave Osiris life in the underworld but prevented him from returning to the terrestrial plain as he was not buried whole. By virtue of his status as a god, he remained in the underworld as its ruler and judge. From the copulation with Osiris' body, Isis eventually gave birth to Horus, a divine son.[295]

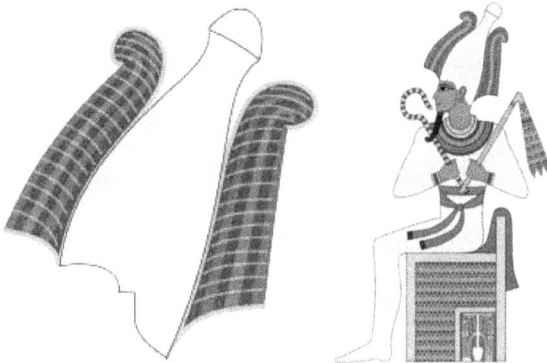

Figure 29 Atef of Osiris

---

[294] Brunson, Margaret, Encyclopaedia of Ancient Egypt, Facts on File Inc., 2014, p.82
[295] Ibid, p.82

| Hedjet | Deshret | Pschent | Khepresh |

Figure 30 Crowns of Egypt

As ruler of the underworld, Osiris is typically shown adorned with an Atef which is a conical, white crown flanked with ostrich feathers. Like a diadem, the crown covered the browband of the head of Osiris. Although no emblem is shown affixed to his headdress, the ostrich feathers themselves were emblematic representations of his position. They represented truth and purity and were emblematic of his role as judge of the underworld. Together with the white crown, the complete headdress identified Osiris as the judge and ruler of the underworld.[296]

While Osiris ruled the underworld in a white crown, another white crown held significance on the terrestrial plain. Prior to 3150 BC, the Hedjet, which was a conical, white crown adorned with a vulture, identified the ruler of

---

[296] Ibid, p.90

Upper Egypt. The vulture symbolized purification and restoration as vultures gain life from death. It also served to symbolize royal protection by the goddess Nekhbet.[297] The red crown of Lower Egypt, the Deshret, was an inverse, bowl-shaped crown adorned with a protruding cobra or uraeus. The cobra symbolized the protection of the ruler by the goddess Wadjet, counterpart to Nekhbet, who was ready to strike with lethal potency with venom or flames in defense of the ruler.[298]

Figure 31 Pschent with Nemes of Amenhotep III

[297] Ibid, p.87
[298] Ibid, p.87

The convergence of the Hedjet and the Deshret into a single crown occurred during the unification of Upper and Lower Egypt in the Early Dynastic period. The Pschent was a double crown incorporating the features of the Hedjet and Deshret as well as the emblems associated with both. In fact, the Deshret surrounded the conical Hedjet. The cobra and vulture, representing the qualities of the goddesses Nekhbet and Wadjet, ensured strong protection over the pharaoh through the end of the Early Dynastic Period (2686 BC).[299]

During the Old Kingdom Period (2686), two cobras or uraei adorned the Pschent. As Nekhbet was also represented as a cobra in Egyptian culture, her influence was not discarded.[300] The uraei remained intact as an emblematic representation through the end of the Second Intermediate Period (1550BC). The Nemes represented a cloth version of a corona. Its heraldic representation of the uraei is consistent with the Pschent. It was a cloth

---

[299] Ibid, p.359 (See sekhem)
[300] Ibid, p.420

representation of the Egyptian corona which also covered the front shoulders and the upper back of its bearer.[301]

The Khepresh was introduced during the New Kingdom (1550 BC). A blue crown, it was a modified design of the Pschent. The conical shape or Hedjet portion of the Pschent became more dome-like as it protruded a bit further towards the front of the crown. The diameter encapsulated the bowl shape of the red Deshret. Colored blue, it was adorned with uraei and solid in recognition of the protection offered by the goddesses. The Khepresh remained the crown of the pharaoh through the end of the Late Period (332 BC).[302]

Figure 32 Amenhotep III, Tutankhamun and Ramesses IX

---

[301] Ibid, p.147
[302] Ibid, p.90

The Greco-Roman influence in Egyptian culture began near 332BC during the Agread and Ptolemaic Dynasties. The Khepresh was re-introduced in the form of a linen, cap-crown of the pharaoh. In addition, a golden diadem with the vulture and cobra was also worn by the ruler. Although not adorned with laurel wreath, the diadem was a golden band with precious stones surrounding the perimeter in decorative elegance. With a band over the top to maintain its station on the head of the pharaoh, the diadem band settled snuggly on his browband encapsulating the head.[303]

The Papal Mitre is derived directly from the head dress of Aaron in the book of Exodus in the Holy Bible:

Exodus 29:5-6: "And thou shalt take the garments, and put upon Aaron the coat, and the robe of the ephod, and the ephod, and the breastplate, and gird him with the curious girdle of the ephod: And thou shalt put the mitre upon his head and put the holy crown upon the mitre."

---

[303] Hill, Marsha, Royal Bronze Statuary from Ancient Egypt, Brill, 2004, p.63

The Israelites were delivered from slavery and fled into the wilderness. In the wilderness God renewed the covenant with Israel declaring them a holy nation and a kingdom of priests.[304] Aaron's coronation at Mt. Sinai as the first high priest was a fulfillment of that directive.

The mitre which served as the basis for Aaron's mitre was Egyptian in nature. At the time of the exodus, the general mitre was the Pschent which is a combination of the hedjet and the deshret. The Israelite version was made of linen and more closely resembled a hedjet with cords.[305] The initial crown was a petalum or band of precious metal.[306] The modern papal mitre and tiara evolved from this source.

By the 8th Century, the design and shape of the mitre took on the form of a bullet with a single crown at its base. By the end of the 10th Century, the shape shifted dramatically from a peaked bullet to a more rounded shape. A vertical band was added prompting a dip in the middle

---

[304] Holy Bible, Exodus 19:5-6
[305] Holy Bible, Exodus 39:28
[306] The Reliquary and Illustrated Archaeologist, Volume 10, 1904, p.6

which created two rounded horns. Peaked horns followed splitting the top of the mitre into halves. By the end of the 10th Century, it morphed into a beehive shape.[307]

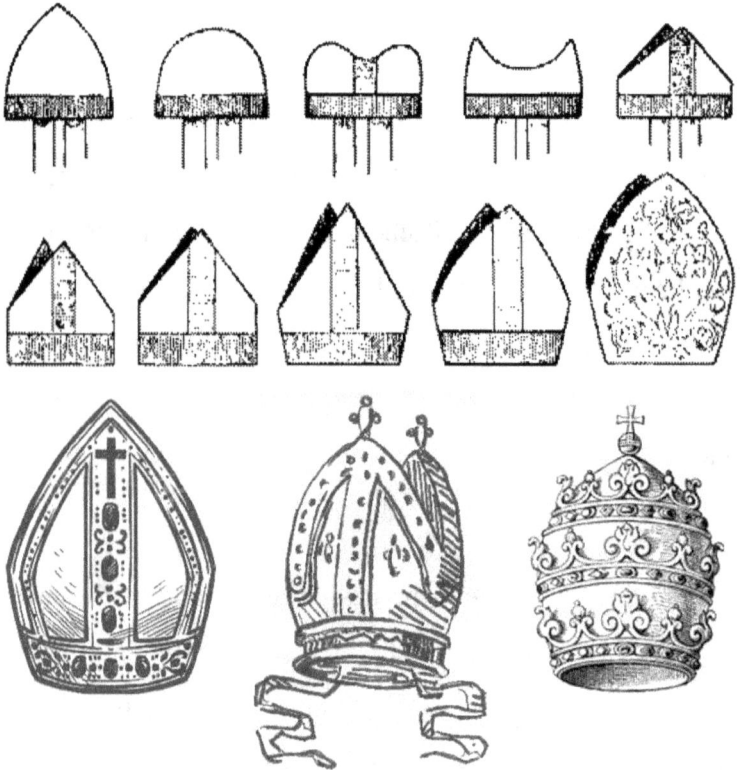

Figure 33 Evolution of the Mitre and Papal Tiara

---

[307] Becerra II, Sergio, The Papal Tiara: The Authority and Power of the Pope, Lulu.com, 2013, p.3

By the end of the 7th Century, the simple mitre had evolved from a plain to a more elaborate representation. Jewels were added to the linen mitre and the empty cross, which was initially affixed to the front and center, moved to the top of the mitre. In the 8th Century, the split mitre was joined together creating a more structured and solid tiara in the shape of a beehive but still with a single crown at the base. Pope Boniface VIII added a second crown towards the end of the 13th Century. In the early 14th Century, a third crown was added completing the evolution of the tiara.[308]

Both the mitre and the tiara were worn as the official headdress of the papacy throughout the centuries. However, the tiara was worn during more formal ceremonies and occasions because of its heraldic value to the papacy. The three crowns represent the three jurisdictions of authority for the pope including spiritual authority as the Vicar of Christ on the earth; temporal

---

[308] The Catholic Encyclopaedia: Simony-Tournaly, Appleton, 1912, pp.714-715

sovereignty over Rome and her Papal States; and historical sovereignty on earth.[309]

Early Romans also integrated Egyptian characteristics in their crowns. In 30BC, Octavian defeated Mark Antony at the Battle of Actium, deposed Pharaoh Cleopatra, adopted her Egyptian regalia to reconcile the citizens of Egypt after annexing Egypt to the Rome. This period not only ushered in an era of Roman control which lasted nearly five hundred years but also started Roman-Egyptian homogenization.[310]

Rome was strengthened greatly under the term of the emperor Constantine who reigned from 306AD to 337AD. He began as a Christian in 312AD and successfully quelled civil wars with Maxentius and Licinius in to become Rome's sole ruler by 324AD. It was during his term that Roman Christianity spread throughout Egypt and Nubia.

---

[309] Clarke, Richard Henry, The Life of His Holiness Pope Leo ZIII, Ziegler, 1903, p.245
[310] Sellars, Ian J., The Monetary System of the Romans, 2013, p.47

Figure 34 Denars of Emperor Constantine the Great

Constantine convened the first Council of Nicea in 325AD and constructed a crown which reflected his faith in a manner similar to the battle-ready Khepresh. Although the shell was smaller, it was plated around the edges of the brow like a golden diadem and ornate with jewels. The Christian Cross was the heraldic representation on display on the front and center as shown on various medals. He also bore a coronatus as shown on denarii.[311] His crown is the basis upon which subsequent crowns were forged.

Battles with external forces opposed to Roman expansion or sore from Roman occupation began to rise to overthrow the empire. These forces included the Huns, Goths, Vandals, Germania and others who fought the

---

[311] Spielman, Marion Harry, The Magazine of Art, Cassell, Petter & Galpin, 1888, p.278

empire. Not since Hannibal had forces wrought such havoc at the gates and sacked the city: [312]

- In 452 AD, the Huns, led by Attila, sacked Italy.
- The Vandals sacked Rome in 455AD and, by 468AD, gained control over its African Empire.
- In 476AD Germanic General Odoacer deposed the last Emperor of Rome, Romulus Augustulus.
- Theodric, the Ostrogoth (Goth of the East), defeated King Odoacer securing the kingship in 493AD.
- Clovis defeated the Visigoths, or Goths of the West, in 507AD and became Christian in 526AD.
- The Byzantines captured the East Roman African Empire in 533AD and invaded Italy two years later.
- In 541AD, the Bubonic Plaque spread across Rome.

The Dark Ages generally covers the period after Clovis took Rome to the 15th Century AD.[313] This period of social, cultural, and economic deterioration was a

---

[312] Ward-Perkins, Bryan, The Fall of Rome and the End of Civilization, OUP Oxford, 2006, pp.188-189

[313] American Encyclopaedic Dictionary, R.S. Peale and J.A. Hill, 1897, p.1272

tumultuous time in which control over the lands where often contested and kings wore crowns that emulate the ancient diadems and coronas to show sovereignty.

The crown of Clovis the Great, first King of the Franks who united the Frankish Tribes in the 5th Century, is made of gold and topped with the Christian Cross in the form of the "fleur-de-lis", a sign of the Holy Trinity (The Father – God, The Son – Jesus, The Holy Ghost).[314] It is slightly flared but emulates the crown of Constantine. Like the uraei on the crowns of the Egyptians, the cross signified divine protection. It also was a clear sign of Clovis' faith. A denarius of King Charlemagne, 8th Century King of the Franks, shows his head adorned with a coronatus.[315] Like Clovis and Charlemagne, the crown of King Richard I was forged from gold and fitted with jewels. His successor's crown, King John, followed suit and the headdress of 14th Century King Edward III incorporates the same characteristics of the crowns of his predecessors. Both bear resemblance to the Nemes and Pschent of Amenhotep.

---

[314] Hickman, Hoyt L., United Methodist Altars: A Guide for the Congregation, Revised, Abingdon Press, 2011, pp.106
[315] Beecher, Matthias, Charlemagne, Yale University Press, 2003, p.17

Figure 35 King Clovis and a Denarius of King Charlemagne

Figure 36 Crowns of Amenhotep III, Richard I & Edward III

The era of the Crusades produced Orders of European Knights which are not limited to but do include:

- The Hospitallers of St. John – Established at the start of the Crusades in 1095AD;[316]

---

[316] Macoy, Robert, The True Masonic Guide: Containing Elucidations of the Fundamental Principles of Freemasonry, Clark, Austin and Smith, 1858, p.250

- The Knights Templar – Founded by veterans of the First Holy War, Hugh De Paynes, Godfrey Adelman and seven others in 1118AD;[317]
- The Knights of St. Lazarus–Founded in 1119AD;[318]
- The Hospitallers of St. Thomas of Canterbury;[319]
- The Teutonic Knights – Founded in 1190AD in Acre, Kingdom of Jerusalem by German Knights.[320]

These orders also recognized heraldic emblems as identifiers of leadership. So, although the period between Egypt royalty and the Crusades represents a difference of more than a millennium, there are clear similarities to the headgear that remain in place in the modern era.

The crown of St. Edward is a modern representation of the days of old. Prior to the middle of the 17th Century, the English monarchy controlled the nation. However, after the conclusion of the First Civil War in 1647 and Second

---

[317] Ibid, p.232
[318] Brewer, Ebenezer Cobham, The Historic Notebook, p.433
[319] Runciman, Steven, The Crusades and Military Orders: Expanding the Frontiers of Medieval Latian Christianity, Department of Medieval Studies, Central European University, 2001, pp.6-17
[320] Nicolaus, A History of the Teutonic Knights in Prussia: 1190-1331, Ashgate, 2010, p.3

English Civil War in 1649, the monarchy had been overthrown, King Charles I beheaded, and the Commonwealth of England established under the leadership of Oliver Cromwell.[321]

Figure 37 Crown of St. Edward

Cromwell's ascension ushered in a period of turbulence culminating in the Third Civil War. It ended in 1652AD with leadership under the form of representative government. It concluded with the restoration of the

---

[321] Cromwell, pp.255-256

monarchy in 1660 under King Charles II.[322] After the death of Charles in 1685AD, Britain began its shift to a limited monarchy. In the modern era, the monarch is crowned with the Crown of St. Edward but undertakes constitutional and representational duties only as the titular head of state.[323]

The modern usage of wreaths to identify sovereignty and membership ranking still serve as signs of faith and fealty while also serving as a totem for divine protection. This concept aligns perfectly with the usages of old. Even their placement either at the center-front of the crown, atop it or clearly visible on the side are quite similar. While the materials are clearly different, most likely due to the cost of production and the cosmopolitan and non-military nature of organizations, they are similarly structured showcasing many of the characteristics of old. As such, it is in this vein that the crowns of the Ancient and Accepted Scottish Rite and the York Rite of Freemasonry find their roots.

The primary heraldic emblem of the Scottish Rite is clearly affixed to the front and center of all caps and

---

[322] Ibid, p.449
[323] https://www.royal.uk/role-monarchy, retrieved 6/14/2023

crowns. Un-wreathed caps represent those who have not been elevated. While elevation to the level of Sublime Prince or 32nd Degree is represented by the gold bands, no wreath is present like the un-adorned diadems of old. Only those who have been coronated are adorned.

York Rite caps and crowns for a similar pattern. Royal Arch Masons who have not been elevated to leadership wear caps with the insignia of a triple-tau, the badge of a Royal Arch Mason, on a red cap.[324] The insignia of a Past Excellent High Priest is further adorned with the breastplate of a high priest but is not wreathed unless the member has been elected to Grand Chapter office.[325] Royal and Select Masters or Cryptic Masons follow a similar pattern.[326] Eminent Priors of the Knights of the York Cross of Honor (KYCH), organized in 1930, showcase a wreathed logo surrounding the letter "G" in the middle of the cross.[327]

---

[324] Mackey, Albert Gallatin, William James Hughan, An Encyclopaedia of Freemasonry, Masonic History Company, 1912, p.210
[325] Ibid, pp.325-326
[326] Ibid, p.191
[327] The New Age Magazine, Volume 54, Supreme Council, Ancient and Accepted Scottish Rite of Freemasonry of the Southern Jurisdiction USA, 1946, p.634

32ⁿᵈ Degree Cap – Wings Up

32ⁿᵈ Degree Cap – Wings Down

33ʳᵈ Degree Cap – Wings Up

33ʳᵈ Degree Cap – Wings Down

Royal Arch Cap

Grand High Priest Crown

Royal & Select Master Cap

Grand Thrice Ill. Master Crown

KYCH Cap

KYCH Eminent Prior Crown

Figure 38 Scottish Rite and York Rite Caps and Crowns

The headgear regalia of a Masonic Knight Templar is a cap with the cross affixed to the center of its front. The cross is the Latin Cross which represents solidarity to the army of Christ and is a direct reference to those soldiers who fought in the Holy Wars. [328]   It is a clear sign of the faith of its bearer. As one advances to leadership, silver edges are transformed to gold emulating the act of coronation. Chapeaus are also made with Ostrich plumes; the same materials utilized in the creation of the Atef of Osiris and host the red cross.[329]

Figure 39 Knights Templar Caps and Chapeaus

---

[328] Hickman, Hoyt L., United Methodist Altars: A Guide for the Congregation, Revised, Abingdon Press, 2011, p.104
[329] Mackey, Albert Gallatin, Edward L. Hawkins, An Encyclopedia of Freemasonry and Its Kindred Sciences, Masonic History Company, 1913, p. 141

Sovereign Grand Commander Crowns

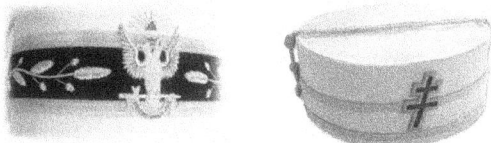

Sovereign Grand Inspector General Crowns (White and Purple)

Figure 40 Supreme Council Member Crowns

The colors of the Scottish Rite crowns are also significant. Purple has traditionally represented royalty while white has represented light. As such, actual members of Supreme Councils wear purple or white crowns like the Hedjet of Upper Egypt. The Cross of Salem identifies the Sovereign Grand Commander despite the color of the crown while the Cross of Lorraine or double-headed eagle adorns the crown of the other actual members.[330]

---

[330] Mackey, Albert Gallatin, Edward L. Hawkins, An Encyclopedia of Freemasonry and Its Kindred Sciences, Masonic History Company, 1913, p.187

Figure 41 Masonic Top Hat and Shriner Fez

The Masonic Top Hat and the Shriner's Fez also conform to a similar structure. Historically, all Master Masons wore top hats without distinction. The jewel of office was the key indicator of sovereignty. In modern Masonic Lodges, the Top Hat is now the premier emblem of leadership. It is the crown of Freemasonry worn only by the leaders of Lodges and Grand Lodges during their respective sessions.[331] He who wears the top hat is in charge and no others are to be worn when the premier leader, the Grand Master, adorns his.

Modern Shriners follow the path of the Freemasons of old as it relates to headgear. Every Shriner adorns a fez which, historically, links to a 14th Century coif worn by

---

[331] Bulletin of the Iowa Masonic Library, Volumes 16-20, Grand Lodge of Iowa, 1915, p.70

Turkish soldiers. A tassel was added to it so that soldiers could be identified on the battlefield.[332] After Mehmed II conquered Constantinople and crushed the Byzantine Empire in 1453, he declared himself Caesar and wrapped his fez in a white turban to signify his sovereignty. The two piece headgear constituted the Tarboosh.[333]

The Tarboosh was not only distinguished as a sign of rank it also became an emblem of affiliation to Islam. This concept transitioned over subsequent centuries but its distinction as a royal headdress faded. By the 19th Century Christians, Jews and other faiths wore it regularly. Ultimately, the terms Tarboosh and Fez had become synonymous. As such, Ottoman Sultan Mahmud II made the plain fez official army issue in 1827 and, in 1829, extended the regulation beyond the military.[334] The 1829 mandate was an effort to homogenize and unify Ottoman citizens. Mahmud intended for the fez to symbolize

---

[332] Edrehi, Moses, History of the Capital of Asia and the Turks, I. Edrehi, 1855, p.125

[333] Dunham, Dilmeran Akgoze, The Hat as a Symbol of Westernization in Turkey, Cornell University, 1985, p.22

[334] Yilmaz, Hale, Becoming Turkish: Nationalist Reforms and Cultural Negotiations in Early Republican Turkey 1923-45, Syracuse University Press, 2013, pp.24-25

equality among all Ottomans under the sultan, but this met with subsequent modifications and contestations of the law over the years that followed. The unrest drove efforts to ban the fez in 1925 as a part of Mustafa Kemal Ataturk's reforms which aligned more with European society.[335]

Figure 42 Mehmed the Conqueror and Mahmud II

The Ancient Arabic Order of the Nobles of the Mystic Shrine (AAONMS) was created in 1871 in the United States. Inspired by a tour of Egypt, William J. Florence was inducted into a Moorish organization in 1870. Upon returning to America, he created an organization of similar

[335] Lynch, Annette, Mitchell D. Strauss, Ethnic Dress in the United States: A Cultural Encyclopedia, Rowman & Littlefield Publishers, 2014, p.121

style and character and gathered Dr. Walter M. Flemings, Albert L. Lawson, Charles T. Mclenachan and William Sleigh Patterson to meet the aim. They established the Order of the Mystic Shrine on June 16, 1871, and translated the Arabic ritual into English.[336]

The AAONMS adopted the fez as its official headgear in 1872 as it is a direct tie to the Arabian linkages of the organization.[337] In addition, it was the likely form of headgear worn during the initiation of Noble Florence in the Arabic rite. It was subsequently adopted by the Ancient Egyptian Arabic Order of the Nobles of the Mystic Shrine (AEAONMS) during its initial organization among African American men in 1893, having received a charter from the Grand Council of Arabia. AEAONMS was reorganized in 1901 during the downward slide of John G. Jones, founder of the organization among African American men.[338]

---

[336] Griffo, Kedar, Michael Berkley, African Origin Found in Religion and Freemasonry, Lulu.com, 2010, p.136
[337] Croly, Herbert David, The New Republic, Volume 35, Republic Publishing Company, 1923, p.96
[338] Andrews, Daryl L., Indignation: A Psychological Profile of the Infamous John G. Jones, AndrewsPress, 2023, pp.88-90

Figure 43 William J. Florence and John G. Jones

Both organizations, AAONMS and AEAONMS, cite a linkage to the Moroccan City of Fez where Christians were slain by Muslim hoards in the early 8th Century.[339] There is no direct evidence that the massacre was the reason for the selection of the fez as headgear. Its association to the Arabian origins of Islam is the likely basis. There is also no evidence that the organization which bestowed degrees upon Florence also adopted the fez as its official headgear. Nonetheless, its tie to Arabia is undeniable.

---

[339] Carlson, Ron, Fast Facts on False Teaching, 2003, p.74

Contrary to the Masonic Top Hat, each member, or Noble dons a fez as all are on equal plane within the Temple. Those who have been elevated to leadership are allowed distinctions in their designs in recognition of the additional duties and responsibilities that they have absorbed. The universal emblem for the organization is its general heraldic representation. The logo is purely Arabian and Egyptian in nature. The basis is a crescent moon centered around a five pointed star with the face of an Egyptian Pharoah situated in the center underneath a scimitar. The crescent moon and star are emblematic of the Islamic influence on the Order.[340]

Figure 44 Shrine Logo

---

[340] Ibid, p.96

The scimitar was the weapon of choice during the Holy Wars. According to legend, the Prophet Muhammad's sword was a scimitar that he wielded at the Battle at Badr also known as "The Day of Criterion" in 624AD.[341] Muhammad lead over three hundred warriors in a raid of a Meccan caravan. Outnumbered, nearly three to one, the Meccans were defeated indicating the effectiveness of Muhammad's tactics and the strength of the scimitar in battle.[342]

Collectively, the combination of the scimitar, crescent moon, star and Pharoah emblems wreak of the divine providence and protection of Allah for believers. It is a clear and present representation that faith base for the organization is Islam. Modern day Shriners adopted this symbology into its dogma during a period in which Orientalism had gained great popularity across the world in the 19th Century.[343] Desiring a linkage to a noble history,

---

[341]Natan, Yoel, Moon-o-theism, Y. Natan, 2006, p.112
[342] El-Neil, Ibn, The Truth About Islam, Strategic Book Publishing, 2008, p.149
[343] Lynch, Annette, Mitchell D. Strauss, Ethnic Dress in the United States: A Cultural Encyclopedia, Rowman & Littlefield Publishers, 2014, p.122

the Nobles of the Mystic Shrine organization adopted the emblem. Yet, like the crowns of the other Masonic Orders, the fez bears a strong resemblance to the crowns of old.

Figure 45 Fez and Scottish Rite Crown Comparisons

The fez (top-right) mimics the Khepresh of Amenhotep III (top-left). Similarly, like the Pschent of Amenhotep III (bottom-left) and the Scottish Rite crown also align. In the current era, the diadems and coronas of old appear to have been, simply, modernized.

All in all, Ancient Egyptian symbology is pervasive throughout the bounds of Freemasonry and other modern-day organizations. Those ancient brethren of Upper and Lower Egypt set a method in motion to identify sovereignty and present emblematic representations that express the core beliefs of their nations. As such, the wreathed coronas of modern Freemasonry along with their emblematic representations have a link to a more ancient past in which similar heraldic symbols not only hold great meanings but also great expectations.

Raiment and Vestments

Historically, raiment has supplemented the corona to comprise full heraldic regalia for pharaohs, emperors, kings, princes, potentates, and commanders. To array oneself with clothing is the definition of the term raiment. In heraldry, it refers to the adornment of all regalia according to one's style or rank of office. While the coat of arms identifies fealty, the raiment is the key identifier of one's level underneath the banner to which allegiance is held.

The way raiment is adorned is based upon the dogma to which heralds pledge themselves. While the specific raiment varies, the practice has been consistent throughout multiple empires over the course of history. Each empire has showcased variations of crowns, jewels, coats, armor, shields and scepters that incorporate symbolism which identify rank and faith. Most were adorned with precious gems and made of materials that are of the highest value. They were constructed to last and ensure that one's royal rank or societal designation was clear. In many instances, they followed the bearers to the grave.

Unfortunately, history's greatest mysteries have been uncovered from the graves of the kings and queens of the past by the hands of grave robbers and archaeologists whose pursuit of precious metals drove them to disturb the bones of those who were resting at peace. For the grave robbers, the searches were purely for personal gain. For archaeologists, it is difficult to conclude their true purposes. Fame, on the one hand, could have been the driver. On the other hand, greed, the continuous search for gold could have been the other. There is no evidence to confirm that all the artifacts gathered were presented to museums for public display or to other institutions for detailed research. Some may have been carefully and quietly placed in private collections. Yet, it is a melancholy truth that the disturbances to the final resting places of pharaohs have yielded valuable details on African societies. They have helped to solve the modern questions of ancient times. Without them, the world may never have known of the treasures of the ancient Egyptians.

In the tomb of King Tutankhamun, Lord George Herbert, the 5th Earl of Carnarvon, found several artifacts that would have been disturbing in the 20th Century because racial theories since the 18th Century supported black inferiority. Constantin François de Chasseboeuf, Count of Volney noted that "the ancient Egyptians were true negroes of the same type as all native born Africans." After subsequent visits in the mid-1780s, he stated "we can see how their blood, mixed for several centuries with that of the Romans and Greeks, must have lost the intensity of its original color, while retaining nonetheless the imprint of its original mold."[344]

German Physician Dr. Johann Friedrich Blumenbach concluded in 1790 that the ancient Egyptians had the countenance of Ethiopians. This theory was derived from his extensive research in physical anthropological comparisons between multiple races. He found that the Egyptian skull and skin tone aligned with a mixture of Caucasoid, Mongolian, Ethiopian, American, and Malayan. The skin tone, which preserved from the Egyptian mumification method, was the driver for the research on race and physiology.[345] His view and the view of Chasseboeuf confirmed their darker hue.

Georges Cuvier and Augustus Bonzi Granville, on the other hand, promoted that the Egyptians were Caucasian. Dr. Samuel Morton of Philadelphia classified the Egyptians as a "subtype of the Caucasian race" despite the negroid

---

[344] Ohaegbulam, Festus Ugboaja, Towards an Understanding of the African Experience from Historical and Contemporary Perspectives, University Press of America, 1990, p.56
[345] Riggs, Christina, Unwrapping Ancient Egypt, p.49

features identified in artifacts and mummies he examined.[346] Considering the day and age, it is no surprise that his view mirrored Blumenbach's and that this became the common view around the world.

Figure 46 Mannequin of King Tutankhamun and Relief

---

[346] Ibid. p.71

While Lord Canarvon and Howard Carter, the British archaeologist who discovered Tutankhamun's tomb, were aware of both sides of the race argument, they were not so different from Blumenbach. The reliefs in the tomb and artifacts provided clear indications of racial origins. Clearly, the king is painted with a brown skin tone when greeting Osiris. Also, a mannequin painted to his likeness was unveiled.[347] Race aside, the contents provide a clear picture of the way Egyptian royalty was regaled.

Relative to other raiment, headgear also identified hierarchical status. The reliefs in the Tomb of King Tutankhamun denote Osiris with the Atef and the king by the Nemes. The king is being ushered to Osiris, judge of the dead. The king, adorned in a khepresh, presents an offering to Osiris. It being accepted, his soul carrying the ankh, symbol for eternal life, meets the Goddess Nut, who commends the body to Osiris and the soul to eternity.[348]

---

[347] Carter, Howard, Arthur Cruttenden Mace, The Tomb of Tutankhamun, Volume 1, Cassell, Limited, 1923, p.120
[348] Smith, Mark, Following Osiris: Perspectives of the Osirian Afterlife from four Millennia, OUP Oxford, 2017, pp.150-151

Figure 47 Zucchetto

The Roman Catholic Church utilizes the papal tiara to identify the pope during specific ceremonies. The mitre, however, is worn more commonly during liturgical services not only by the pope but also by his bishops and abbots. Its sole purpose is for liturgy. The Zucchetto is a small skullcap worn by all ecclesiastics to signify faith and fealty. Its colors are utilized to distinguish ranks in the priesthood:[349]

- White represents the pope who is the head of the church.

- Red represents cardinals, leading bishops, or senior members of the clergy of the Catholic Church. A consortium of cardinals constitutes the College of Cardinals, and it is from this pool that popes are selected.

---

[349] Chico, Beverly, Hats and Headwear around the World: A Cultural Encyclopedia, ABC-CLIO, 2013, pp.497-498

- Purple represents archbishops and bishops. The former oversees large areas of the church called archdiocese and the latter are ministers of the faith.
- Black represents the priesthood.
- Black with purple piping represents monsignors who have been distinguished as such by way of service.

Like a coat of arms, the crown and other headgear represent the crest of the human royal heraldic emblem. Other regalia is selected to support the crest to complete royal attire to clearly identify the fealty of the herald. Despite the era, the patterns have remained consistent throughout the ages across multiple empires. So, that rank which is represented above the neck in the crest is also represented below the neck in similarly regaled attire.

There are many similarities between the vestments of the Egyptians, Catholic Church, and Masonic organizations. Male royals in Egypt wore articles of clothing which covered the lower halves of their bodies. The linen garments protected the phallic region as shown in many hieroglyphs and monuments of ancient Egypt. In times of battle, fitted armor covered the torso for full protection. Each pharaoh wore distinctive garments and armor as a unique identifier of leadership.

The shendyt was the loin cloth worn by Egyptians. These linen or leather garments were opened at the bottom allowing both legs to move freely. The designs of Scottish kilts align with these ancient predecessors and could be considered modern day representations. The tripartite royal shendyt was worn by kings or gods during the Ptolemaic era.[350] The garment provided the ability for uninhibited movement and could have been implemented for more comfort in the specific environments. Tunics were also worn during Greco-Roman times to cover the torso.[351] Tunics were not typically worn by kings of Egypt and were rarely found in their tombs. For the most part, the upper body was left bare during the Old and Middle Kingdoms.[352]

---

[350] Vassilika, Eleni, Ptolemaic Philae, Department Orientalistrek, 1989, p.96
[351] Victoria and Albert Museum, Catalogue of Textiles from Burying Grounds in Egypt, H.M. Stationary Office, 1920, p.31
[352] Mendoza, Barbara, Artifacts from Ancient Egypt, ABC-CLIO, 2017, p.22

Figure 48 Shendyt, Hebrew Ephod, and Assyrian Tunic

Figure 49 Roman Catholic and Orthodox Cassocks

The vestments of the Levite High Priest were elaborate. The base was a robe covered by a broidered coat. The ephod was like the shendyt which served as an apron. A linen apron with suspenders, it was multi-colored in gold, blue, purple, and scarlet. A breastplate affixed with twelve stones representing the Tribes of Israel was also suspended from the shoulders resting across the breast of the high priest. The turban atop as the crest completed the regalia.[353]

Vestments of Assyrian High Priests predate Hebrew vestments. They also wore tunics, made of wool or linen, which extended past the knee under their robes. The fringed robe suspended from the shoulder down to the ankles. A shawl of animal skin was worn atop descending from the left shoulder. Affixed with the headgear, a staff and rod, the priest was regaled.[354] Men of rank dressed similarly but wore sheathed swords, bracelets, and other jewelry linking themselves to membership of a higher caste class.[355]

---

[353] Holy Bible, Exodus 28

[354] Sayce, Archibald Henry, Babylonians and Assyrians: Life and Customs, C. Scribner's Sons, 1899, p.100

[355] Rawlinson, George, Assyrian Empire: Illustrated Edition, e-artnow, 2018, p.159

The ancient Romans adopted a similar style of dress with less ornamentation in the form of a toga. While the shendyt draped from the waist and the Assyrian tunic covered to the torso, the toga was a flowing garment which draped from the shoulders and extended to the ankles. It was typically worn over a tunic. Per Gaius Plinius Secundus, the toga was worn by kings.[356] While casual dress for Roman Catholics incorporated the toga, the basis for the cassock or liturgical robes worn by the clergy of the church was a combination of the toga and Levite vestments.

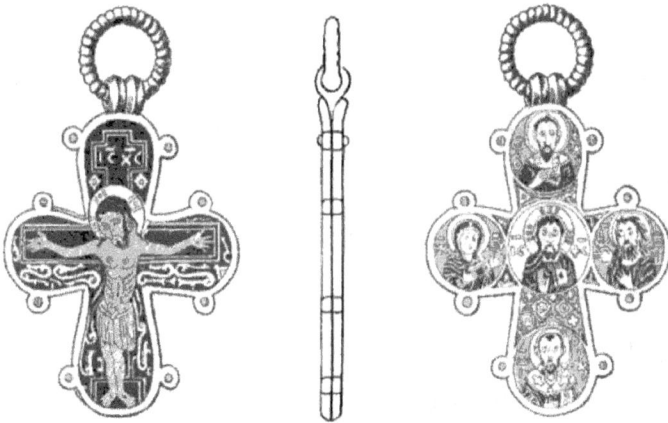

Figure 50 Pectoral Crosses

---

[356] Victoria and Albert Museum, Catalogue of Textiles from Burying Grounds in Egypt, H.M. Stationary Office, 1920, p.31

The cassock is the base garment for vestments. It is a linen gown that drapes over the shoulder and down to the ankles of clergy. An alb which is similar to surplice may also be worn to cover the cassock as a symbol of baptism. Stoles are then worn atop the alb as a symbol of ordination.[357] A mozetta is also worn by cardinals. It is a short red cape that encircles the cardinal's shoulders. It is worn outside of the rochet which is worn over the cassock by cardinals.[358] Upon these layers, rests the pectoral cross.

The pectoral cross is worn on a chain around the neck as a symbol of the Christian faith by many Roman Catholics as well as a heraldic identifier of rank within the Catholic Church. Pope Hilarius is said to have been the first to wear a cross suspended from a chain on his neck in 461 AD. The Emperor Justin presented Pope Gregory I the first pectoral cross in 519 AD which rested upon the chest. "Agnus Dei" or "lamb of God" was placed in the center with representations of Jesus and John the Baptist affixed

---

[357] The Prayer for the Church Militant, and the Surplice, in reply to the Quarterly Review, J.G.F. & J. Rivington, 1843, pp.12-15
[358] Tobin, Greg, Selecting the Pope: Uncovering the Mysteries of Papal Elections, Sterling, 2009, p.73

in the upper and lower portion.[359] For cardinals, the pectoral cross is gold and suspended by a red rope or chain. For all others, it is traditionally suspended by a green rope or chain. Outside of liturgical services, it is silver with a silver rope or chain.[360]

Like the pope and cardinals, the regalia as it relates to jewels for Masonic Officers is either gold or silver. The jewels of Grand Lodge Officers are golden and suspended in a circle or wreath from ornate collars to correspond with the richness and elevation in accountabilities or responsibilities of the Grand Lodge. However, the cross is the single jewel adorned by the Roman Catholic Church leadership as compared to Grand Lodges whose jewels vary. The most important jewel is that of the Grand Master who bears full accountability for the Grand Lodge itself.[361] His jewel and top hat are the key heraldic emblems that show his authority. His Masonic apron, which is like a

---

[359] Seymour, William Wood, The Cross in Tradition, History and Art, G.P. Putnam, 1898, p.251
[360] Tobin, Greg, Selecting the Pope: Uncovering the Mysteries of Papal Elections, Sterling, 2009, p.73
[361] Macoy, Robert, The True Masonic Guide, Clark, Austin and Smith, 1858, p.356

squared shendyt with a bid, is his badge and heraldic emblem of fealty to the fraternity of Freemasons.

In the Scottish Rite, the jewel of the Sovereign Grand Commander is the Cross of Salem which is affixed to an ornate collar in a slanted format. In the York Rite, the unslanted Cross of Salem is worn. The cross symbolizes their roles as the most accountable officers for the Rites. The same symbol is affixed to the crown and chapeau of the Sovereign Grand Commander and the Right Eminent Grand Commander of Knights Templar.

The solidarity of the Scottish Rite is Sovereign Grand Inspectors General who adorn the slanted Cross of Lorraine like Knights Templar who adorn the unslanted version. Sovereign Grand Inspectors General convene like the College of Cardinals serving as senior members of the Scottish Rite. Members of the Active Grade align with archbishops while Emeriti align with bishops. Grand Inspectors General constitute the monsignors of the priesthood while Sublime Princes align with priests.

Except for the Sovereign Grand Commander and elected officers, Scottish Rite jewels are not worn from collars about the neck but are pectoral and placed on the left side over the heart. The Teutonic Cross affixed with the double headed eagle is the base jewel of the Scottish Rite. The quadruple tau cross was the heraldic emblem of the Teutonic Knights. They were organized in 1191AD in Acre by German merchants to aid Christians on their way to the Holy Land and establish hospitals for aid.[362] The cross also pays homage to the German origins of the Scottish Rite degrees.

Grand Commanderies of Knights Templar perform a similar function ensuring that the affairs of this York Rite Body are cared for in due form and fashion. It is the military arm of the York Rite which also represents Grand Chapters of Holy Royal Arch Masons and Grand Councils of Royal and Select Masters. With their hierarchies constructed in a similar fashion to the Knights Templar, their collective purposes ensure that key facets of Judaism

---

[362] Mackey, Albert Gallatin, Edward L. Hawkins, An Encyclopedia of Freemasonry and Its Kindred Sciences, Masonic History Company, 1912, p.781

and Christianity are inculcated and expressed through service to the world.[363]

Scottish Rite Masons wear cassock-like, black robes along with crowns to designate their styles and ranks in the camp. The distinctions between Grand Inspectors General and Sublime Prince are the crowns and jewels of office. The former bears crowned eagles and wreathed crowns while the latter bears an uncrowned eagle on the cap and the cross Teutonic Cross as its jewel. Sovereign Grand Inspectors General wear black robes with blue yoke panels along with wreathed crowns of purple and either the Cross of Lorraine or crowned double-headed eagle. Some jurisdictions grant white crowns to elected Supreme Council officers. The jewel of office is the wreathed Teutonic Cross affixed with the crowned double headed eagle.[364] Sashes are incorporated by some jurisdictions to designate Active from Emeriti which is necessary due to the privileges associated with each role.

---

[363] Ibid, p.871
[364] Mackey, Albert Gallatin, William James Hughan, An Encyclopaedia of Freemasonry, Masonic History Company, 1912, pp.188-189

Knights Templar represent the military arm of the York Rite. Their regalia is reminiscent of the military wear of the ancient brethren without cassocks. Uniforms are affixed with the cross and silver emblems. Grand Commandery officers are affixed with emblem of gold. The priesthood is represented by Holy Royal Arch Masons whose heraldic emblem is the triple tau and primary color is red. Wreathed adornments in gold identify officers of the Grand Chapter.[365] Grand Council officers follow the same pattern. The primary color is purple and this house honors Melchizedek, the Biblical High Priest to whom Abraham paid tithes.[366]

Figure 51 Potentate and Past Potentate Jewels

---

[365] Sheville, John, James L Gould, Guide to the Royal Arch Chapter, Health Research, 1996, pp.136-137

[366] Royal and Select Masters, Grand Council of Minnesota, Proceedings of the Grand Council of Royal and Select Masters of Minnesota, 1871, p.32

Through these channels, both the York Rite and Scottish Rite operate from the spiritual and philosophical perspectives respectively. While the York Rite has specific religious focal points, the Scottish Rite reviews all faiths and promotes understanding from multiple perspectives and conversion of the lessons learned from all faiths into practical action for the betterment of all mankind.

The fez represents the crest for the human coat of arms for Nobles of the Mystic Shrine. The fez for the Imperial Council is more ornate and is wrapped like a turban. It is adorned with jewels at the front and center. The Imperial Divan is adorned with cassock-like, silk robes that extend from the shoulders down to the ankles. Atop this base rests the jewel of office suspended from an ornate collar and resting on the center of the chest. The sun in the pyramid on the jewel represents leadership.[367] It is a direct link to Ra, the Sun God of Egypt.[368]

---

[367] Melish, William B., The History of the Imperial Council, Ancient Arabic Order, Nobles of the Mystic Shrine for North America, 1921, p.149

[368] Owusu, Heike, Egyptians Symbols, Sterling, 2008, p.103

Crook and Flail

In historic and modern times, specific symbols were utilized to represent the dispersal of power from the hands of the sovereign lord. While the crown and other raiment provide a splendid heraldic representation, they do not serve as that mechanism. A wand, for example, is typically associated with the conductor of an orchestra because it is the primary tool for orchestrating the musicians. Likewise, gods and leaders of ancient times had wands of their own.

The Heqa scepter or crook and the flail date to the early dynasties of Egypt as insignias of power. The crook and flail represented godliness or kingship and fertility for the land respectively. Osiris and Khonsu, the moon god, are typically shown with both heqa and crook to symbolize their authority. Kings also adorned both to symbolize their sovereignty.[369] Khonsu is often portrayed with deceased kings as a protector for them in the underworld of Osiris. He empowered kings by taking the souls of other gods by using the flail as a weapon to defeat them and,

---

[369] Wilkinson, Toby A.H., Early Dynastic Egypt, Taylor & Francis, 2002, pp.160-161

subsequently, give the souls to the kings to consume to grant them strength to survive the underworld.[370]

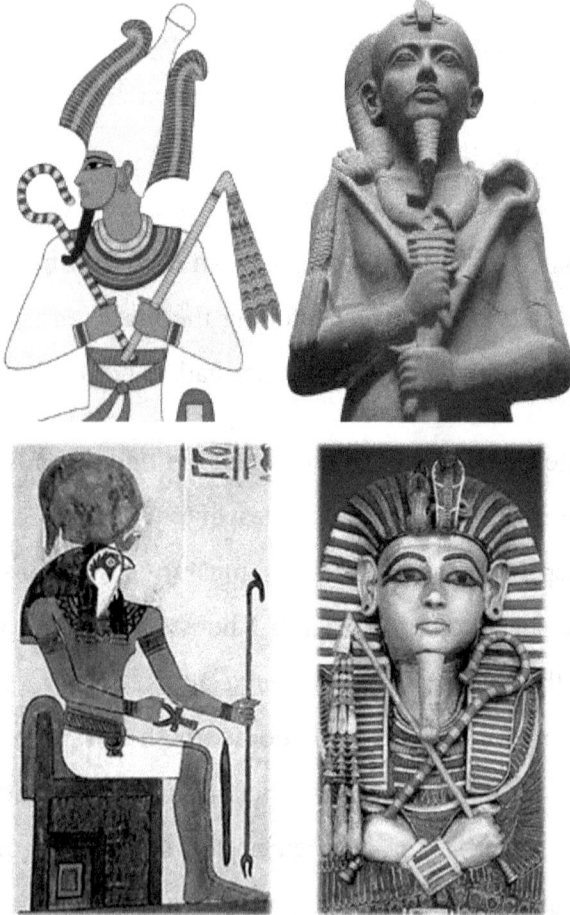

Figure 52 Osiris, Khonsu, Horus and King Tutankhamun

---

[370] Jayne, Walter Addison, The Healing Gods of Ancient Civilizations, Yale University Press, 1925, pp.68-69

The predecessor to the heqa was the Was Scepter which was longer in the form of a rod, typically adorned with the head of a lion or bull at the hook, and had a split end.[371] Khonsu, portrayed with a hawk's head topped by a moon, was armed with it and a bull's tail to show dominion over the beasts of the underworld.[372] Like the crook and flail, they both identified the king as a shepherd of people who is endowed with power over nature which is represented in the form of the bull's tail. Due to the ferocity and strength of a bull, it was also seen as a representation of the degree to which a king should defend his people.

Both the Heqa and the flail as well as the Was and bull's tail also served practical purposes. Shepherds utilized a peasant's Heqa and Was not only to manage and hook cattle when they went astray but also to defend against predators. Both were also used like common canes for support.

---

[371] Wilkinson, Toby A.H., Early Dynastic Egypt, Taylor & Francis, 2002, pp.160-161
[372] Jayne, Walter Addison, The Healing Gods of Ancient Civilizations, Yale University Press, 1925, p.71

The flail was used to thrash crops as a fertilizing lash to deliver their sustenance and rend waste. Bull's tails appear to have been its predecessor driving the creation of the flail as an artificial and stronger form.[373] By that same token, the kings of Egypt were charged to protect their subjects, be the provider of sustenance and be that guide who leads them along the proper paths. Hence, both were revered as insignias of leadership in the Egyptian culture.

The Holy Bible makes continuous references to the use of scepters as symbols of power throughout the Old Testament. Jacob identified Judah as the chief protector of Israel and the bearer of the scepter of leadership:[374]

> *Judah, thou art he whom thy brethren shall praise: thy hand shall be in the neck of thine enemies; thy father's children shall bow down before thee. Judah is a lion's whelp: from the prey, my son, thou art gone up: he stooped down, he couched as a lion, and as an old lion; who shall rouse him up? The sceptre shall not depart from Judah, nor a lawgiver*

---

[373] Ancient Egypt, Macmillan, 1925, p.66
[374] Holy Bible, Genesis 49:8-10

from between his feet, until Shiloh come; and unto
him shall the gathering of the people be.

King Xerxes I wielded his authority over his subjects
including the Jewish Esther using a golden scepter:

All the king's servants, and the people of the king's
provinces, do know, that whosoever, whether man or
woman, shall come unto the king into the inner
court, who is not called, there is one law of his to
put him to death, except such to whom the king shall
hold out the golden sceptre, that he may live: but I
have not been called to come in unto the king these
thirty days.[375]

Now it came to pass on the third day, that Esther
put on her royal apparel, and stood in the inner
court of the king's house, over against the king's
house: and the king sat upon his royal throne in the
royal house, over against the gate of the house. And
it was so, when the king saw Esther the queen
standing in the court, that she obtained favour in his

---

[375] Holy Bible, Esther 4:11

> *sight: and the king held out to Esther the golden*
> *sceptre that was in his hand. So, Esther drew near,*
> *and touched the top of the sceptre.* [376]

She touched the tip acknowledging the king's authority.
Moses' rod was consecrated by God and was the
embodiment of a combined Was Scepter and Bull's tail:[377]

> *And Moses answered and said, But behold, they will*
> *not believe me, nor hearken unto my voice: for they*
> *will say, The LORD hath not appeared unto thee.*
> *And the LORD said unto him, What is that in thine*
> *hand? And he said, A rod. And he said, Cast it on*
> *the ground. And he cast it on the ground, and it*
> *became a serpent; and Moses fled from before it.*
> *And the LORD said unto Moses, Put forth thine*
> *hand, and take it by the tail. And he put forth his*
> *hand, and caught it, and it became a rod in his*
> *hand: That they may believe that the LORD God of*
> *their fathers, the God of Abraham, the God of Isaac,*
> *and the God of Jacob, hath appeared unto thee.*

---

[376] Holy Bible, Esther 5:1-2
[377] Holy Bible, Exodus 4:1-5

Although the priests of the Pharoah Ramesses II were able to turn their rods into serpents, the rod of Moses devoured them further showcasing its dominance.[378]

During the exodus, Moses stretched forth his rod to part the Red Sea. In the wilderness, he tapped the rod on a rock to provide drinking water. During the subsequent attack by the Amalekites, he raised the rod giving the Israelites the victory.[379] For by the holy rod, was God's power revealed. As such, the rod took on the persona of divine providence.

The Staff and the Sword

Lineage remains of the utmost importance particularly with Judaism and Christianity. Jesus is shown as a member of the Abrahamic line, the same line as King Solomon and King David, through Isaac. This lineage ties Jesus directly to the promise of God to Abraham that he would be the father of many nations while also solidifying the prophecies of Isaiah and Micah. The prophecy of Isaiah that Jesus would be born of the line of David from Abraham, Isacc,

---

[378] Holy Bible, Exodus 7:10-12
[379] Holy Bible, Exodus 17

and Jacob.[380] The prophecy of Micah affirmed that Jesus would be born in Bethlehem, of Judah at the time, and be king of the Jews.[381] The staff of Jacob became the manual symbol for the lineage of the line of King David and aligns to Judah as follows:

- Judah received the staff of Jacob at his passing transitioning leadership to him.[382]
- It was the staff and signet of Judah that was passed to Tamar. The widow of two of Judah's sons who died of mysterious causes, she became the mother of Judah's own twin sons Perez and Zerah surreptitiously.[383] By obtaining Judah's staff and signet, she ensured the alignment of herself and offspring with the Tribe of Judah and had evidence of the tie through the heraldic emblems from Judah himself.[384]

---

[380] Holy Bible, Isaiah: 9:6-8
[381] Holy Bible, Micah 5:2
[382] Holy Bible, Genesis 32:9-10
[383] Holy Bible, Numbers 26:20
[384] Holy Bible, Genesis 38:18

- David, a descendant of Perez, used this staff with a sling to slay Goliath.[385] He was elevated to king succeeding King Saul, ushering in a line of kings that lasted until the destruction of the Temple.[386]

The staff was an early heraldic signet of lineage from Jacob to David. Fourteen generations passed from David to Jesus. Both Mary and Jospeh source to David. Mary descends from David's son, Nathan, while Joseph descends from Solomon through Rehoboam. Together, they seal the lineage of Jesus by blood all the way back to Abraham.[387] Christians, however, believe in the immaculate conception which dictates that Mary was not impregnated by Joseph but by divine copulation.[388] Nevertheless, the lineage to Abraham is salvaged through Mary.

Under the Roman Empire, scepters and staffs were also insignias of leadership and tokens of authority. The

---

[385] Sandusky, Michael, Flight from Destiny: Psalmwriter the Chronicles of David Book I, Xlibrus US, 2007, p.21
[386] Eds. Shaw, Jeffrey M., Timothy J. Demy, War and Religion: An Encyclopedia of Faith and Conflict, ABC-CLIO, 2017, p.102
[387] Robertson, T.A., Commentary on the Gospel According to Matthew, Macmillan, 1911, p.55
[388] Holy Bible, Luke 1:26-38

Sceptrum Eberneum was an ivory scepter that marked Roman Consuls and Magistrates. The Sceptrum Augusti was the implement of the emperor. It was gold and ivory tipped with a gold eagle symbolizing the power and sovereignty of the emperor.[389] Thus, both were Sceptrum Regale or royal scepters in heraldic terms.

The origins of the Papal Ferula or scepter links directly the Sceptrum Augusti as well as the Heqa in style and form. Spiritually, it aligns with the rod of Moses as a link to divine power. The pastoral staff or baculus used by the pope was initially hooked like the Heqa with the length of a shepherd's rod. It was abandoned toward the end of the Middle Ages but re-adopted with modifications. Atop the staff is the single-barred cross representing the Christian faith. This design is labelled the "ferula" and it is utilized in modern liturgical ceremonies as the extension of the holy arms of the pope and bishops.[390]

---

[389] The Encyclopedia Britannica, Encyclopedia Britannica Company, 1911, p.309
[390] Lightbrown, R.W., Carlo Crivelli, Yale University Press, 2004, p.213

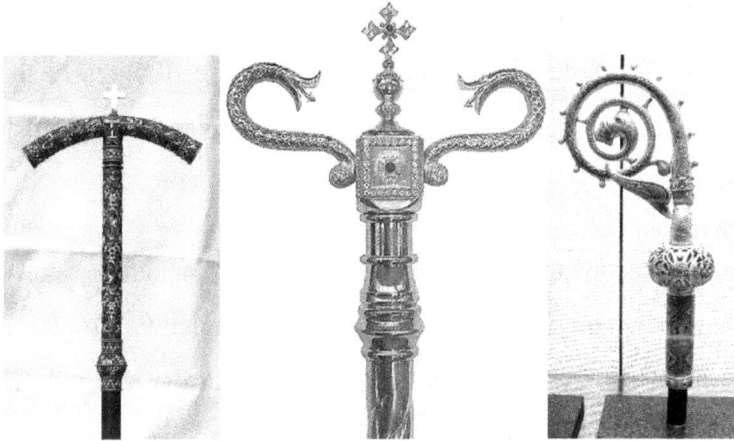

Figure 53 Crosiers of the Orthodox Catholic Church

The Orthodox Catholic Church, which separated from the Roman Catholic Church in 1054AD in the Great Schism, utilizes the crosier or the pastoral staff of clergy. Like the Roman Catholic Church, the staff was also inspired by the extension of God's power through Moses as well as the spiritual shepherding work of Jesus. The crosier of a bishop is topped with the cross flanked by serpents. The pastoral crosier is hooked representing Jesus, the "Good Shepherd". The tau shaped crosier is representative of eternal life through the trinity of the father, son and holy ghost.[391] The Byzantine Empire was associated with the

---

[391] Victoria and Albert Museum, Publication, Issue 162, 1924, pp.9-12

Orthodox faith.[392] Incidentally, the heraldic emblem of the Orthodox faith is the double-headed eagle of Lagash, the same eagle adopted by the Roman Empire and the Scottish Rite.[393]

Ancient and modern Knights Templar also carried baculi as an insignia of leadership. Anciently, it was a golden rod capped by a croix pattée or "rosy cross". In battle, the symbolism of the rod was to empower the master to defend the weak and strike down the vice of delinquents.[394] In doing so, it served as a spiritual symbol and reminder of the solemnity of purpose in service to the army of Christ. But, During times of war, the baculus was exchanged for a sword as evidenced by the Norman Invasion of Ireland in the 12th Century. Monks transitioned to Knights Templar. Having secured Kilmainham, Lord Richard de Clare, Strongbow, erected a castle from which Templars extended their reach in the land against barbaric

[392] Krueger, Derek, Byzantine Christianity, Fortress Press, 2010, p.7
[393] Grierson, Philip, Catalogue of the Byzantine Coins in the Dumbarton Oaks Collection and in the Whittemore Collection, Dumbarton Oaks Research Library and Collection, 1966, p.86
[394] Allan, Brian, Heretics: Past and Present: Can We Now Explain the Unexplainable, John Hunt Publishing Limited, 2010, p.44

tribes. After Strongbow's death in 1177, battles with tribes continued to force monks to transition into military service:[395]

> *"When the blast of war summoned them to the field, these monks laid aside their white mantles and caps; the baculus was exchanged for the lance or sword; and the Templar endued himself with the armour of an ordinary knight, distinguished, however, by having the cross, the badge of his Order, displayed on his breast, and emblazoned on his banners."*

Though the Lord's name may have been utilized for more than missionary work, the belief of the monks was of such a high degree that they were prepared to give their lives militantly for the cause.

While the teachings of Jesus seemed to be geared more commonly towards the savior as the lamb of God in the modern era, portrayal as the lion of the Tribe of Judah was expressed by the Templars in their actions. Muslims approached the subject through Muhammad's example in

---

[395] The Irish Builder, 11/1/1896, p.225

the same manner. Thus, the sword and the scimitar clashed in the name of God and Allah in the region of Palestine during the Crusades.

Prior to the 7th Century, Palestine was under the control of the Byzantine Empire. Jerusalem was captured by the Rashidun Caliphate under the leadership of Omar ibn Al-Khattab in November, 636AD.[396] It remained a Caliphate state until Christian efforts were initiated to secure Jerusalem whose holiness is justified by its consecration history in Judaism, Christianity, and Islam:

1. Moriah is the site where Isaac was to be offered by Abraham, per the command of God as a test of faith marking the initial consecration of Jerusalem.[397]
2. Moriah was also the site of King Solomon's Temple, a house of worship and leadership for a united, Kingdom of Israel. The temple was a permanent replacement of the Tabernacle of David

---

[396] Jerusalem Documents, Palestinian Academic Society for the Study of International Affairs, 1996, p.54
[397] Holy Bible, Genesis 22

which housed the Ark of the Covenant.[398] Solomon built his temple on Mount Moriah because it was the location where God appeared to his father, David.[399] God's communication to David and Solomon, in the tabernacle and, subsequently, the temple further consecrated the ground.[400]

3. Jesus ascended into heaven at Jerusalem after resurrection further consecrating the ground.[401]

4. Muhammad ascended to heaven from Jerusalem marking it as consecrated ground for Islam.[402]

So, the debate for control centered around religious inheritance and the fulfillment of prophecy. As history could not identify who was the most entitled, it had to be decided through bloodshed between descendants of Abraham.

Like Jesus, the bloodline of the Prophet Muhammad is also shown to be linked to Abram or Abraham through

---

[398] Holy Bible, 2 Samuel 2
[399] Holy Bible, 2 Chronicles 3:1
[400] Holy Bible, 1 Kings 6
[401] Holy Bible, John 20:17
[402] Holy Qu'ran, Surah 17:1

Ishmael who was born out of wedlock from Hagar, hand maiden of his wife Sarai.[403] God blessed Ishmael and promised that from him a great nation would be made from twelve princes of his loins.[404] It was not until after the birth of Isaac, that God changed the names of Abram and Sari to Abraham and Sarah.

The sons of Ishmael were Nebajoth, Kedar, Adbeel, Mibsam, Mishma, Dumah, Massa, Hadar, Tema, Jetur, Naphish, and Kedemah.[405] The second son, Kedar, settled in Arabia.[406] His descendant, Adnan, a Kedarite, is considered the patriarch of the Adnanite Arabs of Arabia who settled in Mecca before Islam and still retained a relationship with Judaism.[407] It was from the Jewish perspective that it was prophesied that a "new song" would come from this land of Kedar.[408] Per Islam, the "new song"

---

[403] Holy Qu'ran, Surah 37:105
[404] Holy Bible, Genesis 17:20
[405] Holy Bible, Genesis 25:13-15
[406] Holy Bible, Ezekiel 27:21
[407] Pirnahad, Kamran, Evolution of Humanity: The Path to Independence, iUniverse, 2007, p.51
[408] Holy Bible, Isaiah 42:9-12

was revealed through the Muhammad, a son of Abrahamic lineage and heir to the promised land of Jerusalem.[409]

The Quraysh was a polytheistic, Adnanite Clan from the line of Fihr ibn Malik through his descendant Qusayr ibn Kilab who settled in Mecca.[410] Fihr secured the Kaaba at Mecca as a pagan sanctuary.[411] Control of Mecca passed through six generations to Qusayy who maintained polytheistic beliefs.[412] Under their control, the Kaaba incorporated many pagan idols which, per the prophet Jeremiah, angered God.[413] The Hashim Clan of the Quraysh, a monotheistic clan under Hashim ibn Abdallah Manaf, placed its religious focus on the God of Abraham. It was through Shaiba ibn Hashim, and Muhammad's father, Abdallah Al-Muttalib, that a return to Judaism ensued. But, while the lineage of David passed the staff, the father of Muhammad, Abdallah Al-Muttalib, passed to his son a

---

[409] Rizvi, Sayyid Saeed Ahktar, Prophecies about the Hoy Prophet of Islam in Hindu, Christian, Jewish, and Parsi Scriptures, Bilal Muslim Mission of Tanzania, 2002, p.15

[410] Retso, Jan, The Arabs in Antiquity: Their History from the Assyrians to the Umayyads, Taylor & Francis, 2013, p.33

[411] Holy Quran, Surah 22:25

[412] Retso, Jan, The Arabs in Antiquity: Their History from the Assyrians to the Umayyads, Taylor & Francis, 2013, p.614

[413] Holy Bible, Jeremiah 2:9-13

sword - Al-Ma'thur. This sword was his inheritance prior to receiving his revelations at Mt. Hira and symbol of leadership of the Hashim.[414]

Another sword of Muhammad, Al-Mikhdham, became the quintessential sword of choice for Muslims during the Holy Wars. It was passed from Muhammad, prior to his death in 632AD, to Ali, the first Imam and last Caliph of the Rashidun Caliphate.[415] It was a scimitar.

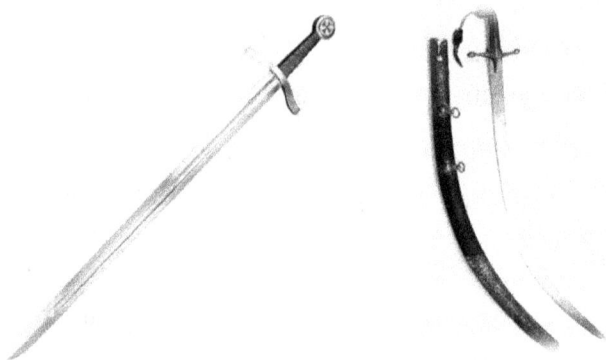

Figure 54 Templar Arming Sword and Scimitar

The two primary weapons utilized on the battlefields were the arming sword and the scimitar. The arming sword

---

[414] Wheeler, Brannon, Mecca and Eden: Ritual, Relics and Territory in Islam, University of Chicago Press, 2006, p.34
[415] Wheeler, Brannon, Mecca and Eden: Ritual, Relics, and Territory in Islam, University of Chicago Press, 2006, p.33

was the primary weapon for Knights Templar while the scimitar was the weapon of choice Muslim soldiers. While both weapons had unique strengths and weaknesses, they were utilized effectively to secure victories.

The arming sword was a short and well balanced, dual edged sword with enough girth to penetrate through chain mail armor. It could be wielded with one hand and was used over multiple centuries in Templar and Crusader battles. Although all Crusaders were not Templars, the sword was forged in the form of a cross to represent Christianity and soldiers who wielded it did so without fear of death.[416]

The scimitar provided an advantage for its wielder on horseback. Its curved blade allowed for slicing with ease for calvary, but it was also a strong, penetrating weapon. As removal after penetration was not a straight retreat, the curved blade could cause additional internal damage. Its spiritual reference was the crescent moon of Islam which was emulated by its curved form. Its alignment with the

---

[416] Campbell, David, Templar Knight vs. Mamluk Warrior, Bloomsbury Publishing, 2015, pp.14-16

weapon of choice of Muhammad also held special significance to the Muslim forces who also fought without fear of death.[417]

The First Crusade was initiated by Pope Urban II in 1095 in response to a request of Byzantine Emperor Alexios I Komnenos for military support to combat the Seljuk Turks, Sunni Muslims, who held control over Jerusalem. After four years of battles and sieges, the Byzantine Empire took control after the Siege of Jerusalem in 1099AD after massacring the Turks. A final defeat of the Turks at the Battle of Ascalon ended the crusade. King Baldwin I was installed as King of Jerusalem and served until his death in 1118AD.[418] After the crusade, Templar armies returned home. By the middle of the 12th Century, Muslims had regained control of Jerusalem.

The Second Crusade was initiated by King Louis VII of France, King Conrad III of Germany and Pope Eugene III in 1145AD in response to the fall of the County of Edessa

---

[417] Hoshour, Ben, Origins of the Minor Arcana, Primedia eLaunch LLC, 2020, p.108

[418] Riley-Smith, Jonathan, The Crusades, Christianity and Islam, Columbia University Press, 2011, p.17

in 1144AD - the first Crusader State established by King Baldwin I in 1098AD. The French and German armies were defeated multiple times by the Turks after crossing into Anatolia which was Byzantine territory. The losses, due to Byzantine withdrawals, significantly depleted the Templar forces. They were ineffective when attempting to regain control of Jerusalem in 1148AD.[419]

The Third Crusade was not a papal crusade but was a Christian effort initiated by King Philip II of France, King Richard I of England and Holy Roman Emperor Frederick I of Germany to recapture Jerusalem. After the Second Crusade, Jerusalem had become a multicultural city housing Muslims, Jews and Christians alike. Balian of Ibelin, a Crusader, had become Lord of Jerusalem, serving as its protector until 1187AD when he surrendered it to Sultan Saladin of the Ayyubid Empire who sought to reclaim the lands in the name of Islam.[420]

The crusader armies took the offensive in 1189AD. By 1190AD, they seized control of Acre and Jaffa but the

---

[419] Peoples, Scott R., Crusade of Kings, Wildside Press, 2007, p.73
[420] Ibid, p.97

battles and death of Frederick in 1190AD after leading his army across Anatolia and the Balkans depleted the German forces to a degree and those remaining fell under the command of the Duke of Austria, Leopold V. The Battle of Arsuf of 1191AD was a substantial victory by the combined crusader armies which secured a significant amount of coastline. However, the forces were insufficient to defeat Saladin which forced the Treaty of Jaffa in 1192AD. The treaty recognized Muslim control of Jerusalem while ceding unarmed Christian visitation to the city for pilgrimage.[421]

Pope Innocent III called for the Fourth Crusade in 1202AD initially to recapture Jerusalem by first capturing Egypt and utilizing it as a base for the attack of Jerusalem. However, due to disputes between the Roman Catholic and Byzantine states, it concluded with the sacking of the Byzantine capital of Constantinople in 1204AD. The disputes were tied to the retractions of agreed upon rates for travel and resources. In response, the Crusaders attacked.

---

[421] Ibid, pp.93-95

eventually partitioned the Byzantine Empire into Crusader States giving rise to the Latin Empire.[422]

To obtain the initial ground set for the Fourth Crusade, the Fifth Crusade starting in 1217AD, also called by Pope Innocent III, briefly succeeded in capturing parts of Egypt. The Siege of Damietta in 1218AD secured a key seaport for the Catholic armies. Rather than discuss terms for peace, the armies sought to capture Cairo. However, defeat at the Battle of Mansurah in 1221AD crushed their forces. The subsequent surrender and peace offered by Sultan Al-Kamil drove all crusader forces off the continent by year's end.[423]

The Sixth Crusade was one of redemption at the hands of Holy Roman Emperor Frederick II. The Ayyubids Empire had become embroiled in civil war after the Fifth Crusade. Al-Kamil, Al-Mu'azzam and Al-Ashraf were jointly responsible for the Muslim victory and wrestled for control of the empire. Amid the civil war, Frederick attacked and forced negotiations with Al-Kamil. Satisfied,

---

[422] Ibid, p.44
[423] Shaw, Jeffrey M., Timothy J. Demy, War and Religion: An Encyclopedia of Faith and Conflict, ABC-CLIO, 2017, p.525

Frederick returned to home in 1228AD to the disdain of Pope Gregory IX. The pope excommunicated him removing military support, to a degree, as he travelled to Jerusalem to assume the kingship of city and the lands ceded in the treaty with Al-Kamil. The lands included Nazareth, Sidon, Jaffa and Bethlehem which became Crusader States.[424]

The Seventh and Eight Crusades were led by King Louis IX of France. Both efforts targeted Egypt as its critical point to solidify it as a base of attack for Jerusalem. His first attempt in 1248AD extended to 1254AD but fell short.[425] His second attempt in 1270AD concluded with his death from dysentery. The Treaty of Tunis ended hostilities on November 1, 1270, with a Muslim victory.[426]

The Ninth Crusade led by Duke Edward of Gascony in 1271AD voided the Treaty of Tunis. It was an attempt to avenge the Eighth Crusade. Internal conflicts in England drove the duke to withdraw and concede through the Treaty

---

[424] Ibid, p.299
[425] Ibid, p.215
[426] Ibid, p.257

of Caesarea in 1272AD.[427] It ushered in a truce of ten years. The concept for a final Crusade was introduced by Pope Gregory X. He was successful in engaging the Mongols for support, but his plans outlived him. He died on January 10, 1276, and King Charles I of Sicily took up the mantle. By 1278AD, he had control of the Templar states of Acre and Achaea as bases of attack on Constantinople. However, internal conflicts in Sicily through 1282AD led to him yielding the throne to King Peter III.[428]

Conflicts between Charles and Philip endured through the death of Charles in 1285AD which halted plans for a final crusade. By the time that plans were reintroduced by Pope Nicholas IV in 1287AD, six popes had passed on to that undiscovered country from whose bourne no traveler returns. The plans were not heavily supported because they were unclear. The preceding popes had passed without fully

---

[427] Ibid, p.215
[428] Selart, Anti, Livonia, Rus' and the Baltic Crusades in the Thirteenth Century, Brill, 2015, p.300

disclosing their efforts.[429] Clarity did not return until 1291AD at the loss of Acre to Muslim Mamluk forces.[430]

Acre was the last major stronghold in the region significantly diminishing the foothold of Christian forces in the Holy Land. Although some forces were maintained in the region in Ruad, they were not sufficient to recapture Acre, failing after multiple attempts. The fall of Ruad in 1302AD was the last stand of the Templars in the region.[431] These final defeats by Muslim forces are considered the conclusion to the Tenth Crusade which ushered in a period of centuries without European incursion in the region.

On the battlefield, the scepter had no place. The sword was the implement of authority. Heraldic diplomacy and internal sovereignty no longer mattered as anyone could be killed in battle. Therefore, in the ranks of Freemasonry and its related bodies, the sword is utilized particularly in orders that are military in nature like the Scottish and York Rites.

---

[429] Crowley, Roger, Accursed Tower, Yale University Press, 2019, p.96
[430] Ibid, p.207
[431] Muir, Diana Jean, TEMPLARS: Who Were They? Where Did They Go?, Volume 2, Lulu.com, 2019, p.474

The Scottish Rite is, in fact, representative of the military arm of Freemasonry. In Scottish Rite Consistories, the sword is the implement that Commanders-In-Chief wield to signify adoption or acceptance of motions and to control meetings. He does this over a camp of Fraters who move the armorial pieces across the battlefield of life.[432]

Figure 55 Scottish Rite Camp

[432] McClenachan, Charles T., Ancient and Accepted Scottish Rite Manual, Masonica, 2020, p.400

It is also the sword that Eminent Commanders of Knights Templar Commanderies wield to direct Knights among their various paths. The slogan on their swords is "Non nobis domine! Non nobis sed nomini tuo da Gloriam!" or "Give Glory, not for us, God, not for us, but for your name!"[433] Lastly, it is the scimitar that is the implement of Potentates of Shriner Temples.[434] It is utilized to slice away ignorance and direct the performance of tasks to resolve the plans on the dias. Like the Consistory and Commandery, the militaristic arms of Philosophy, Judaism, Christianity, and Islam are solidly represented.

The Gavel

Masonic Lodges are not militaristic in nature. Its focus is on construction. As such, a different implement is used for authority. Worshipful Masters, or leaders of Masonic Lodges, wield the gavel, an administrative implement used for the high purpose of building and shaping in accordance with the orders laid out of the Trestle Board of the Lodge.

[433] Masonic Eclectic, Volume 1, 1860, p.409
[434] Eds. Shalem, Avinoam, Christiane J. Gruber, The Image of the Prophet Between Ideal and Ideology: A Scholarly Investigation, De Gruyter, 2014, p.377

Figure 56 Judges' Gavel and Masonry Hammer

The gavel affirms the directives. It is intended to break off the rough edges of ignorance and confusion like a Masonry hammer does to stone and present solid plans to ensure that the objectives of the Lodge are met.[435] It is the only by way of the gavel that stones can be carved for placement in their appropriate places outlined by the plans on the Trestle Board. It is an implement of order.

In the modern era, the gavel is a ceremonial mallet used to punctuate rulings and proclamations and demand attention. It is a symbol of the authority wielded by a presiding officer. Vice President of the United States, John Adams, used a gavel to call order in the first United States

---

[435] Masonic Eclectic, Volume 1, 1860, p.219

Senate in New York in 1789.[436] Since then, it has remained customary to tap the gavel to open and close proceedings.

In American courts of law, judges also wield gavels to symbolize authority, prestige, power, control, and order. The judge's duty is to preside in a court, try lawsuits and make legal rulings based on the evidence submitted. One rap of the gavel follows the announcement of adjournment, the completion of a business item or a message to the members to be seated. Two raps call the meeting to order. Three raps signal all members to stand.[437]

Without order, chaos rules and plans do not get accomplished. The implements of leadership are designed to minimize chaos. In war, implements of combat serve to eradicate enemies. In peace, in times of building and construction, implements that contribute to construction serve to satisfy the designs. So, the establishment of order is critical in securing the needs of the day and age.

---

[436] Byrd, Robert C., The Senate, 1789-1989: Addresses on the History of the United States, U.S. Government Printing Office, 1988, p.425
[437] Records and Briefs of the United States Supreme Court, United States Supreme Court, 1832, p.70

Signets and Landmarks

Signets are implements that are utilized as signatory tools to make a unique mark for the purposes of notarization. A notarization is an endorsement signifying the wishes of the notary. The wishes can be orders or directives from leadership as well as plans for implementation. Once notarized, the notary affirms his or her intentions as laid out in the directives allowing the recipient of the notarized item to progress with full endorsement.

As signets are manual implements, landmarks are monuments that help to identify ownership of domains. They too carry unique marks and verbiage for the official designation of specific ownership. Many also incorporate other figurative emblems that provide further background on the owners. With all emblematic representation arranged on the monuments themselves, the heraldic symbol was meant as a permanent marker for the respective domain.

Seals

The unique marks have varied over the ages but have traditionally aligned with heraldic emblems or coats of arms that denote specific entities. Many royals carried rings or other implements with variations of seals. They indicated either individual or corporate endorsements of approved plans or directives. In the modern era, for example, states in the United States of America utilize unique seals for certification on documents like birth and marriage certificates to affirm that the birth of a child or marriage was affirmed within its boundaries. The seal of the President of the United States affirms the originator of the approval. The official seal of the United States of America affirms corporate endorsement as put forth by its representatives. As such, the seal affirms individual and corporate interests.

The term signature derives from the word signet. Written signets also serve as unique identifiers that carry the wishes of the notary. The prophet Daniel affirmed that signature was utilized in biblical times when King Darius signed a decree.[438] Checks and other promissory notes require a signature from financial institutions for processing. Electronic signatures and personal identification numbers are also an implementation in the

---

[438] Holy Bible, Daniel 6:8-10

modern era along that are forms of acceptable signets. Yet, no signet is like the fingerprints of individual citizens. A fingerprint is as unique to an individual as deoxyribonucleic acid (DNA).[439] There is only one per person and cannot be exactly duplicated.

The need for authentication was pervasive particularly in ancient times not only for endorsements but also to identify lineage. Lineage determined royalty in many societies and unique implements were passed between generations to affirm affiliation to royal houses. This format was utilized to keep and transition power within bloodlines. The common manual implements were cylinders and rings.

The substances utilized to capture the stamp and seal the media were wax, lead, or clay. The substance had to be soft enough to capture the imprint of the stamp but also able to harden. The hardening served as a very effective lock particularly on documents to ensure that they could not be opened without being noticed. Heat was required for

---

[439] Watson, James D., Andrew Berry, DNA: The Secret of Life, Knopf Doubleday Publishing Group, 2009, p.275

softening wax and lead in the substances in the sealing process. Both were heated and placed on documents before a stamp could be pressed. Clay, on the other hand, had to be wet before stamping an impression and took much longer to harden.[440] Of the processes, clay sealing is the oldest.

The earliest known signet implement was the cylindrical seal of ancient Sumer. The cylinder was engraved with written characters and figures for unique identification. It would be pressed and rolled across wet clay to transfer the shapes to the medium.[441] Upon drying, the signet seal was permanently affixed on the tablet. Figures on the seals incorporated words as well as emblematic representations since the First Dynasty of Babylon.[442] The seal of Bashu-Enzu, the first king of the 4th Kish Dynasty near 2900BC, incorporated the representation of the goddess Ningal. It also incorporates a bull which further alludes to his devotion to the moon good.

---

[440] Oikonomides, Nicolas, Byzantine Lead Seals, Dumbarton Oaks, 1985, p.3
[441] Handcock, Percy S.P., Mesopotamian Archaeology: An Introduction to the Archaeology of Ancient Mesopotamia, Good Press, 2021, p.107
[442] Legrain, Leon, The Culture of the Babylonians from Their Seals in the Collections of the Museum, University Museum, 1925, pp.8-9

Gilgamesh is also shown kneeling while the king communicates with the goddess.[443] This combination of imagery and wording completed Bashu-Enzu's unique seal.

Figure 57 Sumerian Basha-Enzu Seal and Egyptian Cylinder

Sumerian cylinders were made by burguls who utilized copper tools to shape stones, bones, or other materials into cylindrical forms. Once formed, they carved emblems to produce the seals so that they would roll over clay tables

---

[443] Ibid, pp.210-211

and create a unique signature. Holes atop the cylinder were drilled to affix to a cord for the bearer to wear.[444]

Ancient Egyptian civilization was also known to utilize cylindrical seals in the same manner since its 1st Dynasty using similar materials. Hieroglyphics and symbolic animal forms were affixed to the cylinder to create unique signatures for nobility. Seal cutters were also employed to carve the emblems into the materials and clay was the primary media upon which the cylinders were rolled.[445]

Stamp seals were forged during the same period as cylinder seals with the same symbolism. In Sumerian society, stamp seals were smaller than the cylinders which were three to four inches in length and had become more pervasive in usage than the cylinders by 1000BC.[446] In Egyptian society, Scarab Seals were utilized. Much smaller than the cylinder seals, they also were carved by seal

---

[444] Bertman, Stephen, Handbook to Life in Ancient Mesopotamia, OUP USA, 2005, p.233

[445] Kemp, Barry J., Ancient Egypt: Anatomy of a Civilization, Routledge, 1991, p.90

[446] Makkay, Janos, Early Stamp Seals in South-east Europe, Akademiai Kiado, 1984, p.78

cutters and provided a unique impression of its bearer.[447] Because of their size, they became more convenient.

Figure 58 Sumerian, Egyptian Scarab, and Hebrew Seals

---

[447] Teissier, Beatrice, Egyptian Iconography on Syro-Palestinian Cylinder Seals of the Middle Bronze Age, University Press, 1996, p.9

Hebrew seals followed along the same paths. They were heavily utilized since 900BC and were not only associated with men but also with women. This was in contrast Mesopotamian societies in which the authorization laid specifically in the hands of men. The Hebrew seals contained characters denoting familial heritages and images associated with their faith community.[448]

This practice carried through to the Medieval Era with the exception being the specific media upon which the seals were pressed. The Romans utilized bulla and bitumen seals. Bulla refers to inscribed clay or a soft metal like lead or tin. Although strong enough to maintain a seal, it was soft enough to receive an impression.[449] Bitumen is a sticky substance which is the residue of burnt coal or wood. Although the substance was used to seal ships and other cargo containers, it was also used to affix seal impressions

---

[448] Zerbe, Alvin Sylvester, The Antiquity of Hebrew Writing and Literature, Central Publishing House, 1911, pp.121-122
[449] Rich, Anthony, A Dictionary of Roman and Greek Antiquities with Nearly 2000 Engravings on Wood from Ancient Originals Illustrative of the Industrial Arts and Social Life of the Greeks and Romans, D.Appleton, 1874, pp.91-92

when softened on documents.[450] Both was and bitumen hardened creating a solid, signet seal.

By the time of the Byzantine Empire, lead seals were prominent. While bitumen and wax seals sufficed on paper documents, they were not strong enough to maintain on cargo were not strong enough to withstand the pressures of transit. As such, lead was utilized as a more effective seal particularly for items of high quality and had been heavy utilized for that purpose through the 7th Century.[451]

Figure 59 Seals of King Henry VI and King Henry VIII

---

[450] McGeough, Kevin M., The Romans: An Introduction, OUP USA, 2009, p.232
[451] Oikonomides, Nicolas, Byzantine Lead Seals, Dumbarton Oaks, 1985, p.3

The bouleuterion was created as an alternative method for sealing documents at a lower risk by the Byzantine Empire. These iron pliers or bouleuteria were created to secure lead disks to both sides of the document, connecting them like buttons or sandwiching the document itself. They were, then, rolled and wrapped with cording to secure the document. Gold disks along with a red of purple cord adorned sealed documents from the emperor.[452]

Rings

Rings have also historically been utilized as signets that defined lineage, rank, and nationality of the bearers. In addition, they were utilized to affix a seal of authorization to documents, denote social status, and represent fealty to specific nations or entities. Although they may have initially been ornamental, they evolved to become key indicators of authentication all over the world.

The rings of the ancient Egyptians varied in form and style and were constructed of various materials including gold, silver, bronze, brass, ivory, and porcelain. While ivory

---

[452] Ibid, pp.4-6

and porcelain were rings worn by lower classes, gold was on the opposite end of the spectrum. The left hand was the primary hand of ring adornment and most rings served for decorative purposes. Silver rings were occasionally adorned while brass rings were primarily utilized as signets.[453]

The ancient Assyrians and Greeks followed a similar custom which was sourced from the Egyptians. Trade between Assyria and Egypt was intact during the era of the biblical prophet Isaiah near 700BC. But due to its opulence, Egypt was seen as a nation trending towards weakness and the prophet predicted that Egypt would eventually serve Assyria which came to pass.[454] From 671BC to 655BC, Assyria ruled Lower Egypt under the hands of King Esarhaddon who defeated the Pharoah Taharqa. Pharoah Tanutamani lost control of Upper Egypt from 664BC to

[453] McClintock, John, James Strong, Cyclopedia of Biblical, Theological and Ecclesiastical Literature: Rh-St, Harper, 1880, p.31
[454] Holy Bible, Isaiah 19:23

653BC.[455] Despite the transition in power, Egyptian customs remained in place as it related to rings.

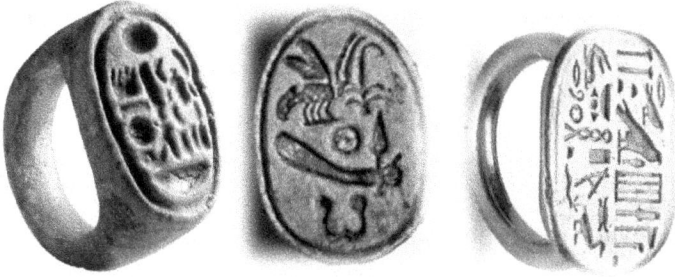

Figure 60 Rings of Tutankhamun, Amenhotep I and Sa-Neith

The wedding ring has its root in Egypt. The bridegroom placed a plain, gold band on the bride's finger which signified that all his possessions were entrusted to his bride.[456] The Romans followed suit with a ring of iron.[457] Those with precious stones were also attributed to contain curative qualities. Diamonds, for example, were believed to be antidotes to poison. Engraving the names of Jesus, Mary and Joseph on rings were believed to prevent the plague.

---

[455] Rice, Michael, Who's Who in Ancient Egypt, Taylor & Francis, 2002, p.30

[456] Cumming, Constance Frederica Gordon, Via Cornwall to Egypt, Chatto and Windus, Piccadilly, 1885, p.251

[457] Mackey, Albert Gallatin, Edward L. Hawkins, An Encyclopedia of Freemasonry and Its Kindred Sciences, Masonic History Company, 1913, pp.708-709

Gemstones attached mystical powers to the ring like those of the zodiac.[458]

These concepts and practices have transitioned into the modern era through zodiac birthstones. Signet rings, however, were extremely unique as they were carved with identifiers like the name and rank of the wearer. While some were more elaborate, they were usually made in an oblong shape of gold, and when dipped into soft wax, could be used to seal documents as a signatory representation of the bearer or the entity whom the bearer represented. The rings of King Tutankhamun, who reigned Egypt from 1332BC to 1323BC and King Amenhotep I, who reigned Egypt from 1525BC to 1504BC, hold animal representations and markers that identify their royal status. Tutankhamun's ring contains the scarab which is a representation of the sun god and a symbol of leadership as pharaoh. Amenhotep's ring contains the glyph of the "reed and the bee" which symbolizes that he was Pharoah of Upper and Lower Egypt. The ring of Sa-Neith contains

---

[458] Cumming, Constance Frederica Gordon, Via Cornwall to Egypt, Chatto and Windus, Picadilly, 1885, p.251

markers that identify him as a member of the priestly class denoted by the falcon which represents Horus.[459] These representations are unique signets of each.

Figure 61 Signets of Marcus Antonius, Tiberius, and Akakios

The materials utilized in the creation of early Roman rings were key indicators of status. Iron was the prevailing material utilized as compared to gold which was utilized for upper class citizens. Glass jewels were common in iron rings while real jewels bedazzled upper class versions. Both had unique characteristics that could identify the class and household. Soldiers were also presented gold bands as rings for laudable military service.[460] While the rings were

---

[459] Rossini, Stephanie, Egyptian Hieroglyphic: How to Read and Write Them, Dover Publications, 1989, pp.6-7
[460] Chisholm, Hugh, The Encyclopedia Brittanica, Volume 24, 1910, p.539

plain, they stood out as symbols of valor. However, they were not unique to the bearer. So, while some rings did, in fact, seal documents like the rings of Marcus Antonius and the Emperor Tiberius. Others were worn for adornment.

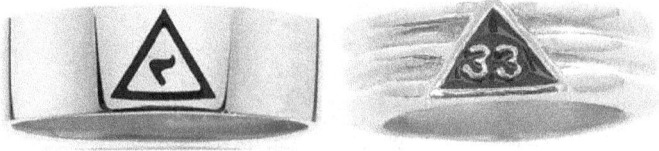

Figure 62 14th Degree Ring and 33rd Degree Ring

Rings in Freemasonry are not commonly issued by Masonic bodies to its membership. There is no specific ring for Symbolic Lodge membership but there is a specific emblem for a Master Mason. Many individual members have customized rings constructed that vary in size and design, but they are typically adorned with the emblem of Freemasonry – the Square and Compass.

Contrary to the Symbolic Lodge, there is one specific Masonic body that does have two official rings along with rules and regulations for their manners of wear. The two rings are the 14th Degree Ring and 33rd Degree Ring. When a member attains the 14th Degree, he is entitled to wear the ring which symbolizes the completion of the Lodge of

Perfection. It is a plain, flat band of gold, five-sixteenths of an inch in width, having engraved or enameled an equilateral triangle surrounding the Hebrew letter yod representing the first letter of the name of the Supreme Being. The motto of the degree, "Virtus junxit, mors non separabit" is engraved in Latin which translates to "whom virtue unites, death cannot separate" in English.[461]

A Scottish Rite Mason who has been coronated has the right to wear the 33rd Degree ring. The ring consists of three plain, half-round gold rings united into one, not exceeding five-sixteenths of an inch in width. The equilateral surrounds the number 33 in Arabic characters. It is engraved with the motto of the 33rd Degree, "Deus meumque jus" which translates to "God and my right" in English.[462]

While the 14th Degree ring can be earned after progressing through the Scottish Rite Degrees, the 33rd Degree cannot be so earned. It can only be worn by one who has been coronated. To be considered for coronation, a

---

461 Fox, William L., pp.216-217
462 Ibid, p.216

32nd Degree Scottish Rite Mason must first be found worthy of nomination. Once approved by a Supreme Council, the Sublime Prince may be eligible to receive the degree. Only after coronation, can the 33rd Degree ring be worn.

Rings of the York Rite and Shrine organizations follow the same pattern as rings for the Symbolic Lodge. There are no specific rings endorsed by the organization. Members create customized rings showcasing the emblems of the respective organizations. While ornate and exquisite, there are no rules of wear or design for them. However, for those that are corporately controlled, exposure of the emblematic representations is limited only to those who need to know to prevent the risk of counterfeiting. As such, protection of heraldic emblems is of the utmost importance.

Monuments

Landmarks refer to stationary identifiers which proclaim ownership of specific meaning to its constructor. While rings and other signets were manual totems, monuments were stationary and utilized on continents across the globe as visual representations of kinship or nationality. As such, the stationary signet has not historically represented singular persons but has represented clans, sects, and nations. Hence, its greater visibility in the respective domains.

Figure 63 Totem Poles

Indigenous peoples of the Americas constructed totem poles to define kinship and boundaries of a domain. Many contained human, animal, and supernatural forms which defined the spiritual linkage of the clan to the domain.[463]

[463] Johansen, Bruce E., Barry M. Pritzker, Encyclopedia of American Indian History, Volume 1, ABC-CLIO, 2008, p.478

Distinct figures were commonly found on totem poles echoing the nature of the totem including:[464]

- Raven - a psychic symbol of the creator;
- Eagle – a symbol of leadership and divinity;
- Killer Whale - a symbol of strength;
- Thunderbird – a symbol of mystical leadership and protection against evil spirits;
- Crow – a magical symbol of spiritual strength and the only bird who dares to attack an eagle;
- Beaver – a symbol of determination;
- Bear – a symbol of protection;
- Badger – a symbol of aggressiveness, passion, and drive;
- Wolf – a symbol of intuition and spirit of freedom;
- Butterfly – a symbol of metamorphosis and rebirth;
- Frog – a symbol of medicine and fertility.

Colors also hold deeper meanings. Red, the color of blood, represents war or valor. Blue represents the skies and

---

[464] Encyclopaedia of Religion and Ethics: Picts-Sacraments, T&T Clark, 1908, pp.97-98

waters. White represents the clouds or the heavens. Yellow represents the sun which brings light and happiness. Black represents power.[465] When combined with the animal symbols, the totems carried great meaning and became unique identifiers for the territorial jurisdiction of clans.

Figure 64 Obelisk at Temple of Seti I at Abydos

Ancient Egyptians utilized obelisks or tekhenu and pyramids for a similar purpose. The obelisks were stone pillars, typically having a square or rectangular cross section and a pyramid top, served as landmarks as well as

---

[465] Halpin, Marjorie M., Totem Poles: An Illustrated Guide, University of British Columbia Press, 1981, p.13

monuments.[466] Although the timeline of their genesis is unknown, they have been traced to the Old Kingdom of Egypt where their initial purpose seemed to be commemoration for the dead.

Over time, the obelisk took on several meanings but one of the most common references equated it to the representation of the lost phallus of Osiris. Isis was able to recover all the mutilated pieces of Osiris except for the phallus which had been eaten by fish in the Nile River. Not being completely whole, Osiris was limited to the underworld after being resurrected. So, the obelisk, in this regard, became a symbol that was associated with the realm of death and a mortuary monument.[467]

Obelisks were later utilized as monuments to other gods in complexes across Egypt and boundary markers for the controlling dynasties. The complexes themselves also incorporated pyramids and temples not only for

---

[466] Budge, Sir Ernest Alfred Wallis, Cleopatra's Needles and Other Egyptian Obelisks: A Series of Descriptions of all the Important Inscribed Obelisks with Hieroglyphic Texts, Translations, Etc., 12-13
[467] Eds. Zahi A. Hawass, Lyla Pinch Brock, Egyptology at the Dawn of the Twenty-First Century: Language, Conservation, Museology, American University in Cairo Press, 2003, pp.324-325

worshipping Osiris but others in the pantheon of Egyptian gods. The common factor on the reliefs on the walls of the edifices and throughout the boundaries of the complexes is the belief in death as a transitory state to an afterlife that is controlled by the gods.

The complex of Pharaoh Pepi I was built in Saqqara after his death and named Men-nefer-Pepo or "Pepe's splendour is enduring". The complex contained obelisks, a large pyramid for his tomb, and smaller pyramids for consorts. The obelisks were situated at the best angles to attract the rays of the sun as energy for resurrection of the deceased.[468] Thus, ensuring safe travel to the gods into eternal life.

The complex of Pharoah Seti I at Abydos is similarly aligned. He ruled Egypt during the 19th Dynasty from Memphis. His temple complex was ornate incorporating obelisks and a pyramid with beautifully adorned halls

---

[468] Verner, Miroslav, The Pyramids: The Mystery, Culture, and Science of Egypt's Great Monuments, Grove Atlantic, 2007, p.351

showcasing frescos of Seti interacting with the gods.[469] The obelisk was not a token to honor Seti but Ra, the sun god. Like Pepi's complex, the power of the sun was necessary to deify Seti. This concept is reiterated on scenes on the chapel walls of the second hall which depict the transformation of Seti as a resurrected Osiris.

Abydos had long been a landmark city for the Cult of Osiris which had been established since the Middle Kingdom era. The cult worshipped Osiris as protector and patron of the departed for the promise of resurrection and eternal life. This privilege was initially only associated with pharaohs and elites, but the cult believed resurrection to be universal for all which drove their worship and practices to Osiris. Thus, Seti's complex in Abydos, which was completed by his son Ramesses II and dedicated to Osiris, became a site of pilgrimage for the cult.[470]

---

[469] Kemp, Barry J., Ancient Egypt: Anatomy of a Civilization, Taylor & Francis, 2007, p.62
[470] Ibid, p.140

Figure 65 Relief of Seti communing with Amun-Ra

King Piye ruled over Egypt during the 25th Dynasty and was renowned for being the first Kushite King to push deeply into the Nile Delta. Piye was a worshipper of Amun-Ra who, by the time of 1600BC was the product of a fusion between Amun, god of the air, and the sun god, Ra. To the Greeks and Romans, Amun-Ra was personified as Zeus Ammon and Jupiter Ammon respectively.[471] To commemorate Amun-Ra and monuments to Egyptianize his leadership in conquered areas, Piye initiated construction projects particularly in the Middle Nile Region. An obelisk made of black granite was erected at Kadakol near 747BC inscribed with a description characterizing the king as a strong bull, the seizer of every land, and a son of Amun-Ra.[472]

Prior to this era in Egypt, the complexes were not as elaborate. The mastaba was a rectangular superstructure constructed with mud brick or stone. It was formed with sloping walls and a flat roof. The burial chamber descended

[471] Nardo, Don, Egyptian Mythology, Greenhaven Publishing, 2013, p.11
[472] Harkless, Necia Desiree, Nubian Pharaohs and Meriotic Kings: The Kingdom of Kush, AuthorHouse, 2006, p.141

deeply underground and was accessible via shafts. It was a stand-alone structure and tomb for the dead.[473]

Figure 66 Mastaba and Ziggurat

---

[473] Bauer, Susan Wise, The History of the Ancient World: From the Earliest Accounts to the Fall of Rome, W.W. Norton, 2007, pp.79-80

The ziggurat of Mesopotamia, though, was a larger and more ornate step pyramid which served the same purpose as the mastaba. It was also built with a core of mud brick and bears the appearance of stacked mastabas to a degree that culminate into a larger, pyramid-like structure.[474] There were no major complexes surrounding them, but a temple was incorporated.

Obelisks were transported to multiple lands after the fall of the Egyptian Empire as a sign of dominion over the continent. Caesar Augustus did so after disposing of Cleopatra to align himself with the lineage of Egyptian royalty but also, ironically, to show that he was victorious by the divine providence of Amun-Ra. They were transported from Heliopolis to Rome and placed in the Caesareum in 12BC. Additional obelisks were transported to Rome in 10BC. Caligula imported an Obelisk in 37AD which still resides in the Vatican today.[475] The obelisk of Theodosius I was the last transport from Egypt. The 4th

---

[474] Ibid, p.80
[475] Kleiner, Diane E.E., Cleopatra and Rome, Harvard University Press, 2009, pp.164-166

Century transport became the resident of Constantinople. It remains a fixture in the Hippodrome.[476]

Figure 67 Washington Monument

---

[476] LePree, James Francis, Ljudmila Djukic, The Byzantine Empire: A Historical Encyclopedia, ABC-CLIO, 2019, p.160

These and many others were transported initially as a sign of mastery over the African continent but evolved to become a symbol of power by many nations. The Washington Monument in Washington, District of Columbia, United Staes of America, for example, was erected in the form of an obelisk in honor of George Washington's leadership of the nation as its first President. The 555 foot marble obelisk was completed in 1885 and is topped with a pyramid resembling the obelisks of old.[477]

As Washington was also a prominent Freemason, several stones reflect Masonic emblems forever cementing Washington's link with the fraternity. The laying of the cornerstone was performed in true Masonic fashion in 1845. Forty years later, a special session was held at its dedication.[478] This structure remains the tallest, freestanding stone obelisk in the world.

Although Egyptian complexes incorporated obelisks and pyramids, they also contained temples. The temples at

---

[477] Gordon, John Steele, Washington's Monument: And the Fascinating History of the Obelisk, Bloomsbury USA, 2016, p.8
[478] Illustrated Masonic Secrets of America's Founding Fathers, Bottletree Books, 2008, pp.170-172

Abydos are considered some of the most renown but are slightly different than those of the ancient Hebrews. While the presence of deities was generally acknowledged in Egyptian temples at the sites of the temple grounds after the death of the Pharaohs or other prominent citizens, God's physical presence in the Hebrew tabernacles and temples in the face of the living consecrated them. The difference being that the consecration was witnessed by those in the land of the living while Egyptian sanctuaries were memorials and pathways for the dead to travel to eternity.

During the exodus of the Israelites from Egypt, they were instructed to build the Ark of the Covenant as a dwelling place for God and tabernacles as temporary structures for its rest and as a place of worship. Detailed instructions were provided to Moses for the construction of the tabernacle. It was to be an oblong square, with an inner and outer court. An altar of sacrifice was to be incorporated into the outer court and an altar of incense in the inner court which served as the sanctuary in which God dwelled by way of the Ark of the Covenant behind a veil.[479]

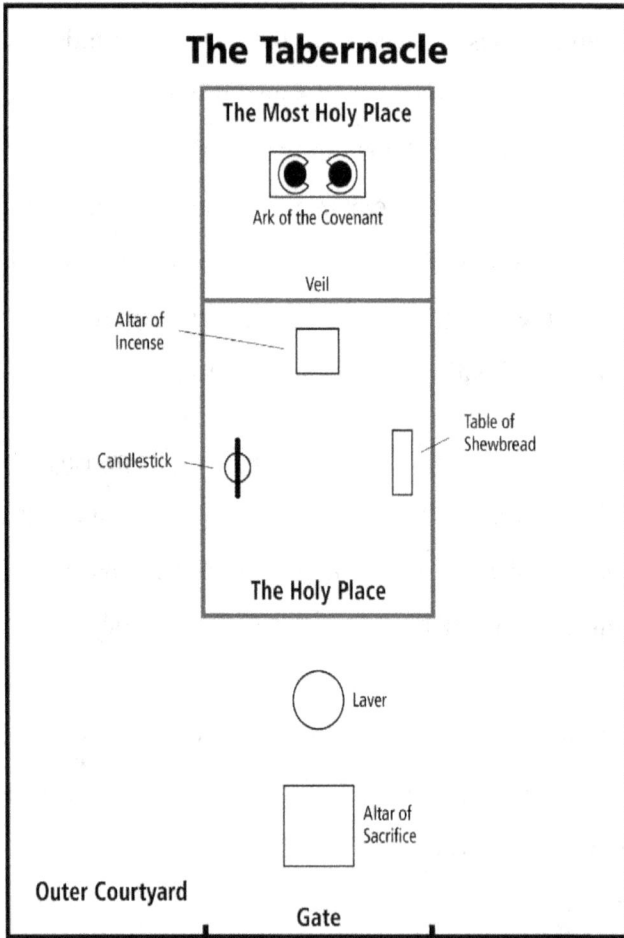

The Tabernacle

The Most Holy Place

Ark of the Covenant

Veil

Altar of Incense

Candlestick

Table of Shewbread

The Holy Place

Laver

Altar of Sacrifice

Outer Courtyard

Gate

Figure 68 Tabernacle of Moses

---

[479] Holy Bible, Exodus 25

Levite priests were also commissioned to maintain the grounds of the tabernacle. Their primary task was to ensure its construction was in accordance with the details laid out by out wherever the Israelites settled. After being built, they were charged to maintain its ordinances and sanctity ensuring compliance with the statutes that were granted.[480]

The tabernacle system remained intact for nearly five hundred years after Israelite settlement in Canaan. Judges were instituted to maintain control over the nation during this period which did not provide a stable resting place for the tabernacle. This was not resolved until the implementation of the era of the kings. King Saul settled the nation in its initial capital of Gibeau. His successor, King David, settled in Jerusalem.[481] His successor, King Solomon, erected the first temple in Jerusalem which, in effect, ended the need for the tabernacle system.

King Solomon's Temple was a permanent replication of the tabernacle. It was constructed with the same sections in

---

[480] Holy Bible, Leviticus 6
[481] Andrews, Daryl L., Valiance: Dynamics of True Faith and Brotherhood in a Changing World, Andrews Press, 2015, pp.5-9

place including the inner and outer courts affixed with the same internal structure as the tabernacle. A permanent structure, columns and other implements were required to physically support it. It was ornately designed and furnished, making it a spectacle for the ages. As it was primarily a permanent dwelling place for God whose presence was witnessed by King Solomon himself in a pillar of fire, it was considered consecrated ground as a result and a prime landmark for the Kingdom of Israel.[482]

The first temple remained intact through the Babylonian Conquest where it was sacked and destroyed. However, by the benevolence of King Cyrus, it was rebuilt in 515BC. The conquests of Jerusalem, however, according to several sources saw its decline as by 20BC it had become dilapidated. Herod the Great, King of Judea, saw to its dismantling but also saw to the construction of a new temple to replace it. The new temple became the site of pilgrimage for Hebrews and Christians until it was finally destroyed by Rome in 70AD. Despite its destruction, the ground was still revered as holy not only

---

[482] Ibid, pp.10-12

because of God's manifestation on the site but also through Jesus' presence and activities there.[483]

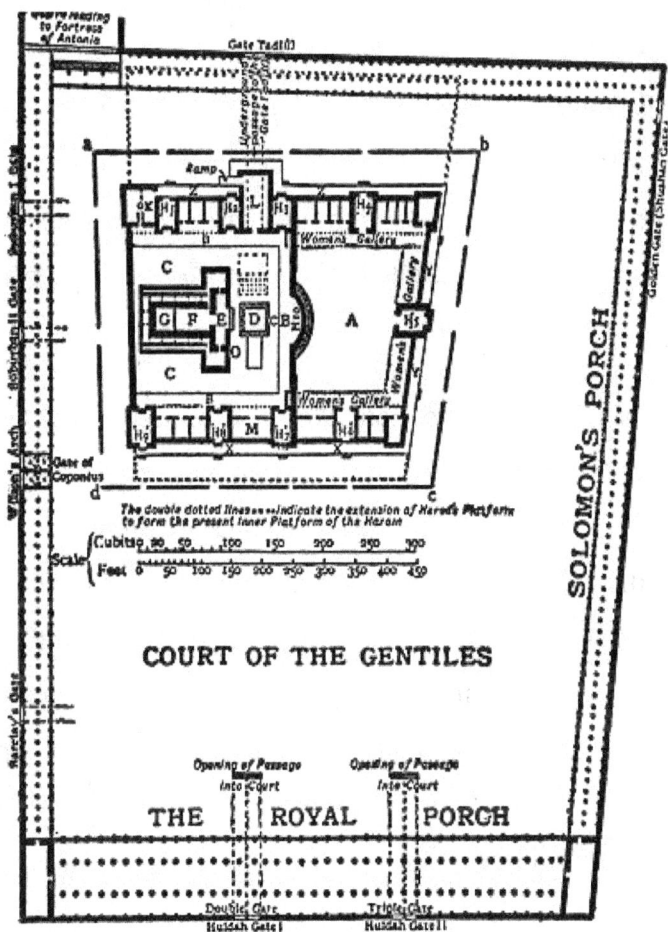

Figure 69 Herod's Temple

---

[483] Ibid, pp.13-14

Six hundred years after the destruction of Herod's Temple, the site was further consecrated through the Isra and Miraj of Muhammad. So, by the Middle Ages, the ground had become a landmark of faith for Judaism, Christianity, and Islam which, unfortunately, was disputed during the Crusades. However, the temple concept, as a home for the various orders of Freemasonry, translated well as all faiths are represented. Though different, they operate in peace.

It is important to note that a Freemason or Mason cannot be an atheist but must be one who believes in the concept of a supreme being without reference to one specific faith or theology. As multiple faiths can claim a lineage to the holy ground of Jerusalem, men of different faiths can attain membership in the order. The temple, therefore, is that ground, that consecrated ground upon which all Masons can meet equally and work accordingly for the aims of the order.

The oldest female appendant body of Freemasonry meets in courts which pay homage to the outer court of the second temple. Within the outer court was contained the

Court of Women, Court of Gentiles, and the Court of Men. The Heroines of Jericho bodies meet in courts for this reason. This order reveres Rahab, the heroine who hid Israelite spies at the Battle of Jericho, whose bravery set the stage for victory for Joshua and the nation of Israel.[484]

The male counterparts to the Heroines of Jericho are Holy Royal Arch Masons who revere Joshua, Zerubbabel, and Haggai. The male advisor to a Heroines of Jericho Court is personified by Joshua whom the Rahab aided. Zerubbabel represents the King of Judea who rebuilt the second temple and incorporated a court for women. Haggai represents the high priest through whom God communicated.[485] Although other female appendant bodies do exist, they do not hold the same biblical lineage as the Heroines of Jericho:

- The Order of the Eastern Star has its roots in the 19th Century and is an adoptive rite of the Masonic

---

[484] Holy Bible, Joshua 2:1-22
[485] Morris, S. Brent, The Complete Idiot's Guide to Freemasonry, Alpha Books, 2006, pp.93-94

Order. They congregate in chapters and their parent organization reports to Masonic Grand Lodges.[486]

- The Ladies of the Circle of Perfection are counterparts to the Royal and Select Masters or Cryptic Rite who revere Menelik, the high priest to whom Abraham paid a tithe. They congregate in courts while their counterparts congregate in councils. As the tabernacle system was not implemented until millennia later, there is no linkage to the courts of Herod's temple.[487]

- The Heroines of the Templar Crusades or Cyrenes are counterparts to the Knights Templar who are dedicated to Christianity. They congregate in guilds to signify their support of the Knights Templar and their own participation in the Holy Wars. The Knights congregate in commanderies.[488]

- An honorary order, the Princesses of the York Cross of Honor are counterparts to the Knights of the York Cross of Honor. They congregate in priorates or

---

[486] Ibid, pp.84-85
[487] Ibid, p.65
[488] Ibid, p.65

nunneries which signify their service as past leaders of Heroines of Jericho Courts, Ladies of the Circle of Perfection Courts, and Crusade Guilds. Their service from Jericho to the Holy Wars sets them aside as the quintessential women of faith. Their counterparts congregate in priories.[489]

- The Order of the Golden Circle is the female counterpart to the Scottish Rite. They congregate in Assemblies supporting Scottish Rite Consistories in their respective Valleys. The parent organizations report to Supreme Councils.[490]

- The Daughters Auxiliary is the counterpart to the Shrine which is dedicated to Islam. They meet in courts and align with Shrine Temples.[491]

The temples are landmarks for the specific organizations which are subordinate to a parent organization. The parent organizations maintain headquarters or grand temples or Holy Sees which serve as

---

[489] http://www.tucker-coffeegrandcourtpych.com/pych-history.html, retrieved 8/5/2023
[490] Morris, S. Brent, The Complete Idiot's Guide to Freemasonry, Alpha Books, 2006, p.65
[491] Ibid, p.56

the highest landmark for the orders. For example, Masonic Lodges are subordinate to a Grand Lodge within a specified jurisdiction. The authority of a Grand Lodge, however, does not extend beyond its defined boundaries.[492]

Grand bodies also exist for Chapters, Councils, Courts, etc. for the same purpose within specific regions. Those classified as appendant are extensions of their designated counterparts and fall under their authority. Concordant bodies have their own authoritative structure but are related to Grand Lodges by mutual agreements.[493]

While the regions in the United States of America are typically defined by state lines, they may vary in other parts of the world to include the nation themselves. They serve as the highest authority for the bodies and keepers of the rules and regulations of the orders under the leadership and heraldry designated by their respective constitutions and

---

[492] Ibid, p.71
[493] Ibid, pp.117-118

bylaws.[494] Thus, each organization is regulated and monitored to ensure compliance.

Lodge

Chapter

Royal Arch Masons

Heroines of Jericho

Royal and Select Masters

Circle of Perfection

Knights Templar

Heroines of the Templar Crusades

Knights York Cross of Honor

Princesses York Cross of Honor

Scottish Rite

Order of the Golden Circle

Shrine

Daughters

Figure 70 Logos for Masonic Bodies

---

[494] Ibid, p.279

Emblematically, the parent organizations are typically affixed with wreaths. Although there are some exceptions, the wreath symbolizes the corporate coronation of the parent organization which holds the full accountability for the organization. The headquarters of each parent organization also represents their physical seats of power making them unique monuments of power for representation to the world.

Castles and camps were designed to secure monuments and maintain seats of power. Medieval knights operated from castles or fortified walls to defend against enemy forces. The complex of Herod could be considered a castle as its outer walls fortified the second temple. The Maccabeans of the 2nd Century BC could certainly have been considered knights for Judaism having fortified ground to secure the faith community from the Seleucids. In this instance, their fortress or castle served as the headquarters for their operations.

Camps were formed to satisfy objectives outside of the walls of the fortress. These objectives are not limited to but do include pursuit of enemy forces, travel for communications and gathering resources, and laying siege or executing raids against enemy castles or camps. Knights were utilized in both circumstances to meet the desired aims. Muhammadean conquests in the 7th Century AD during the initial promotion of Islam were done primarily from camps which served as temporary fortresses for the horsemen. These oases provided the security and sustenance needed to maintain ranks.[495]

It is for this reason that the orders of knighthood in the York Rite and Scottish Rite have direct links to Freemasonry as a whole. York Rite Knights secured temple grounds through commanderies. The commandery, therefore, became a protectorate of the region.[496] Scottish Rite Knights were akin to warrior priests and secured camps in consistories.[497] In doing so, the valleys they secured comprised the orient under the holy empire to whom fealty was pledged. Muhammad's horsemen also have a direct link to the Shrine. They were renowned for

---

[495] www.merriam-webster.com/dictionary/oasis, retrieved 8/9/2023
[496] www.merriam-webster.com/dictionary/commandery, retrieved 8/9/2023
[497] www.merriam-webster.com/dictionary/consistory, retrieved 8/9/2023

securing desert grounds and surviving in harsh conditions in oasis camps. All these factors may have served as the logical source for the namesake characterizations adopted by their modern, Masonic representations.

Empire	Region	Conclaves	Heralds
General Grand Conference of Knights Templar	Grand Commandery	Commandery	Knights
	*The Right Eminent Grand Commander of a Grand Commandery is the chief executive officer over local Commanderies of Knights Templar.*		
Supreme Council of a Holy Empire	Orient	Consistory (Valley)	Fraters
	*The Sovereign Grand Commander of the Supreme Council is the chief executive over Orients and their subordinate Valleys of Fraters.*		
Imperial Council	Desert	Temple (Oasis)	Nobles
	*The Imperial Potentate of the Imperial Council is the chief executive over Deserts and their subordinate Oases of Nobles.*		

Figure 71 Security for the Rites

As monuments are stationary landmarks, signets are portable landmarks. The wearer, in essence, becomes the land that is marked by the signet and the way bearers conduct themselves in times of peace and war creates the terms of engagement with the entity for which the signet represents. As such, honor and integrity in deeds and works are critical factors in the development of a positive reputation for individuals, organizations, and nations. As reputation typically proceeds engagements, a strong, positive reputation could be the factors that determine one's ability to successfully secure the landmarks that are held near and dear.

Afterword

The practice of heraldry is as ancient as the days. It is significantly older than the Crusades and the pyramids and has been intact for millennia. Often, the pursuit of glory and recognition is a common friend to heraldry. According to Ralph Waldo Emerson, the "whole of heraldry and of chivalry is in courtesy. A man of fine manners shall pronounce your name with all the ornament that title of nobility could ever add." Yet, along with the glory comes the expectation for heralds to meet or exceed the standards of predecessors. So, is the practice a blessing or a curse?

"He stands for fame of his forefather's feet, by heraldry, proved valiant or discreet!" - Edward Young

For some, the weight to uphold historical standards is a heavy load to carry. Consider that Alexander the Great was reared to either equal or surpass the accomplishments of his father, Philip II, King of Macedon. Alexander's training not only consisted of the most noted scholars of the age but also the most accomplished warriors to ensure that he would be ready to lead and succeed when the time called.[498]

Alexander certainly followed in the footsteps of his father. Yet, in his goings and comings he came to understand that the initial curse or the circumstances of nobility that he was forced to endure could become a blessing of his own during his tenure of leadership. He truly embraced the words of Hosea Ballou who said, "it is better to be the builder of our own name than to be indebted by descent for the proudest gifts known to the books of heraldry."[499]

Pharoah Amenhotep IV was the successor to Amenhotep III whose reign over Egypt was considered one of the prosperous dynasties in the history of the nation. The father was a noted polytheist whose diplomatic relations were extensive due to the wealth of Egypt in gold. His relationships with other nations including Assyria, Mittani,

---

[498] Art Institute of Chicago, Philip II, Alexander the Great, and the Macedonian Heritage, University Press of America, 1982, p.86
[499] Ballou, Maturin Murray, Treasury of Thought: Forming an Encyclopedia of Quotations from Ancient and Modern Authors, J.R. Osgood, Company, 1872, p.22

Babylon, and others were of a superior state. Letters found at Amarna to him found nations desperately seeking to wed into his family line and obtain assets of gold.[500] He, clearly, set an extreme standard for his seed.

Amenhotep IV succeeded his father near 1350BC but sought his own path. After years following the path of his forefather, he made a major theological shift which caused a rift through the nation. For the first time in the history of Egypt, he shifted the nation from polytheism to monotheism preferring the god Aten, the sun god, over all others. Further, he changed his name from Amenhotep to Akhenaten in reverence to his god a shifted the capital to Amarna, the city he built for the worship of Aten.[501] These moves were massive shifts from the expected path, but it was more important for him to build his own legacy for eternity's sake rather than for the laurels of man. His Tutankhaten, restored the polytheism of his grandfather and

---

[500] Eds. O'Connor, David B., Eric H. Cline, Amenhotep III: Perspectives on his Reign, University of Michigan Press, 2001, p.225
[501] Ibid, p.271

changed his name to Tutankhamun in reverence to the gods of old.[502]

> *"In the heraldry of heaven, goodness precedes*
> *greatness; so, on earth it is more powerful. The*
> *lowly and the lovely may frequently do more in*
> *their own limited sphere than the gifted."*
> - Thomas Hartwell Horne

Like Akhenaten, Alexander took a different path relative to faith. Instead of attempting to thrust a religious belief down the throats of conquered nations, he allowed them to proceed without impact. He even became absorbed with Mesopotamian theism himself which was in stark contrast to Grecian beliefs. Akhenaten's tale is even more remarkable as Tutankhamun and other successors sought to remove his legacy from the historical record. Yet, both examples survived leaving indelible legacies that lasted for a time but did not extend, as it relates to their continued practice, beyond the grave.

---

[502] Ibid, p.9

"The boast of heraldry, the pomp of power, and all that beauty, all that wealth ever gave, awaits alike the inevitable hour. The paths of glory lead but to the grave." - Thomas Gray

The grave is the great leveler. In the grave, all ranks are levelled, all titles are done away with, all accomplishments are history, and laurels can no longer be granted in person. All that remains in the land of the living is the historical record and reputation that was left behind. These lasting remnants can either set the stage upon which succeeding generations can build or a measuring stick against which they will be judged. Nonetheless, they build the reputation associated with the respective heraldic representations. So, heraldry can be an asset for the promotion of positivity and redemption, a stage for the construction of higher edifices of praise, or, as James Planche asserts, "the science of fools with long memories."[503]

---

[503] Seton, Robert, Shane Leslie, Memories of Many Years (1839-1922), Long, 1923, p.225

Appendix

1. Roman Legion Heraldic Inspirations I

2. Polytheistic Deities with Commonalities III

3. Leaders of Masonic Bodies and Counterparts IV

4. General Timeline of Ancient Empires VIII

Empire	Timeline	Page
Egyptian	7000BC – 30BC	VIII
Mesopotamian	6200BC – 1924AD	XIII
Chinese	5000BC – 1949AD	XXV
Indus Valley	3200BC – 1526AD	XXXIII
Grecian	3200BC – 393AD	XXXVI
Roman	1250BC – 536AD	XLII
Japanese	50BC – 1910AD	LVI

5. Timeline of the Origins of Major Faiths LXI

6. "De Insigniis et Armis" Translation IXIII

Roman Legion Heraldic Inspirations

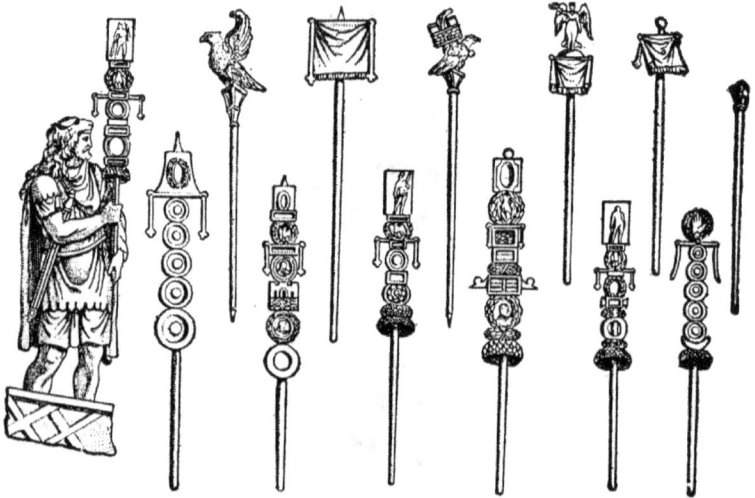

Legion	Unit(s)	Animal	Mythical	God
I	Adiutrix		Capricorn & Pegasus	
	Italica	Boar & Bull		
	Minervia	Ram		Minerva
II	Adiutrix	Boar	Pegasus	
	Augusta		Capricorn & Pegasus	Mars
	Italica	She-wolf	Capricorn	
	Trajana			Hercules
III	Gallica	Bull		
	Italica	Stork		
IIII	Flavia	Lion		
	Macedonica	Bull & Ram	Capricorn	
	Scythica	Ram	Capricorn	
V	Alaudae	Elephant		
	Macedonica	Eagle & Bull		

VI	Ferrata	She-wolf	Twins	
	Victrix	Bull		
VII	Claudia	Bull		
	Germina Pia Fidelis		Castor & Pollux	
VIII	Augusta	Bull		
VIIII	Triumphalis Macedonica Hispana			Neptune
X	Fretensis	Bull, Boar, & Dolphin		Neptune
	Gemina	Bull		
XI	Claudia	Dolphin & She-wolf	Capricorn & Twins	Neptune
XII	Fulminata		Lightning Bolt	
XII	Gemina	Lion & Eagle	Capricorn, Castor & Pollux	
XIIII	Gemina		Capricorn	
XV	Apollinaris			Apollo
XVI	Flavia	Lion	Pegasus	
	Gallica	Lion		
XX	Valeria Victrix	Boar	Capricorn	
XXI	Rapax		Capricorn	
XXII	Deiotariana	Wolf		
	Primigenia	Bull	Capricorn	Hercules
XXVIIII		Eagle with Lion in talons		
XXX	Ulpia	Dolphin	Capricorn	Jupiter & Neptune

Polytheistic Deities with Commonalities

Attributes	Greco	Roman	Egyptian	Babylonian
King of the gods - sky and thunder	Zeus	Jupiter	Amun	Marduk
Queen of the Gods - marriage, and womanhood	Hera	Juno	Isis / Hathor / Mut	Ishtar
God of the sea	Poseidon	Neptune	Hetmehit (goddess)	Tiamut (goddess)
Goddess of the harvest	Demeter	Ceres	Isis	Nabu (god)
Goddess of wisdom and war	Athena	Minerva	Neith/Isis	Nabu (god)
God of light, sun, archery, and arts	Apollo	Apollo	Horus	Shamash
Goddess of the hunt	Artemis	Diana	Bastet	Ninurta (god)
God of war	Ares	Mars	Anhur	Nergal
Goddess of love	Aphrodite	Venus	Hathor/Isis	Ishtar
God of the Underworld	Hades	Pluto	Osiris	Nergal
God & Goddess of fire and craftsmanship	Hephaestus & Hestia	Vulcan & Vesta	Ptah / Anuket	Enki
Messenger of the Gods	Hermes	Mercury	Anubis / Thoth	Nabu
God of festivity	Dionysus	Bacchus	Shezmu	Ishtar

Leaders of Masonic Bodies & Counterparts

Freemasons and Eastern Stars

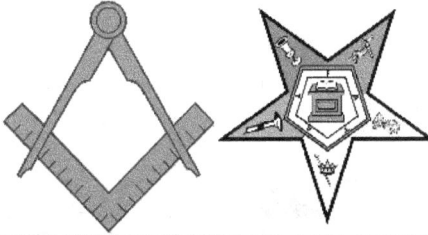

Organization	Leader
Grand Lodge	Grand Master
Subordinate Lodge	Worshipful Master
Grand Chapter	Grand Matron (female)
	Grand Patron (Male)
Subordinate Chapter	Worthy Matron
	Worthy Patron (Male)

Royal Arch Masons and Heroines of Jericho

Organization	Leader
Grand Chapter	Grand High Priest
Subordinate Chapter	High Priest
Grand Court	Most Ancient Grand Matron
	Most Worthy Grand Joshua (Male)
Subordinate Court	Ancient Matron
	Worthy Joshua (Male)

Royal & Select Masters and Ladies Circle of Perfection

Organization	Leader
Grand Council	Grand Thrice Illustrious Master
Subordinate Council	Thrice Illustrious Master
Grand Court	Royal Grand Perfect Matron
	Royal Grand Advisor (Male)
Subordinate Court	Royal Perfect Matron
	Royal Advisor (Male)

Knights Templar and Heroines of the Templar Crusades

Organization	Leader
Grand Commandery	Right Eminent Grand Commander
Subordinate Commandery	Eminent Commander
Grand Guild	Noble Grand Princess Captain
	Sir Knight Grand Advisor (Male)
Subordinate Guild	Princess Captain
	Sir Knight Advisor (Male)

Knights and Princesses of the York Cross of Honor

Organization	Leader
Grand Priory of Knights of the York Cross of Honor	Grand Master General
Subordinate Priory	Eminent Prior
Grand Priorate of Princesses of the York Cross of Honor	Regal Grand Prioress Sir Knight Grand Advisor (Male)
Subordinate Priorate	Eminent Prioress Sir Knight Advisor (Male)

Ancient and Accepted Scottish Rite

Organization	Leader
Supreme Council of the Scottish Rite	Sovereign Grand Commander
Subordinate Orient	Deputy or Most Illustrious Commander-In-Chief
Subordinate Consistory	Commander-In-Chief
Grand Assembly of the Order of the Golden Circle	Grand Loyal Lady Ruler Grand Advisor (Male)
Subordinate Assembly	Loyal Lady Ruler Advisor (Male)

The Mystic Shrine

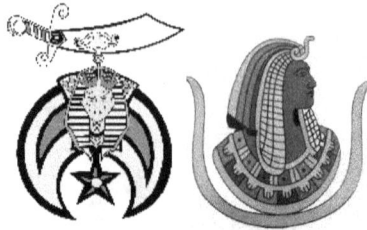

Organization	Leader
Imperial Council of the Shrine	Imperial Potentate
Subordinate Temple	Potentate
Imperial Court of Daughters	Imperial Commandress Imperial Advisor (Male)
Subordinate Court	Commandress Advisor (Male)

General Timeline of Ancient Empires

𝕰𝕘𝖞𝖕𝖙𝖎𝖆𝖓 𝕿𝖎𝖒𝖊𝖑𝖎𝖓𝖊

❖ Pre-Dynastic Period (7000BC – 3150BC)

- o 7000BC – Neolithic Period

  Nile Valley settlement

- o 4500BC – Badarian (Middle/Upper Egypt)

- o 3900BC – Naqadan Periods (Upper Egypt)

  - ▪ Naqada I (3900-3650BC)

  - ▪ Naqada II (3650-3300BC)

  - ▪ Naqada III (3300-3100BC)

❖ First Dynastic Period Begins (3100BC -2675BC)

- o 3100BC –Dynasty 1 (Thinis)

  - ▪ King Narmer (Menes) established government at Thinis

  - ▪ Upper and Lower Egypt unite

- o 2880BC –Dynasty 2 (Thinis)

  - ▪ King Hotepsekhemwy, first ruler, established Horus as patron god

❖ Old Kingdom Period (2686BC – 2150BC)

- o 2686BC – Dynasty 3 (Memphis)

- Pharaoh Djoser, first ruler, shifted capital to Memphis
- Constructed step pyramid and sent expedition to Sinai Peninsula
    - 2625BC – Dynasty 4 (Memphis)
    - 2500BC – Dynasty 5 (Memphis)
    - 2350BC – Dynasty 6 (Memphis)
        - 2180BC – Egypt splits between Memphis (Lower) and Thebes (Upper)
    - 2170BC – Dynasty 7 & 8 (Memphis)
        - 2160BC – Capital shifted to Heracleopolis Magna by Pharoah Meryibtawy
- ❖ First Intermediate Period (2130BC – 2030BC)
    - 2130BC - Dynasty 9 (Heracleopolis Magna) & 10 (Thebes)
        - 2130BC – Egypt reunites under Pharaoh Intef and shifts capital to Thebes
    - 2080BC – Dynasty 11 (Thebes)
- ❖ Middle Kingdom (1980BC – 1640BC)
    - 1938BC – Dynasty 12 (Itjtawy)

- Pharaoh Amenemhat shifts capital to Itjtawy
  - 1759BC – Dynasty 13 (Itjtawy) & 14 (Avaris)
    - 1725BC – Second seat of power established in Lower Egypt in Avaris
- ❖ Second Intermediate Period (1650BC – 1540BC)
  - 1650BC – Dynasty 15 (Avaris)
    - 1650BC – Hyksos invasion (Avaris)
    - 1650BC – Abydos dynasty established concurrently with Hyksos
  - 1649BC – Dynasty 16 (Thebes) - concurrent
  - 1580BC – Dynasty 17 (Thebes)
- ❖ New Kingdom (1550BC – 1070BC)
  - 1550BC – Dynasty 18 (Thebes)
    - 1540BC – Hyksos expelled
    - 1470BC – Ruled by first female pharaoh, Queen Hapshepsut
    - 1350BC – Akhenaten monotheism
      - 1346BC – Akhenaten moved capital to Amarna
    - 1334BC – Tutankhaten polytheism

- 1334BC – Tutankhaten changes name to Tutankhamun
- 1332BC – Capital shifted back to Thebes
- 1292BC – Dynasty 19 (Thebes)
  - Capital shifted from Thebes to Memphis to Pi-Ramesses
  - 1274BC – Battle of Kadesh (Hittites defeated)
  - 1220BC est. - Israelite Exodus
- 1190BC – Dynasty 20 (Pi-Ramesses)
- 1075BC – Dynasty 21 (Tanis)

❖ Third Intermediate Period (1070BC – 664BC)
- 943BC – Dynasty 22 (Tanis)
  - Capital shifted to Bubastus under Pharaoh Shoshenq, Libyan ruler
- 837BC - Dynasty 23 (Thebes) – Libyan rule
  - Dynasty 24 (Sais) - concurrent
- 744BC – Dynasty 25 (Memphis) – concurrent
  - Nubian Pharaoh King Piye rules
  - 721BC – Capital shifted to Napata
  - 671BC – Assyria conquers Egypt

- ❖ Late Period (664BC – 332BC)
  - o 664BC – Dynasty 26 (Sais)
    - ▪ 653BC – Egypt expels Assyria
  - o 525BC – Dynasty 27 (Babylon)
    - ▪ 525BC – Persian conquest of Egypt
    - ▪ 522BC – King Darius of Persia is the first Persian to be declared Pharaoh
  - o 404BC – Dynasty 28 (Sais)
    - ▪ Egypt defeats Persians and conquers Palestine
  - o 399BC – Dynasty 29 (Mendes)
  - o 380BC – Dynasty 30 (Sebennytos)
  - o 343BC - Dynasty 31 (Babylon)
    - ▪ Persia re-conquers Egypt
- ❖ Greco- Roman Period *(See Grecian and Roman Timelines for details)*
  - o 332BC – Macedon (Alexander) conquers Egypt
  - o 304BC – Ptolemy rules Egypt (Greek)
  - o 30BC – Roman conquest

Mesopotamian Timeline

- ❖ Early Mesopotamia (6200BC – 2900BC)
    - o Nineveh founded prior to 6000BC
    - o Ubaid period
        - ▪ 5500BC – City of Sumer founded
            - • First Ziggurats constructed
        - ▪ 5400BC - City of Eridu founded
        - ▪ 4500BC – City of Uruk founded
        - ▪ 3800BC – City of Ur founded
        - ▪ 3000BC - Ziggurat of Uruk completed
        - ▪ 2900BC – City of Mari founded
- ❖ Uruk, Kish and Lagash Dynasties (2900-2350BC)
    - o 2800BC – Gilgamesh rules Uruk
    - o 2700BC –Kish conquer Elamites
    - o 2700BC – City of Assur founded
    - o 2600BC – City of Adab founded (Lagash rule)
    - o 2500BC – Mari rebuilt and populated
    - o 2450BC –Lagash defeats Mari and Elam
    - o 2358BC – Uruk conquers Lower Mesopotamia
    - o 2350BC – Uruk Conquers Kish
    - o 2350BC – First code of laws (Lagash)

- ❖ Akkadian and Gutian Periods (2334BC – 2050BC)
  - o 2334BC - Sargon I of Akkad begins the Akkadian rule in Mesopotamia
    - ▪ 2300BC – Adab conquered
    - ▪ 2300BC – Assur conquered
  - o Akkadian Rulers (2278-2154BC)
    - ▪ 2278-2270BC – Rimush
    - ▪ 2269-2255BC - Manishtushu
    - ▪ 2254-2218BC – Naram-Sin
      - • 2240BC – Elam declares independence
    - ▪ 2217-2193BC – Shar-Kali-Sharri
    - ▪ 2192-2169BC – Dudu
    - ▪ 2168-2154BC – Shu-turul
  - o 2154BC - Gutians of Adab conquer Akkadia
  - o 2153BC –Akkadian Empire under Shar-Kali-Sharri declines (2153-2129BC)
  - o 2141BC – Capital shifted to Adab
  - o 2055BC – Gutians conquered by Uruk
- ❖ Third Sumerian dynasty of Ur (2125BC - 1750BC)
  - o 2100BC – Assur conquered
  - o 2050BC – Code of Ur-Nammu introduced

- o 2047BC – King Ur-Nammu defeats barbarians
- o 2025BC – Assyria founded as an independent city-state with capital at Assur
- o 2004BC – Elamites sack Ur
- o 2002BC – Elamites conquer Sumer
- o 1940BC – Elamites conquer Ur
- o 1930BC – Laws of Eshunna introduced
- o 1870BC – Codex of Lipit-Ishtar introduced
- o 1808BC – Assyria conquered by Amorites
- o 1760BC – Hammurabi drives Elamites out of Southern Mesopotamia establishing Babylonian control
    - 1754BC – Code of Hammurabi
    - 1750BC – Elamite invasion of Sumeria
- ❖ Babylonian, Assyrian and Kassite Periods (1750BC – 1170BC)
    - o 1750BC – Death of Hammurabi
    - o 1700BC – Assyria re-established as an independent state
    - o 1680BC – Hurrians occupy Assyria
    - o 1595BC – Hittites conquer Babylon
    - o 1531BC – Kassites sack Babylon

- o 1500BC – Kassite peace treaty with Assyria
- o 1480BC – Kassites conquer Babylon
- o 1472BC – Mittani annexes Assyria
- o 1400BC – Kassite Sutean campaign
- o 1400BC – Assyria regains independence
- o 1375BC – Dur-Kurigalzu founded
- o 1360BC – Assyria defeats Mittani to restoring independence
- o 1330BC – Kassite Battle of Sugagi against Assyria
- o 1254BC – Nippur revolts (1254-1246BC)

❖ Assyrian, Israelite and Babylonian Periods (1250BC

- o 1250BC – Assyria conquers Mittani
- o 1230BC – Israelites conquer Canaanite lands of Palestine after exodus from Egypt
- o 1208BC – Assyria conquers Hittites
- o 1200BC – Othniel becomes first Judge of Israel
- o 1157BC – Babylon conquered by Elamites
- o 1155BC – Kassites deposed from Babylon
- o 1115BC – Assyrian conquest of Phoenicia (1115-1076BC)

- 1072BC – Peace treaty between Babylon and Assyria by Kings Marduk-shapik-zeru and Ashur-bel-kala
- 1050BC – Assyrian civil war and Babylonian independence
- 1050BC – Philistines conquer Israelite Shiloh capturing the Ark of the Covenant
- 1020BC – Israel anoints King Saul
- 1000BC – Israel is ruled by King David
- 1000BC – Jerusalem becomes Israelite capital
- 960BC – King Solomon of Israel builds first Temple
- 931BC – King of Israel is divided between Israel and Judah
  - Kingdom of Judah (Rehoboam)
    - Tribes of Judah and Benjamin
  - Kingdom of Israel (Jeroboam)
    - Asher, Dan, Ephraim, Gad, Issachar, Manasseh, Naphtali, Reuben, Simeon, and Zebulon
- Reign of Sargon II (722BC – 705BC)

- 722BC – Assyria conquers Kingdom of Israel defeating 10 Tribes of Israel (Lost Tribes) (722-720BC)
- 706BC – Dur-Sharrukin becomes Assyrian capital
- Reign of Sennacherib (705BC – 681BC)
  - Capital shifts to Nineveh
  - 701BC – Levantime War
  - 700BC – Assyria controls Southern Mesopotamia
  - 698BC – Expedition against Kirua to quell Cilician revolt
  - 695BC – Campaign against Tegarama
  - 694BC – Invasion of Elam
  - 689BC – Destruction of Babylon
- Reign of Esarhaddon (681BC – 669BC)
  - 681BC – Quelled Assyrian civil war over leadership
  - 671BC – Assyria conquers Egypt
- Fall of Assyria (668BC – 612BC)
  - 654BC – Egypt expels Assyrians
  - 650BC – Zoroastrianism introduced

- 631BC – Death of Ashurbanipal
- 626BC – Split of Assyria
  - Assur-etil-Ilani ruled South
  - Sin-sumu-Lisir ruled North until defeated by Asur-etil-Ilani
- 612BC – Death of Sin-sumu-Lisir

❖ Babylonian Rule (612BC – 549BC)
  - 612BC - Fall of Assyrian Nineveh to Babylon under King Nabopolassar
  - 604BC – Conquest of Philistia
  - 586BC – Conquest of the Kingdom of Judah

❖ Persian Conquest (549BC – 480BC)
  - 549BC – Persian conquest of Assyria (549-539BC)
  - 546 BC - Conquest of Lydia and the Greek cities of Asia Minor by Cyrus
  - 525BC – Conquest of Egypt
  - 499BC - Rebellion of Greek cities against Persian rule (499-494BC)
  - 490BC - Darius I invades Greece (490–489BC)
  - 479BC - Defeat of Persian armies under Xerxes by the Greeks

- ❖ Macedonian and Seleucid Rule (338BC – 129BC)
  - o 332BC - Alexander the Great conquers Persia
  - o 330BC – General Seleucus appointed to rule Persian lands
  - o 329BC – Alexander conquers Bactria
  - o 326BC – Alexander conquers through India
  - o 323BC – Death of Alexander the Great
  - o 250BC – Manichaeism introduced
  - o 129BC – Eastern Seleucid Empire becomes Parthian Empire
- ❖ Roman and Sassanid Rule (115AD-632AD)
  - o 115AD – Rome conquers Mesopotamia
  - o 224AD – Sassanian Empire defeats Persia
  - o 256AD – Sassanian Empire conquers Antioch
  - o 260AD – Battle of Edessa
    - ▪ King Shapur captures Emperor Valerian
  - o 296AD – Sassanian defeat of Rome against Galerius at Callincium
  - o 298AD – Roman victory at Nisibis
  - o 325AD – Shapur II secures areas now known as Afghanistan and Pakistan
  - o 370AD – Loss of Bactria to Huns

- o 421AD – Sassanid War with Rome (421-422AD)
- o 427AD – Hephthalite invasion crushed
- o 440AD – Second Sassanid War with Rome forced Rome to retreat to combat Roman invasion of the Vandals
- o 451AD – Battle of Avaryar against Christians
- o 451AD - Battle of Vartanartz against Christians
- o 483AD – Huns defeated Sassanids
- o 502AD – Sassanids conquer Theodosiopolis in Armenia
- o 522AD – Roman conflicts (522-531AD)
- o 541AD – Lazic War between Sassanids and Rome (541-562AD)
- o 577AD – Armenian Revolt quelled by Sassanids
- o 591AD – Battle of Blarathon
- o 598AD – Southern Arabia annexed
- o 600AD – Byzantine control of the Balkans restored via partnership with Persia
- o 610AD – Muhammad receives revelations at Mt. Hira starting the Muslim faith
- o 611AD – Persian conquers Syria

- o 614AD – Persian invasion of Palestine (Israel and Judah)
- ❖ Muslim – Quraysh War (624-630AD)
  - o 624AD - Battle of Badr (Muslim victory)
  - o 625AD - Battle of Uhud (Quraysh victory)
  - o 627AD - Battle of the Trench (Quraysh victory)
  - o 628AD - Treaty of Hudaybiyyah
  - o 629AD - Battle of Mutah (Muslim victory)
  - o 630AD – Meccan Conquest (Muslim victory)
  - o 632AD - Death of Muhammad
- ❖ Rashidun Caliphate (632-661AD)
  - o 632AD – Caliph Abu Bakr (632-634)
    - ▪ 633AD – Muslim Mesopotamia invasion
    - ▪ 634AD – Compiled Holy Qu'ran
    - ▪ 634AD – Battle of the Bridge (Sassanian victory)
  - o 634AD - Caliph Umar ibn Al-Khattab (634-644)
    - ▪ 636AD – Battle of Qadisiyyah
    - ▪ 637AD – Battle of Jalula
    - ▪ 638AD – Battle of Khaniqeen
    - ▪ 642AD – Muslim conquest of Egypt
    - ▪ 644AD – Umar assassinated

- o 644AD - Caliph Uthman ibn Affan (644-656)
  - 650AD – Muslim conquest of Assyria
  - 651AD – Sassanian Empire defeated and expelled from Mesopotamia
  - 656AD – Death of Uthman
  - 656AD – Battle of the Camel to determine Caliph
- o 656AD - Caliph Ali ibn Abi Talib (656-661)
  - 657AD – Battle of Siffin to quell usurpation by Syrian Council
  - 661AD – Ali assassinated

❖ Umayyad Caliphate (661–750)
  - o 661AD - Sufyanid Rule (661-684AD)
  - o 661AD - Capital shifted to Damascus
  - o 684AD – Marwanid Rule (684-750AD)
  - o 691AD – Dome of the Rock built at Jerusalem
  - o 750AD – Battle of the Great Zab River

❖ Abbasid Caliphate (750–1517)
  - o 750AD – Caliph Al-Saffah became first Caliph
  - o 755AD – Remaining Umayyads settled in Spain (Umayyads of Cordoba)
  - o 786AD – Rebellion of Idrisids

- o 788AD – Idrisid Dynasty founded in Morocco by Idris I (rebellion from Abbasids)
- o 789AD – City of Fez founded by Idris
- o 808AD –Idrisid capital shifts to Fez
- o 869AD – Turks control Idrisid Dynasty
- o 909AD – Fatimid Dynasty founded (rebellion from Abbasids) and Mahdia selected as capital
- o 969AD – Fatamids conquer Egypt
- o 974AD – Idrisids fall to Umayyads of Cordoba
- o 983AD – Fatamid capital shifted to Cairo
- o 1031AD – Umayyads of Cordoba fall to Berbers
- o 1171AD – Fatamids fall to Abbasids
- o 1206AD – Genghis Khan founds Mongol Empire
- o 1250AD – Mamluks (mercenaries) seize Abbasids Sultanate
- o 1258AD – Mongol conquest of Baghdad
- o 1261AD – Abbasid capital shifted back to Cairo
- o 1517AD – Sword and mantle of Muhammad surrendered to Ottomans
- ❖ Ottoman Caliphate (1517–1924)
  - o Caliphate abolished March 3, 1924

Chinese Timeline

- ❖ 5000BC - Yangshao culture in China (5000-3000BC)
- ❖ 3500BC - Longshan culture in China (3500-2200BC)
  - o 3000BC - Silk manufacturing
  - o 2215BC – Yellow River Floods
- ❖ 2200BC - Xia Dynasty (2200-1766BC)
  - o 1766BC – Tang overthrows Xia ruler
- ❖ 1766BC - Shang Dynasty (1766-1046BC)
  - o 1766BC - Capital at Bo
  - o 1700BC – Bronze weapons and tools
  - o 1300BC – Capital shifted to Yin
  - o 1046BC – Slave revolt
  - o 1046BC - Shang overthrown by Zhou
- ❖ 1046BC – Zhou Dynasty (1046-250BC)
  - o 1046BC - Capital in the West at Haojing
  - o 1046BC – The Mandate of Heaven
  - o 771BC – Quanrong attack on capital
  - o 770BC – Capital shifted to Luoyang in the East
  - o 650BC – Chinese coin minting system
  - o 594BC – Lu state adopts land taxation system
  - o 551BC – Confucius born

- o 550BC – The Laozi
- o 550BC – Emergence of four major states
  - Qin (west), Jin (central), Chu (south), Qi (east)
- o 510BC – Sun Tzu authors "The Art of War"
- o 500BC - Crop cultivation in rows in China
- o 500BC - Iron plow in China
- o 403BC – Jin partitioned into Han, Zhao, Wei
- o 400BC - Trace harness in China
- o 400BC - Zhuangzi (Chuang-tzu)
- o 338BC – Reformist Shang Yang executed
- o 338BC – Qin reforms based on Shang's ideals
- o 334BC –Qin declares independence
- o 334BC – Wei declares independence
- o 316BC – Qin conquers Shu and Ba
- o 300BC - Wrought iron in China
- o 300BC - Xunzi (300-237BC)
- ❖ 250BC - Legalist Regime (250-208BC)
  - o 247BC – Ying Zheng (Qin) assumes throne
  - o 229BC – Qin Shi Huang seizes Zhou territory
  - o 221BC - Standardization of weights and measures, coinage, writing system (221-206BC)
  - o 221BC – Qin conquers all five Zhou states

- ❖ 221BC - Qin Dynasty (221-206BC)
  - o 210BC – Mass revolt destroys Imperial library
- ❖ 206BC - Han Dynasty in China (206BC-220AD)
  - o 206BC – Han capital at Chang'an
  - o 202BC – Liu Bang seizes emperorship
  - o 200BC - Use of the seed drill in China
  - o 179BC - Dong Zhongsho (179-104BC)
  - o 145BC - Sima Qian (145-86BC)
  - o 141BC - Emperor Han Wudi (141-87BC)
  - o 140BC - First Chinese ambassadors to India
  - o 138BC – Silk Road (138-114BC)
  - o 111BC - Expansion to South China Sea
  - o 111BC - Expansion to Vietnam
  - o 9AD – Wang Mang usurps Han Dynasty throne
  - o 23AD – Red Eyebrow Revolt
  - o 100AD - Invention of the Rudder in China
  - o 100AD – First Chinese dictionary by Xu Shen
  - o 105AD – Invention of paper by Cai Lun
  - o 130AD – Trade opened with the West
  - o 184AD – Yellow Turban Rebellion in China
  - o 200AD - Porcelain in China
  - o 220AD - Buddhism reaches China

- ❖ 220AD - Three Kingdoms Era (220-280AD)
  - o 220AD – Han divided into three kingdoms - Wei, Shu, Wu
  - o 222AD – Battle of Xiaoting (Wu defeats Shu)
  - o 222AD – Wei invasion of Wu (222-225AD)
    - ▪ 222AD – Battle of Dongkou (Wu)
    - ▪ 223AD – Battle of Jiangling (Wu)
    - ▪ 223AD – Battle of Ruxu (Wu)
    - ▪ 225AD – Incident at Guangling (Wei)
  - o 225AD – Shu rebellion quelled
  - o 228AD – Wei rebellion quelled at Xincheng
  - o 231AD – Battles at Hefei (231-233AD) (Wei)
  - o 234AD – Battle of Wuzhang Plains
  - o 244AD – Battle of Xingshi (Shu defeats Wei)
  - o 253AD – Battle at Hefei (Wei defeats We)
  - o 263AD – Shu falls to Wei
  - o 265AD – Jin Empire established
  - o 266AD –Wei falls to Jin
  - o 280AD – Wu falls to Jin
- ❖ 300AD - Barbarian invasions of China (300-500AD)
  - o 405AD - Adoption of Chinese writing in Japan
  - o 500AD - Glass and magnetic compass created

- ❖ 581AD - Sui dynasty in China (581-618AD)
    - o 581AD – Great Wall of China construction
    - o 583AD – Capital shifts to Chang'an
    - o 589AD – China unified under Sui rule
    - o 595AD – Zhaozhou Bridge construction begins
    - o 603AD – Turkish invasion subdued
    - o 604AD – Secondary capital at Luoyang
    - o 608AD – Tuguhun invasion subdued
    - o 612AD – Korean expedition fails
    - o 618AD –Emperor Yangdi murdered
- ❖ 618AD - Tang Dynasty in China (618-907AD)
    - o 618AD – Li Yuan establishes Tang Dynasty
    - o 626AD – Mutiny of Xuanwu
    - o 638AD –Christianity and Buddhism sponsored
    - o 650AD – Islam introduced in China
    - o 657AD – Tang conquers Turkish frontier
    - o 710AD – Liu Zhiji authors "Shitong"
    - o 755AD – An Lushan Rebellion
    - o 843AD – Buddhism persecution (843-845AD)
    - o 858AD – Great Flood - Grand Canal
    - o 875AD – Huang Chao Revolt (875-883AD)
    - o 900AD - Woodblock printing of books

- o 907AD – Forced abdication of throne
- ❖ 907AD - The Era of the Five Dynasties (907-960AD)
  - o 907AD – Hou Liang Dynasty established
  - o 923AD – Hou Tang Dynasty established
  - o 936AD - Hou Jin Dynasty established
  - o 947AD - Hou Han Dynasty established
  - o 951AD - Hou Zhao Dynasty established
- ❖ 960AD - Song dynasty in China (960-1279AD)
  - o 1127AD – Song split into North and South
  - o 1150AD - Explosive powder used in weapons
  - o 1200AD – Smallpox inoculation
  - o 1205AD - Genghis Khan raids (1205-1207AD)
- ❖ 1279AD - Mongol dynasty in China (1279-1368AD)
  - o 1300AD - Marco Polo travels in China
- ❖ 1368AD - Ming dynasty in China (1368-1644AD)
- ❖ 1644AD - Manchu Dynasty (1644-1911AD)
  - o 1839AD – First Opium War with Britain (1839-1842AD)
    - ▪ 1839AD – China confiscates and destroys British opium
    - ▪ 1839AD – British sailors kill Chinese Villagers

- ▪ 1841AD – British occupy Canton
- ▪ 1842AD – British repel Chinese attack
- ▪ 1842AD – Treaty of Nanjing
- ○ 1843AD – Treaty of the Bogue granted Britain extra-territorial rights
- ○ 1850AD – Taiping Rebellion
- ○ 1856AD – Second Opium War with France (1856-1860AD)
  - ▪ 1856AD – Trading with Britain ceased after further expeditions in China
    - ● France joined Britain after death of a French missionary in China
  - ▪ 1857AD – Franco-British allies capture Canton
  - ▪ 1858AD – Franco-British assault of Tianjin
    - ● Forced Treaty of Tianjin allowing Christin missionaries freedom to roam China
  - ▪ 1859AD – Chinese naval blockade at Dagu after Chinese refusal to ratify Tianjin Treaty

- 1860AD – Blockade and batteries at Dagu destroyed
- 1860AD – Chinese Convention ratified Treaty
- ❖ 1911AD – Xinhai Revolution against Manchu (Qing)
- ❖ 1912AD - Republic of China Period (1912-1949AD)
  - o 1912AD – Sun Yat-Sen elected President by Nanjing Assembly
  - o 1913AD – Yuan Shikai elected President after successfully exiling Qing royalty
  - o 1915AD – Yuan self-declared as Emperor
  - o 1916AD – Yuan abdicates and dies of natural causes causing provinces under warlord rule to declare independence
  - o 1919AD – May Fourth Movement at Tianamen in protest to the Treaty of Versailles which concluded World War I
  - o 1926AD – Northern Expedition to route out warlords and communists and reunify China
  - o 1927AD – Chinese Civil War (1927-1949AD)
- ❖ 1949AD – Communist Revolution

Indus Valley Timeline

❖ 3300BC - Indus Valley civilization (3300-1600BC)
  o Early Harrapan Period (3300-2600BC)
  o Mature Harrapan Period (2600-1900BC)
  o Late Harrapan Period (1900-1500BC)
❖ 1500BC - Vedic Society (India) (1500-500BC)
  o 1500BC – Aryan migration to Indus Valley
  o 1500BC - Rigveda (1500-1100BC)
  o 1200BC - Samaveda (1200-800BC)
  o 1100BC - Yajurdeda (1100-800BC)
  o 1000BC - Atharveda (1000-800BC)
  o 800BC - Upanishads in India (800-600BC)
  o 563BC - Life of Gautama, the Buddha (563-483BC)
  o 540BC - Life of Mahavira, founder of Jainism in India (540-468BC)
  o 513BC - Persian conquest of northwestern India and Indus Valley
  o 400BC – First Buddhist Council
  o 400BC - Mahabharata and Ramayana reach final form in India (400-200BC)

- o 373BC – Mencius (373-288BC)
- o 334BC - Conquests of Alexander the Great (334-323BC)
- o Mauryan Empire founded
- o 323BC - Death of Alexander, division of his empire
- o 322BC - Maurya dynasty in India (322-183BC)
- o 273BC - Reign of Emperor Ashoka in India (273-232BC)
- o 261BC - Ashoka conquers Kalinga, leading to spread of Buddhism in India
- o
- o 183BC - Greek Invasion of India (183-145BC)
- o 0BC - Shaka and Kushan invasions in northern India (0-100BC)
- o 25AD - Kushan rule in northwestern India (25-300AD)
- o 78AD - Kushan Emperor Kanishka promotes Buddhism in India
- ❖ 300AD - Classical age of Hindu culture in India (300-800AD)
  - o 320AD - Gupta dynasty in India (320-467AD)

- 380AD - Kalidasa, India's greatest poet (380-450AD)
- ❖ 550AD - Great stone temple architecture in India (550-1250AD)
  - 600AD - Sanskrit drama in India (600-1000AD)
  - 606AD - King Harsha in India (606-648AD)
  - 751AD - Battle at Talas River ends Islamic penetration of Central Asia
  - 1000AD - Muslim invasions of India (1000-1500AD)
    - 1192AD - Destruction of Buddhism in India
- ❖ 1206-1526 Turkish Sultanate at Delhi
  - 1290AD - Sultanate of Delhi (1290-1320AD)
  - 1370AD - Persian poetry of Hafiz
  - 1398AD - Sack of Delhi by Timur the Lame (Tamerlane)
  - 1498AD - Portugal gains control of East Indian spice trade (1498-1511AD)
    - 1500AD - Founding of Sikh religious sect

Grecian Timeline

- ❖ The Bronze Age (3200BC – 1200BC)
  - o 3200BC – Cycladic settlement in Central Greece
  - o 3000BC – Monian settlement in Central Greece
  - o 1627BC – Eruption of Thera volcano
- ❖ The Iron Age (1200BC – 550BC)
  - o 1200BC - Trojan War (1200-1184BC)
  - o 776BC - The first Olympics takes place at Olympia.
  - o 750BC - Homer writes the Iliad and the Odyssey.
  - o 750BC – Greek colonization of Sicily and Southern Italy
  - o 734BC – Naxos founded
  - o 733BC – Syracuse founded
  - o 730BC – First Messenian War (730 – 710BC)
  - o 650BC - The Period of Greek Tyrants
  - o 640BC – Second Messenian War (640 – 630BC)
  - o 550BC – Peloponnesian Legue formed under the leadership of Sparta

- ❖ 508BC - Athens develops the first democracy
- ❖ Greco-Persian Wars (500BC - 449BC) between Persian King Darius/Xerxes and the Peloponnesian League
  - o 499BC-493BC – Ionian Revolt (Persian victory)
  - o 490BC - Battle of Marathon (Greek victory)
  - o 486BC – Death of Persian King Darius due to failing health and ascension of his son, King Xerxes
  - o 480BC – Battle of Thermopylae (Persian victory)
  - o 480BC – Battle of Salamis (Greek victory)
  - o 479BC – Battle of Platea (Greek victory)
  - o 477BC – Delian League formed between Greek Allies under the leadership of Athens
- ❖ Peloponnesian and Corinthian Wars (460BC – 380BC)
  - o 460BC – Battle of Oenoe (Delian League victory over the Peloponnesian League)
  - o 451BC – Treaty between Athens and Sparta
  - o 450BC – Pericles ascended to ruler of Athens ushering in the Golden Age
    - ▪ 447-432BC - Parthenon is constructed
  - o 449BC – Treaty between Athens and Persia

- o 446BC – 30 Year peace treaty between Athens and Sparta
- o 432BC – Revolt of Potidea (Athenian siege and victory of a city under its domain) triggered Peloponnesian War
- o 431BC – Thebes, a Spartan ally, attacked Platea, an Athenian ally
- o 429BC – Pericles dies of plague.
- o 428BC – Revolt of Mitylene (Athenian victory)
- o 427-413BC – Athenian expedition to Sicily (near Sparta)
- o 421BC – Nicias Peace Treaty in Sicily between Athens and Sparta
- o 416BC – Athens conquers Melos
- o 415-413BC – Spartans expel Athenians from Sicily
- o 405BC – Battle of Aegospotami destroys Athenian fleet (Spartan victory)
- o 404BC – Athens surrenders and Pro-Spartan Oligarchy implemented (Thirty Tyrants)

- o 403BC – Thirty Tyrants overthrown by Spartan King Pausanias who restored democracy and control to Athens
- o 399BC – Socrates tried and executed
- o 395BC - Battle of Haliartus sparks Corinthian War between Sparta and Athenian allies (including Persia)
- o 386BC – Peace treaty between Sparta and Persia, who switched sides, sealed the fate of Athens (Spartan victory) and released Spartan and Athenian claims from lands in Asia
- ❖ Second Athenian League (380BC – 338BC)
  - o 380BC – Plato establishes Athens Academy
  - o 379BC – Boetian War (379-371BC)
    - ▪ 378BC – Second Athenian League formed (Athens, Thebes, et. al) for security against Sparta and Persia
    - ▪ 371BC – Sparta defeated by Thebes
    - ▪ 371BC - Thebes leaves League
  - o 362BC – Thebes defeats Sparta at Mantinea
  - o 359BC – Philip II becomes King of Macedon
  - o 357BC – The Social War (357-355BC)

- 357BC – Athens defeated at Chios
- 356BC – Battle of Embata (Athens victory)
- 355BC – Disintegration of the Second Athenian League into independent states at the threat of war from Persia

❖ Macedonian Rule (338BC – 323BC)

- o 338BC - Athens and Thebes are defeated by Phillip II of Macedonia.
- o 336BC - Alexander the Great becomes king
- o 332BC - Alexander conquers Egypt and Asia recovering lands ceded to Persia during Corinthian War including Palestine
- o 329BC – Alexander conquers Bactria (Afghanistan)
- o 326BC – Alexander conquers through India
- o 323BC - Alexander the Great dies

❖ Hellenistic Period (323BC – 30BC)

- o 322BC – Lamian War (Macedon conquers Athens)
- o 307BC – Athenian democracy restored by Macedonian King Demetrius Poliorcetes

- o 305BC – General Ptolemy rules Egypt
- o 284BC – Achean League founded (reformation of Pelopponesian League)
- ❖ Gallic Period (279BC - 238BC)
  - o 279BC – Gallic invasion of Greece
  - o 267BC – Chremonidean War secured control of all Greek city-states for Macedon (267-261BC)
  - o 238BC – Gauls expelled from Greece
  - o 222BC – Sparta crushed at Battle of Sellasia
- ❖ Roman Period (214BC-30BC)
  - o 214BC - Macedonian Wars
    - ▪ 214BC – First Macedonian War
    - ▪ 200BC – Second Macedonian War
    - ▪ 172BC – Third Macedonian War
      - • 167BC – Macedon divided into four provinces
    - ▪ 150BC – Fourth Macedonian War
      - • 146BC - Roman conquest
  - o 86BC - Athens is burned by Roman soldiers
  - o 30BC - All of Greece becomes part of the Roman Empire after Marc Antony is defeated at the Battle of Actium (31-30BC)

Roman Timeline

- ❖ Latin Origin Legend (1200BC – 750BC)
    - o 1200BC – Alba Longa founded
    - o 1184BC - Aeneas survives Trojan War; escapes to Crete, Sicily, Carthage; and settles in Latium
    - o 1181BC – Aeneas marries Lavinia, daughter of King Latinus, and later founds Lavinium, and becomes King of Latium after death of Latinus
    - o 1176BC – Aeneas dies in Italian Wars and is succeeded by his son King Ascanius
    - o 1151BC - Alba Longa becomes Latium capital
    - o Successors of King Ascanius:
        - ▪ 1139BC –Silvius (Ascanius' brother)
        - ▪ 1110BC – Aeneas Silvius
        - ▪ 1079BC – Latinius Silvius
        - ▪ 1028BC – Alba Silvius
        - ▪ 989BC – Atys Silvius
        - ▪ 963BC – Capys Silvius
        - ▪ 935BC – Capetus Silvius
        - ▪ 921BC – Tiberinus Silvius
        - ▪ 914BC – Agrippa Silvius

- 873BC – Romulus Silvius
- 854BC – Aventinus Silvius
- 817BC – Procas
- 794BC – Numitor
- 794BC – Amulius overthrew Numitor
- 752BC – Numitor restored by Romulus and Remus
- 750BC – Romulus founds Rome outside of Alba Longa after killing Remus

❖ The Kingdom of Rome (750BC – 509BC)
  o King Romulus (750-716BC)
  o King Numa Pompilius (716-672BC)
  o King Tullis Hostilis (672-640BC)
  o King Ancus Marcius (640-616BC)
  o King Lucius Tarquinius Priscus (616-578BC)
    - 600BC – Rome conquered Alba Longa
  o King Servius Tullius (578-534BC)
  o King Lucius Tarquinius Superbus (534-509BC)

❖ The Republic of Rome (SPQR - Senate Populus Que Romanus) (509BC – 31BC)
  o 509BC – Rome defeats Etruria after Monarchy
  o 508BC – Rome defeats Clusium

- o 504BC – Rome defeats Sabines
- o 498BC – Rome defeats Latins
- o 483BC – Fabian War (483-476BC)
- o 437BC – Veientine War (defeats Etruscans)
- o 400BC – Mithraism introduced
- o 396BC – Rome captures Etruscan Veii
- o 390BC – Battle of Alia
  - ▪ Gauls sack Rome
- o 343BC – Samnite Wars (343-290BC)
  - ▪ First War (343-341BC)
  - ▪ Second War (326-304BC)
  - ▪ Third War (298-290BC)
- o 280BC – Pyrrhic War (defeats Greek Epirus)
  - ▪ Battle of Heraclea (280BC)
  - ▪ Battle of the Strait of Messina (276BC)
  - ▪ Battle of Beneventum (275BC)
- o 264BC – First Punic War with Carthage
  - ▪ 264BC – Conflict in Sicily
  - ▪ 262BC – Rome attacks Agrigentum
  - ▪ 260BC – Battle of Mylae
  - ▪ 259BC – Naval battle at Corsica
  - ▪ 258BC – Naval battle at Sulcis

- 257BC – Naval battle at Tyndaris
- 255BC – Defeat at Tunis
- 254BC – War at Sicily (254-250BC)
- 249BC – Defeat at Drepana
- 242BC – Naval battle at Lilbaeum
- 241BC – Carthage surrenders
- 227BC – Annexation of Sardinia and Corsica
- 226BC – Ebro Treaty with Carthage
- 219BC – Second Punic War with Carthage
  - 219BC - Hannibal attacks Sagunthm violating Ebro Treaty
  - 218BC – Hannibal crosses Alps and defeats Roman army at River Trebia
  - 217BC – Defeat at Lake Trasimene
  - 216BC – Defeat at the Battle of Cannae
  - 215BC – Macedon allies with Carthage
  - 214BC – Macedon conquered
  - 211BC – Scipio brother killed in Spain
  - 209BC – Battle at Cartago Nova
  - 208BC – Battle at Baecula
  - 206BC – Scipio Africanus conquers Spain and continues into North Africa

- 202BC – Battle of Zama
- 201BC – Carthage surrenders
○ 214BC – First Macedonian War (concurrent with Second Punic War)
  - 214BC - Macedon navy defeated at Illyria
  - 212BC – Rome defeated at Illyria
  - 211BC – Aetolian alliance with Rome
  - 205BC – Peace of Phoenice
○ 200BC – Second Macedonian War
  - 200BC – Macedonian siege of Abydos
  - 199BC – Roman invasion of Macedonia
  - 198BC – Roman invasion of Thessaly
  - 197BC – Battle of Cynoscephalae
○ 192BC – Roman Seleucid War
  - 191BC – Battle of Thermopylae
  - 190BC – Battle of Magnesia
  - 188BC – Peace of Apamea
○ 172BC – Third Macedonian War
  - 171BC – Battle of Callinicus
  - 168BC – War in Illyria
  - 168BC – Macedon partitioned

- o 150BC – Fourth Macedonian War
  - ▪ 149BC – Andriscus raises army and invades Macedon
  - ▪ 148BC – Battle at Pydna
- o 150BC – Third Punic War (concurrent with Fourth Macedonian War)
  - ▪ 150BC – Carthage attacks Numidia
  - ▪ 149BC – Roman siege of Carthage
  - ▪ 146BC – Carthage destroyed
- o 146BC – Achean War
  - ▪ Battle of Scarpheia
  - ▪ Sack of Corinth
- o 91BC – Marsic War (The Social War)
  - ▪ 91BC – Etruria and Umbria rebellion
  - ▪ 89BC – Marsi supports rebellion
  - ▪ 88BC – Revolt quelled by Pompey Sarbo
- o 86BC - Athens (Greece) sacked and burned
- o 80BC – Volterra (Etruia) conquered
- o 69BC – Armenian Campaign (69-66BC)
  - ▪ 69BC – Tigranocentra conquered
  - ▪ 66BC – Armenia becomes a protectorate

- o 63BC – Syria conquered
- o 58BC – Conquest of Gaul (58-51BC)
  - ▪ 58BC – Julius Caesar attacks Helvetti
  - ▪ 56BC – Gallic naval battle on Atlantic
  - ▪ 55BC – Britan Expansion (55-54BC)
  - ▪ 53BC – Battle of Carrhae
  - ▪ 52BC – Defeat by Vercingetorix
  - ▪ 51BC – Vercingetorix surrenders
- o 49BC – Massilia (Gaul) sieged
- o 36BC – Battle of Naulochos
- ❖ The Empire of Rome (31BC - 324AD)
  - o 31BC - Battle of Actium
    - ▪ Marc Antony is defeated (31-30BC)
    - ▪ Death of Cleopatra (30BC)
  - o 31BC – Octavian crowned Emperor of Rome
  - o 27BC – Cantabrian War (27-19BC)
    - ▪ Conquest of Iberian Peninsula
  - o 9AD – Battle of Teutoburg
    - ▪ Rhine River established as boundary
  - o 15AD – Germanicus quells Rhine mutinies
  - o 43AD – Roman conquest of Brittain (43-77AD)
    - ▪ 43AD - Maiden Castle captured

- ▪ 77AD –Northern Tribes conquered
- o 54AD – Armenian Campaign (54-60AD)
- o 58AD – Roman-Parthian War (58-63AD)
- o 60AD – Boudicca's Revolt
- o 64AD – Great Fire of Rome
- o 66AD – Jewish Revolt
  - ▪ 67AD – Galilee conquered
  - ▪ 68AD – Rebels driven to Jerusalem
  - ▪ 70AD – Jerusalem captured
  - ▪ 72AD – Siege at Masada (72-73AD)
- o 101AD – Conquest of Dacia (101-106AD)
- o 114AD – Annexation of Armenia
- o 132AD – Bar Kochba Revolt
  - ▪ 132AD – Simon Bar Kocha rebels
  - ▪ 134AD – Assault on Judea
  - ▪ 135AD – Judea captured
- o 167AD – Marcomannic Wars (167-180AD)
- o 192AD – Roman Civil War (192-197AD)
  - ▪ 192AD - Emperor Commodus murdered
  - ▪ 193AD - Lucius Septimius Severus, Emperor of Rome from North Africa

stabilizes Rome after defeating rivals
(193-211AD)

- 194AD – Battle of Issus (Severus defeats
  Roman Generals Niger and Albinus)
- 194AD – Osrene annexed
- 197AD – Battle of Lugdunum (Albinus
  conquered and Severus is sole ruler)
- 197AD – Rome defeats Parthians
- 198AD – Caracalla, son of Severus, named co-
  Emperor
- 202AD – Garamantes defeated in North Africa
  extending Roman Empire
- 209AD – Caledonia conquered
- 209AD – Geta, son of Severus also named co-
  Emperor
- 211AD – Death of Severus
- 211AD – Murder of Geta leaving sole rulership
  to Caracalla
- 216AD – Parthian Campaign of Caracalla
  - 217AD - Caracalla murdered
  - 217AD – Macrinus succeeds Caracalla
    as Emperor

- 218AD – Macrinus captured at the Battle of Antioch, executed by Parthians and succeeded by Elagabalus
- 222AD – Elagabalus assassinated by Praetorian Guard
- 230AD – Roman- Persian Wars
- 235AD – Mutiny at Mainz results in death of Emperor Alexander Severus
- 238AD – Year of the Six Emperors
  - Gordian I and Gordian II co-emperors of Africa (both killed at Battle of Carthage in April by Maximinius)
  - Pupienus and Halbinus elected co-emperors by the Senate
  - Maximinius murdered at the Mutiny at Aquileia
  - Pupienus and Halbinus murdered by Praetorian Guard and succeeded by Gordian III

- 244AD – Battle of Misiche results in death of Gordian III who is succeeded by Philip the Arab
- 249AD – Decius defeats and kills Philip
- 251AD – Battle of Arbitus
- 253AD – Mutiny at Terni
- 256AD – Sassanids conquer Antioch
  - 260AD – Valerian taken captive and dies in captivity in 264AD
- 267AD – Palmyrenes split from Rome under Zenobia
- 269AD – Palmyrenes conquer Egypt
- 272AD – Battle of Chalons
- 273AD – Palmyrene rebellion destroys Palmyra

❖ 276AD – Roman Empire split into West and East
  - o 276AD – Death of Emperor Tacitus split power between Probus in the East and Florianus in the West
    - 276AD - Probus defeats Florianus reconciling the initial split

- 282AD – Probus assassinated by the Praetorian Gurad and was succeeded by Carus
  - 283AD- Carinus (West) and Numerian (East) succeed Carus
  - 284AD – Diocletian succeeds Numerian
  - 285AD – Battle of Margus found Diocletian victorious over Carinus
  - 286AD – Diocletian declares Maximian ruler of the West while maintaining control of the East
  - 305AD – Diocletian abdicates
  - 306AD – Declaration of Emperors
    - Constantius I, emperor of the West
    - Galerius, emperor of the East
    - Maxientius, self-declared emperor of Italy with Praetorian Guard support
  - 311AD – East split between Licinius and Maximinius after death of Galerius
  - 312AD – Battle at Milvian Bridge
    - Constantine, successor to Constantius, defeated Maxientius (West)
  - 313AD – Licinius defeats Maximinius (East)

- o 315AD – Battle at Mardia
  - ▪ Failed attempt by Licinius to consolidate
- o 324AD – Battle at Adrianople (Chrysopolis)
  - ▪ Constantine defeats Licinius consolidating sole emperorship
  - ▪ Capital shifted to Byzantium
- ❖ Holy Roman Empire
  - o 324AD –Rome declared a Christian state
  - o 325AD – First Council of Nicea
  - o 330AD – Byzantium renamed to Constantinople
  - o 337AD – Death of Constantine
  - o 361AD – Emperor Julian restored polytheism
  - o 363AD – Emperor Jovian restored Christianity
  - o 367AD – Rome attacked by Barbarians
  - o 368AD – General Theodosius defeats Barbarian Tribes
- ❖ 375AD - Split of Holy Roman Empire (East and West)
  - o Valentenian rules Western Empire
  - o Valens rule Eastern Empire
  - o 375AD – Gratian and Valentinian II succeed Valentinian as co-rulers in the West
  - o 379AD –Theodosius succeeds Valens in the East

- 382AD – Theodosius secures truce with Goths
- 387AD – First Roman Civil War (West)
  - 387AD –Magnus Maximus usurps Valentinian II who escapes to the East
  - 388AD – Battle of Poetovio
    - Theodosius defeats Maximus securing sole rulership of Rome
- 390AD – Massacre at Thessalonica
- 392AD – Second Roman Civil War
  - 392AD - Death of Valentinian II who was found hanged
  - 393AD - Olympic games are ended
  - 394AD – Battle of Frigidus ends Second Civil War with Theodosius victorious
- 395AD – Rome re-divided to West and East
- 402AD – Battle of Verona (Visigoths repelled)
- 410AD – Roman withdrawal from Britain
- 410AD – Visigoths sack Rome
- 452AD – Atilla the Hun sacks Rome
- 455AD – Vandals sack Rome
- 472AD – Siege of Rome by Germanic Tribes
- 476AD –Germanic Odoacer conquers West

𝔍𝔞𝔭𝔞𝔫𝔢𝔰𝔢 𝔗𝔦𝔪𝔢𝔩𝔦𝔫𝔢

- ❖ 300BC – Yayoi Period
  - o Migrants from China and Korea settle
- ❖ 57BC - Beginning of the Japanese state
- ❖ 180AD – Japanese Civil War of Wa
- ❖ 200AD - Creation of the Yamato state (200-300AD)
- ❖ 210AD - Yamato Period (210-710AD)
  - o 405AD - Adoption of Chinese writing in Japan
  - o 552AD - Spread of Buddhism in Japan
  - o 604AD - Shotoku's Seventeen Article Constitution
  - o 645AD - Taika Reform Edict in Japan
- ❖ 710AD – Nara Period (710-794AD)
  - o 710AD - Nara established as first capitol
  - o 784AD – Capital moved to Nagaoka-kyo
- ❖ 794AD - Heian Period (794-1185AD)
  - o 794AD – Capital shifts to Heian (Kyoto)
  - o 1159AD – Heiji War in Japan
  - o 1180AD – Gempei War in Japan
    - ▪ 1185AD – Minamoto clan rule Japan
- ❖ 1185AD - Kamakura Shogunate (1185-1333AD)

- o   1185AD – Capital at Kamakura
- o   1192AD - Establishment of Shogunate in Japan
- o   1200AD - Zen Buddhism in Japan
- o   1221AD – Jokyu Disturbance
- o   1232AD – Joi Shikimoku legal code introduced
- o   1274AD – Mongols under Kublai Khan failed invasion
- o   1281AD - Mongols failed second invasion

❖ 1333AD – Kemmu Restoration - Kamakura government falls to Imperial rule (1333-1336AD)

❖ 1336AD – Ashikaga Period (1336-1568AD)

- o   1336AD – North and Southern Courts split
    - ▪ Northern Imperial Court in Kyoto established by Ashikaga Takauji
    - ▪ Southern Imperial Court in Yoshino established by Emperor Go-Daigo
- o   1338AD – Muromachi Government established
- o   1368AD – Trade with Ming Dynasty becomes extensive (1368-1644AD)
- o   1392AD – Northern and Southern Courts reunified
- o   1467AD – Onin War (1467-1477AD)

- o 1549AD - Christianity and firearms introduced
- ❖ 1568AD – Azuchi-Momoyama Period (1568-1600AD)
  - o 1575AD – Battle of Nagashino
  - o 1590AD – Japan reunited
  - o 1600AD – Battle of Sekigahara
- ❖ 1603AD – Tokugawa Period (1603-1868AD)
  - o 1603AD – Tokugawa government established
  - o 1688AD – Genroku Era in Japan (1688-1703AD)
  - o 1854AD – Commodore Perry and Japan Trade
- ❖ 1868AD – Meiji Period (1868-1912AD)
  - o 1868AD – Meiji Restoration
  - o 1869AD – Capital shifted to Tokyo
  - o 1873AD – Land Tax reform
  - o 1874AD – Rebellion Era against government (1874-1888AD)
    - ▪ 1874AD - Saga Rebellion
    - ▪ 1876AD – Akizuki Rebellion
    - ▪ 1876AD – Hagi Rebellion
    - ▪ 1876AD – Shinpuren Rebellion
    - ▪ 1877AD – Satsuma Rebellion
    - ▪ 1878AD – Takebashi Incident

- 1888AD - Chichibu Rebellion
- 1890AD – Constitution of Japan established the nation as a monarchy with a representative democracy
- 1894AD – Sino-Japanese War (Japan victory)
  - Treaty of Shimonoseki with China over Korea
- 1895AD – Tiawan Invasion
- 1896AD – Sanriku earthquake
- 1902AD – Russo-Japanese War (1902-1905AD) (Japan victory)
- 1910AD – Annexation of Korea
- 1912AD – Taisho succeeds Emperor Meiji
- ❖ 1912AD – Taisho Period (1912-1926AD)
  - 1914AD – Siege of Qingdao (World War I)
  - 1918AD – Race Riots of 1918
  - 1919AD – Samil Movement promoting independence of Korea
  - 1919AD – Provisional government of Korea founded as independent state
  - 1923AD – Great Kanto earthquake causes great financial crisis

- o 1926AD – Hirohito succeeds Meiji and his father Yoshihito
- ❖ 1926AD – Showa Period
  - o 1930AD – Wushe Rebellion in Taiwan
  - o 1931AD – Invasion of Manchuria
    - ▪ 1932AD - Machukuo established as a Japanese state
  - o 1937AD – Second Sino-Japanese War (1937-1945AD) (China victory) and World War II (1939-1945AD) (Allied victory)
    - ▪ 1941AD – Japan attacks United States at Pearl Harbor
    - ▪ 1945AD – United States bombs Hiroshima and Nagasaki with Atomic Bomb forcing surrender
    - ▪ 1945 – Japanese surrender to China (Sino-Japanese War)
    - ▪ 1945AD – South Korea shifts to United States as independent
    - ▪ 1945AD – North Korea shifts to Soviets
  - o 1947AD – Japanese Constitution changes the Empire of Japan to the State of Japan

Timeline of the Origins of Major Faiths

- ❖ Prehistoric Period (Pre-3300BC)
  - o Kemetism (African)
  - o Zoroastrianism (Mesopotamian)
  - o Jainism (Indian)
- ❖ Bronze Age (3300–1200BC)
  - o 1800BC – Judaism (Abrahamic origins)
  - o 1500BC – Hinduism (Vedic Period)
    - 1500BC - Rigveda (1500-1100BC)
    - 1200BC - Samaveda (1200-800BC)
    - 1100BC - Yajurdeda (1100-800BC)
    - 1000BC - Atharveda (1000-800BC)
- ❖ Iron Age and Pre-Hellenistic Periods (1200–332BC)
  - o 500BC – Buddhism
    - 483BC – Death of Gautama
    - 400BC – First Buddhist Council
- ❖ Hellenistic and Roman Periods (332BC - 324AD)
  - o 27AD – Christianity
    - 27AD – Ministry of Jesus (27-30AD)
    - 30AD – Crucifixion, Resurrection, and Ascension of Jesus
    - 39AD – Introduction of Annon Domino

- o 228AD – Manichaeism
  - 228AD – Mani receives first vision
  - 240AD – Mani receives second vision
  - 242AD –Mani produces Shabuhragan
- ❖ Byzantine and Arab Periods (324–1616AD)
  - o 609AD – Islam
    - 609AD – Muhammed's first revelation
    - 613AD – Public spread of Islam
    - 620AD – Isra and Miraj
    - 632AD – Death of Muhammad
  - o 1526AD – Sikhi
    - 1526AD - Guru Nanak Dev Ji found colony of Sikhs

"De Insigniis et Armis" Translation

The Tractatus De Insginiis et Armis is traditionally thought to have been started by Bartolus de Saxoferrato after he was granted arms King Charles IV in 1355AD. Saxoferrato completed the first part of the full treaty prior to his death in 1357AD. His son-in-law Nicolò Alessandri completed and published the full manuscript in 1358AD after adding pictorial displays and explanations of emblems and colors. The completed work has been cited multiple times to resolve heraldic disputes. The first part is translated as follows:[504]

> *Let us consider the insignia and coats of arms that are borne on banners and shields.*
>
> *First, whether it is permitted to bear them, and second, if it is permitted, how they are to be painted and borne.*
>
> *I say that some insignia are proper to a rank or office, and that anyone may bear them if he holds that rank or office, as for example the insignia or proconsuls or legates, or, as we can see today, the insignia of bishops. And anyone who has that rank can bear these insignia. This is not permitted to others, and if someone who is not entitled to them bears them,*

---

[504] www.Heraldica.org/Bartolo.htm, retrieved 8/15/2023

he incurs the charge of fraud. And so I think that those who bear the insignia of the doctor of law when they are not doctor are liable to that penalty.

Some insignia are proper to anyone of a particular rank---for example, any king, prince, or other potentate has his own coat of arms and insignia, and is is permitted to no one else to bestow them or depict them on their own belongings. I believe that this means that one cannot copy the insignia as such; however, it is not prohibited to use such insignia as an accompaniment---for instance, to place the insignia of a king, lord, count, or commune on one's own coat of arms as a sign of subjection. And this is common practice.

Some insignia or coats of arms belong to private persons, either nobles or commoners, and some of these have coats of arms and insignia which they bear by the grant of an emperor or other lord. I have seen the Serene Prince Charles IV, Emperor of the Romans and King of Bohemia, grant many insignia and coats of arms. Among other concessions, the prince gave me (his counselor) and my agnates a red lion on a golden field. And there is no doubt that it is permitted to such persons to bear such insignia, for it is sacrilegious to question the power of a prince. If something is forbidden without the authority of a judge, then it is certainly permissible by his authority.

Some assume coats of arms and insignia on their own initiative, and we should consider whether they are permitted to do it. I think that they are permitted. Just as names are created to identify persons, so insignia and coats of arms are devised for this purpose. Anyone is permitted to use such names for himself, and thus anyone can bear these insignia and depict them on his own belongings, but not on another's.

I ask whether someone is permitted to bear the same coat of arms or insignia as another or whether he can be prohibited. It seems that he is permitted because anyone can assume the name of another, and many may have the same name. Therefore, anyone can assume the coat of arms of another, and many can bear the same insignia and place them on their belongings since this is done for the purpose of identification. It also seems, however, that he can be prohibited, for if we were the first to adopt the sign and thus it belongs to us, it cannot be taken away except by our own consent. But this fundamental principle of ownership cannot be applied here. It applies when several persons cannot use the same object at the same time; however, it does not apply to the use of a facility such as a square, a bath, or a theater.

Furthermore, the sign that someone bears is not really identical to the same sign borne by another; rather, they are different, although they might appear alike. Therefore, concerning the initial question, I say first that one can prohibit or seek to prohibit another from using his sign if he is injured by it because the other party bears the coat of arms with contempt or treats it shamefully.

Second, a third party who is harmed can lodge a complaint about the improper use of the coat of arms, and by his petition the bearer can be prohibited from using it.

Third, if a judge, by virtue of his office, sees that such use may cause public scandal and confusion among the subjects, he can prohibit it lest the people be deceived.

Having established these three points, I make the following distinctions. Sometimes one assumes a coat of arms that another has borne from antiquity and it does not affect or damage the original bearer, nor can he be harmed because of the likeness. For example, a German went to Rome at the time of the jubilee (1350), where he found a certain Italian bearing a coat of arms and insignia of his ancestors, and he wanted to lodge a complaint against the other bearer. Certainly, he could not do it, for the distance between their respective permanent places of residence is so great that the original bearer could not be harmed by the other. Therefore, as in those cases in which someone uses a facility accessible to all, a complaint cannot be lodged without a good reason.

Sometimes it may happen that the use of a coat of arms or insignia by one individual may impinge on another who uses the same insignia. If a person who has many enemies and against whose life many are plotting assumes the coat of arms and insignia of another peaceful or quiet person, certainly it matters much to the latter, and he can see to it that the former is prohibited. Just as a complaint can be lodged against someone who bears a coat of arms or insignia contemptuously, all the more can a complaint be lodged to prevent one from being mistakenly killed or injured in place of another who has adopted the identical coat of arms. Similarly, one can appeal to a judge whose concern is the peace of the people, if the person assuming the coat of arms of another is a public threat.

Next, I ask what are the advantages of having coats of arms by imperial grant. There are many.

First, they are of greater dignity, as we say in the case of a testament made before the emperor.

Second, one cannot be prohibited by another from bearing such coats of arms.

Third, if two persons assumed the same coat of arms and it is not clear who had them first, the one who had them from the prince is preferred.

Fourth, if a question of precedence arises regarding military persons on the battlefield or somewhere else, then the coat of arms granted by the prince should have precedence. The aforesaid applied when all other things are equal---namely, when those who have coats of arms are of equal rank; otherwise, the coat of arms of the one of greater dignity should have precedence.

Other Titles by Daryl Lamar Andrews

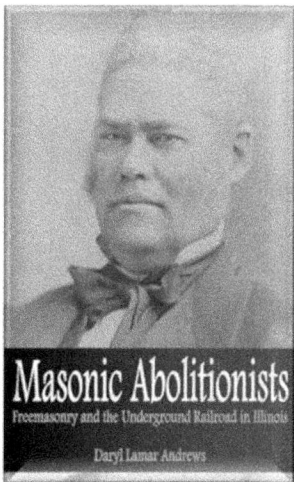

Masonic Abolitionists
Freemasonry and the Underground Railroad in Illinois
Daryl Lamar Andrews

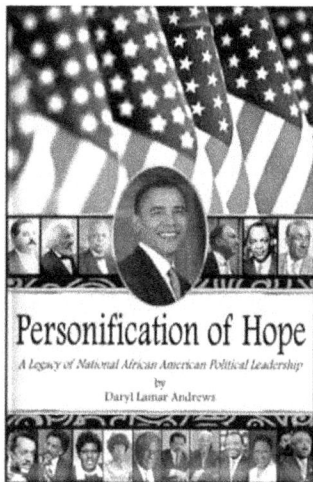

Personification of Hope
A Legacy of National African American Political Leadership
by
Daryl Lamar Andrews

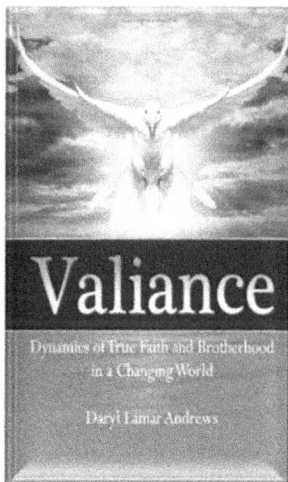

Valiance
Dynamics of True Faith and Brotherhood
in a Changing World
Daryl Lamar Andrews

Indignation
A Psychological Profile of the Infamous John G. Jones
Daryl Lamar Andrews

www.AndrewsPress.com

About the Author

Daryl Lamar Andrews is a noted author on Freemasonry, history, and faith. He is a married father of three, and an ordained Deacon residing in Chicago, Illinois. He has served at local, state, and national levels in multiple bodies of the Masonic diaspora in ritualistic and administrative positions. An author and publisher, he has utilized his skillset in information technology and publishing to serve as the editor for several Masonic publications in Illinois and beyond including the Prince Hall Masonic Journal, Scottish Rite Clarion Newsletter, and the Bulletin for the Northern Jurisdiction of Scottish Rite Freemasonry. He has contributed over two hundred articles about history and faith to multiple publications. In 2010, he was elected an Actual Fellow of the Phylaxis Society, the premier research organization for Prince Hall Freemasonry in the world.

www.ingramcontent.com/pod-product-compliance
Lightning Source LLC
Chambersburg PA
CBHW072010270326
41928CB00009B/1609